读美句·学单词

Learning English Vocabulary Through Authentic Sentences

周正履　张　悦　李海芳　编著

杨　跃　审定

西北工业大学出版社

西安

【内容简介】 本书涵盖大学生应掌握的核心词汇，以单元的模式进行编排，从句子到单词，再将单词还原到句子中，充分体现"语境"在词汇习得中的作用。书中的例句丰富，来源广泛，均为真实语料中的自然语言。所选例句不仅仅包括单词的典型用法，还体现一定的翻译方法和技巧，将为学习者习得词汇、感受语言之美、启迪智慧提供有益帮助。

本书可作为高等院校学生学习英语词汇、培养翻译能力、感受语言魅力的工具书，也可供各层次的英语学习者使用，通过此书来学语言、习文化、观世界。

图书在版编目（CIP）数据

读美句·学单词/周正履，张悦，李海芳编著. —西安：西北工业大学出版社，2023.9
ISBN 978-7-5612-8747-7

Ⅰ.①读… Ⅱ.①周… ②张… ③李… Ⅲ.①英语-词汇-高等学校-教学参考资料 Ⅳ.①H319.34

中国国家版本馆CIP数据核字（2023）第094239号

DU MEIJU · XUE DANCI

读美句·学单词

周正履 张悦 李海芳 编著

责任编辑：杨 军 张 炜		策划编辑：张 炜	
责任校对：胡莉巾		装帧设计：侣小玲	
出版发行：西北工业大学出版社			
通信地址：西安市友谊西路127号		邮编：710072	
电　　话：（029）88491757，88493844			
网　　址：www.nwpup.com			
印 刷 者：陕西向阳印务有限公司			
开　　本：720 mm×1020 mm		1/16	
印　　张：23.875			
字　　数：545千字			
版　　次：2023年9月第1版		2023年9月第1次印刷	
书　　号：ISBN 978-7-5612-8747-7			
定　　价：65.00元			

如有印装问题请与出版社联系调换

  2020年教育部颁布的《大学英语教学指南》指出，英语课程是高等学校人文教育的一部分，兼有工具性和人文性双重性质。对语言学习来说，词汇学习贯穿整个过程，学习者的词汇习得会对其听、说、读、写等语言能力的发展产生极大影响。语言学家Wilkins（1972）认为：如果没有语法，很多东西无法表达；但如果没有词汇，任何东西都无法表达。这一论断说明词汇在语言学习中的基础性和重要性，而现实情况是学生的词汇量往往不达标，或者虽能识记但没有深度掌握。

  为了应对这一问题，专家学者们编写了较多词汇书。这些书大多采用传统的词汇记忆方法，边读边记，直到单词的读音与拼写在脑海中形成条件反射式的一一对应。书本的编排有的采用词典方式，将应掌握的词汇按字母顺序排列，这样容易导致记忆混乱。也有采用乱序法编写的词汇书，但往往仅限于词汇层面，给出拼写、读音和汉语意思。学习者通过简单重复来记单词，实际上，重复是一种低效率的处理方式，记忆效率较差。将单词的意思置于短语和上下文中来记忆则是一种深度处理，在具体的语境中记忆单词比单纯的背诵和重复高效得多。此外，一个单词通常有多种意思，只有当它和其他单词共现时，才被赋予确切的意义。

  鉴于此，本书作者根据长期的一线教学经验，编写了《读美句·学单词》一书，以单元的模式进行编排，涵盖大学生应掌握的核心词汇，从句子到单词，再将单词还原到句子中，充分体现"语境"在词汇记忆中的作用。这里的语境指的是语言使用的环境，可以使学习者更好地记忆和理解词汇的意义，进而激发他们对英语词汇的学习兴趣。本书的语境包含多层含义：其一，单词由句子引出，而非将单词直接列出；其二，对单词的释义采用柯林斯词典模式，用完整的英文自然句子解释词条，充分反映单词在语境中的典型意义及用法；其三，每个核心单词都会通过例句来展示其用法，所有例句均选自真实语料，是英语母语者产生的自然语言，具有很好的示范性和典型性，且难易程度适中。本书对"语境"的充分阐释正好契合了其标题中的"美句"二字，所选例句不仅代表单词的典型用法，往往还体现一定的翻译方法和技巧，为学习者习得词汇、感受语言之美、启迪智慧提供有益的帮助。书中的例句丰富，来源广泛，涵盖政治、经济、科技、教育、商业、文化、体育等众多领域，涉及60多个国家和地区，谈及的人和事体现了文化多样性和包容性。因此，本书看似词汇读本，实则是语言与文化、翻译与哲思的小百科全书。

本书由30个单元构成，每单元体例相同，包括10个主题句，每个主题句引导出2个核心单词，全书含600个核心词汇，加上联想记忆、例句展示和常规词汇，基本涵盖了大学阶段应掌握的词汇。本书由周正履、张悦和李海芳共同编著，三位作者倾注了大量心血，尤其是例句的选取和翻译。本书例句的基本属性是科学性，主要体现为可理解性、典型性、示范性和启发性，往往需要精心挑选。例如，在讨论动词 undergo 时，示范的是其最典型的搭配 undergo surgery（进行手术）和 undergo changes（发生变化），在讨论形容词 detrimental 时，例句展示了其典型用法 be detrimental to，同时也包含做定语的用法。例句的翻译需要反复思考，有时为了打磨译文，作者们需要反复查证和研讨，甚至找到句子所在的原文来佐证，确保呈现在读者面前的是一部有价值的英语工具书。

英语单词的记忆和学习非一朝一夕之事，而是一个长期坚持和积累的过程。著名的艾宾浩斯遗忘曲线告诉我们，遗忘的进程不是匀速而是先快后慢。因此，短时记忆之后，及时复习必不可少，要在大量阅读和经常运用的基础上探索适合自己的记忆方法。

本书是全国翻译专业学位研究生教育指导委员会项目（MTIJZW202165）、陕西省社科联项目"以国际传播为导向的翻译教材建设研究"（2023HZ0994）和山西省教育科学规划项目"新文科视域下地方应用型高校英语专业教学创新研究"（GH220423）的部分成果。

本书可作为高等院校学生学习英语词汇、培养翻译能力、感受语言魅力的工具书，也可供各层次的英语学习者使用。希望广大学习者通过此书学语言、习文化、观世界，倘若如此，写作过程中的辛劳便有所值了。

西安电子科技大学杨跃教授审阅了全书并提出了修改建议，林六辰教授对本书编写的整体思路和编写理念提供了指导，美国亚利桑那州立大学英语系Kerry Fine教授对例句的选取和优化提出了宝贵意见，在此一并表示感谢。在本书的撰写过程中，参考了部分工具书和著作等文献，向其作者表示深深的谢意。

书中如有不当或疏漏之处，敬请专家和读者批评指正。

周正履

目录

Unit 1 001	Unit 18 192
Unit 2 012	Unit 19 203
Unit 3 023	Unit 20 215
Unit 4 034	Unit 21 226
Unit 5 045	Unit 22 238
Unit 6 056	Unit 23 250
Unit 7 067	Unit 24 261
Unit 8 079	Unit 25 272
Unit 9 090	Unit 26 283
Unit 10 101	Unit 27 294
Unit 11 112	Unit 28 306
Unit 12 123	Unit 29 317
Unit 13 135	Unit 30 328
Unit 14 146	
Unit 15 157	参考文献 339
Unit 16 168	附录Ⅰ 参考答案 340
Unit 17 180	附录Ⅱ 词汇索引 361

Unit 1

★ 本单元核心词汇 ★

enroll	departure	associate	surgery	sever
trail	participant	option	intimate	hiker
pursue	furious	potential	survey	optimistic
negligence	tornado	anniversary	exhaust	ditch

★ 本单元拓展词汇 ★

inquiry	scheme	lounge	physician	album
routine	protest	cuisine	allegation	cord
latent	segment	fatigue	potent	quest
centennial	deploy	avalanche	pessimistic	summit
register	provoke	clinical	diabetes	pitch
exodus	dissect	trajectory	tramp	cyclone
diplomatic	shovel	solicitor	rage	

读美句·学单词

1. When I ***enrolled*** at Columbia University in 1975, my mother exercised her parental right to express her worry at my ***departure***.

单词	释义
enroll	*v.* If you enroll or are enrolled at an institution or in a class, you officially join it. 注册；入学

双语例句

He enrolled in a public speaking course and dropped out before it even started.（他注册了一门公共演讲课程，还没开始上课就放弃了。）

In some countries plenty of workers fail to enroll in pension schemes and suffer as a result.（在一些国家，很多工人没有参加养老金计划，因此而遭受损失。）

联想记忆

enrollment *n.* 登记；注册人数
register *v.* 登记，注册 *n.* 登记表；寄存器

单词	释义
departure	*n.* Departure is the act of going away from somewhere. 离开；出发
	n. If someone does something different or unusual, you can refer to their action as a departure. 背离

双语例句

Passengers can buy perfumes in the departure lounge after passing through airport security.（旅客通过机场安检后可以在候机厅购买香水。）

The new album is not a radical departure from the band's previous work.（这张新专辑没有完全背离该乐队之前的风格。）

联想记忆

depart *v.* 离开；出发；背离
exodus *n.* 大批离开

2. The result was a ***severed*** spinal cord, a ***surgery***-filled hospital stay and the rest of his life in a wheelchair.

单词	释义
sever	*v.* To sever something means to cut it completely off. 切断，切掉
	v. If you sever a relationship or connection that you have with someone, you end it suddenly and completely. 断绝（关系、联系）

双语例句

After much heavy labor with trucks and shovels, the severed roads have been reconnected.（经过用卡车和铲子进行艰苦施工后，切断的道路又连通了。）

The two countries established diplomatic relations, which had been severed since the 1967 war.（两国自1967年的战争后就断交了，现在又建立了外交关系。）

联想记忆

dissect *v.* 解剖；剖析

单词	释义
surgery	*n.* Surgery is medical treatment in which someone's body is cut open so that a doctor can repair, remove, or replace a diseased part. 外科手术

双语例句

The doctors are monitoring Harris to see whether he is in good condition for surgery.（医生们正在对哈里斯进行监测，看他的身体状况是否适合手术。）

The Brooklyn resident checked into the hospital for routine surgery to repair a broken shoulder.（这位布鲁克林居民入院接受例行手术，修复肩膀骨折。）

联想记忆

surgeon *n.* 外科医生
physician *n.* 内科医生

3. The weekend was designed to let *participants* experience a section of Detroit on more *intimate* terms.

单词	释义
participant	*n.* The participants in an activity are the people who take part in it. 参加者

双语例句

In the early 1990s, Samsung was a weak participant in segments of the electronics industry.（20世纪90年代初，三星在电子行业的某些领域处于弱势。）

The participants were asked to list all the animals they could think of in a one-minute period.（参与者要在一分钟内列出他们能想到的所有动物。）

联想记忆

participate *v.* 参加，参与
participatory *adj.* 参与式的

participation *n.* 参与；分享

单词	释义
intimate	*adj.* If you have an intimate friendship with someone, you know them very well and like them a lot. 亲密的；私下的
	v. If you intimate something, you say it in an indirect way. 暗示

双语例句

Each program is limited to 15 campers ensuring an intimate experience with the animals.（每个项目仅限15名营员，确保他们能与动物亲密接触。）

Mr. Freeman intimated that the newspaper is working towards shutting its print edition down altogether.（弗里曼先生暗示，报社正着手完全关闭印刷版业务。）

联想记忆

intimacy *n.* 亲密；隐私
cozy *adj.* 舒适的；友好的，亲密无间的

4. The Ruta de Cares is said to be one of the busiest *trails* in Spain with up to 3,000 *hikers* each day in summer.

单词	释义
trail	*n.* A trail is a rough path across open country or through forests.（乡间或林中的）崎岖小路；路径
	n. Trail is a series of marks or other signs of movement or other activities left by someone or something. 痕迹

双语例句

The woodland area provides a great opportunity for hiking and walking, and there are many trails to explore.（林区提供了远足和散步的绝佳机会，有许多小径可以探寻。）

Trekking along muddy jungle paths, we follow a trail of fresh jaguar paw prints.（我们在泥泞的丛林里艰难跋涉，紧跟着一些新留下不久的美洲豹爪印。）

联想记忆

trailer *n.* 拖车
trajectory *n.* 轨迹；弹道

单词	释义
hiker	*n.* A hiker is a person who is going for a long walk in the countryside for pleasure. 远足者

双语例句

Another person, described as a 60-year-old male hiker, is missing after a separate avalanche nearby.（另一名60岁的男性徒步旅行者在附近另一起雪崩后失踪。）

The Tasman Coast makes a satisfying end point, with dolphins and penguins often greeting hikers on their arrival.（塔斯曼海岸是一个好去处，旅行者到来时海豚和企鹅经常会迎接他们。）

联想记忆

hike *v.* 徒步旅行 *n.* 远足
tramp *v.* 长途跋涉；重步行走 *n.* 徒步旅行；流浪汉

5. Her mother contacted Morrish Solicitors four years ago to *pursue* a claim for medical *negligence* against the hospital.

单词	释义
pursue	*v.* If you pursue a particular aim or result, you make efforts to achieve it, often over a long period of time. 追求；努力实现
	v. If you pursue an activity, interest, or plan, you carry it out. 执行，贯彻

双语例句

We also continue to pursue our goal of deploying a nationwide wireless network for public safety.（我们也继续追求为了公众安全建立全国性无线网络的目标。）

After college Brown was still undecided as to what career she wanted to pursue.（大学毕业后，布朗仍无法决定自己要从事什么职业。）

The officer said Japan would continue to pursue the policies laid down at the London Summit.（这名官员表示，日本将继续贯彻伦敦峰会上确定的方针。）

联想记忆

pursuit *n.* 追赶；追求；职业
quest *n.* 寻求，探求 *v.* 探寻

单词	释义
negligence	*n.* If someone is guilty of negligence, they have failed to do something which they ought to do. 疏忽；渎职

双语例句

Lawyers handling claims for patients said poor communication was a major factor in most negligence cases.（为病人处理索赔的律师表示，沟通不畅是大多数医疗

过失案件的主要原因。)

Mr. Neale faced 35 charges of clinical incompetence, professional negligence and extreme rudeness. (尼尔先生面临35项指控，包括临床能力不足、玩忽职守和态度蛮横。)

联想记忆

negligent *adj.* 疏忽的，粗心大意的

6. Wednesday marks the second *anniversary* of the *tornado* that struck Joplin, killing at least 158 people.

单词	释义
anniversary	*n.* An anniversary is a date that is remembered or celebrated because a special event happened on that day in a previous year. 周年纪念日

双语例句

Celebrating its 100th anniversary this year is Zion National Park, in the western state of Utah. (位于美国西部犹他州的锡安国家公园今年迎来了100周年纪念。)

One couple booked their 25th wedding anniversary celebration in a village, but split up before the big day. (有对夫妇在一个度假村预订了结婚25周年纪念活动，但在这天来临之前便劳燕分飞了。)

联想记忆

centennial *n.* 一百周年；百年纪念 *adj.* 一百年的

单词	释义
tornado	*n.* A tornado is a violent wind storm consisting of a tall column of air which spins around very fast and causes a lot of damage. 龙卷风

双语例句

Dozens of tornado warnings were issued for central Oklahoma and parts of Missouri. (俄克拉荷马州中部和密苏里州部分地区发布了数十次龙卷风警告。)

Around 300 people were killed by tornadoes across seven states two weeks ago, more than 200 in Alabama alone. (两周前，龙卷风导致七个州约300人死亡，仅阿拉巴马州就有200多人死亡。)

联想记忆

hurricane *n.* 飓风
cyclone *n.* 旋风

7. A new home owner *furious* at faults with the construction has put up a warning notice to other *potential* buyers.

单词	释义
furious	*adj.* Someone who is furious is extremely angry. 狂怒的，生气的
	adj. Furious is also used to describe something that is done with great energy, effort, speed, or violence. 激烈的；玩命的；迅猛的

双语例句

The miners were furious about the outdated facilities and threatened to walk out. （矿工们对陈旧的设备感到愤怒，威胁要罢工。）

The press release provoked furious protests from the Gore camp and other top Democrats. （新闻发布会引发了戈尔阵营和民主党其他高层的强烈抗议。）

联想记忆

fury *n.* 狂怒，暴怒
rage *n.* 狂怒，狂暴 *v.* 发脾气；（战斗、争论等）激烈进行

单词	释义
potential	*adj.* You use potential to say that someone or something is capable of developing into the particular kind of person or thing mentioned. 潜在的
	n. If someone or something has potential, they have the necessary abilities or qualities to become successful or useful in the future. 潜力

双语例句

Priceline.com CEO blamed on-going fiscal problems worldwide for keeping potential travelers stuck at home. （普利斯林首席执行官认为，潜在的游客待在家里应归咎于全球持续的财政问题。）

In clinical trials these substances have showed potential in preventing cancer and fighting heart disease. （在临床实验中，这些物质表现出了在预防癌症和治疗心脏病方面的潜能。）

联想记忆

potent *adj.* 强大的；有强效的
latent *adj.* 潜在的，隐藏的；潜伏的

8. After four 12-hour days of sandbagging, Trish Connelly, 57, was *exhausted* but *optimistic* the town would beat back the river.

单词	释义
exhaust	*v.* If something exhausts you, it makes you so tired, either physically or mentally, that you have no energy left. 使精疲力竭
	v. If you exhaust something such as money, you finish it all. 用完，耗尽
	n. Exhaust is the gas or steam that is produced when the engine of a vehicle is running. 废气，（汽车）尾气

双语例句

They have traveled by foot through the mountains for as long as five days, arriving exhausted.（他们徒步穿越山区长达五天，到达时已筋疲力尽。）

He has been looking for natural gas in the Gulf of Mexico, a basin that was given up as exhausted just a few years ago.（他一直在墨西哥湾寻找天然气，这个盆地在几年前因为枯竭而被放弃开采。）

A class of chemicals found in French fries and car exhaust may contribute to Alzheimer's.（炸薯条和汽车尾气里的一系列化学物质会导致阿尔茨海默病。）

联想记忆

exhaustion *n.* 枯竭；耗尽；精疲力竭
fatigue *n.* 疲劳；疲乏 *v.* 使劳累

单词	释义
optimistic	*adj.* Someone who is optimistic is hopeful about the future or the success of something in particular. 乐观的，乐观主义的

双语例句

People who are optimistic are less likely to have high blood pressure or diabetes.（乐观的人不太可能患高血压或糖尿病。）

Last week Japan posted weak manufacturing reports, and analysts aren't optimistic about upcoming data.（上周日本公布了疲弱的制造业数据，分析师对接下来的数据也不乐观。）

联想记忆

optimism *n.* 乐观；乐观主义
optimize *v.* 优化；持乐观态度
pessimistic *adj.* 悲观的

9. According to the latest *survey* from the National Center for Health Statistics, nearly 35 percent of people have *ditched* their landlines for a cell phone.

单词	释义
survey	*n.* If you carry out a survey, you try to find out detailed information about a lot of people or things, usually by asking people a series of questions. 调查
	v. Survey is also a VERB. 调查；勘测

双语例句

Technology and the fast pace of life are killing off romance in Britain, according to a survey.（据一项调查显示，科技和快节奏的生活正在扼杀英国人的浪漫。）

Eighteen percent of those surveyed said they would take a trip during Thanksgiving week and weekend.（18%的受访者表示，他们将在感恩节和周末去旅行。）

联想记忆

inquiry *n.* 调查；审查；询问

单词	释义
ditch	*v.* If you ditch something, you get rid of it because you no longer want it; if you ditch someone, you end a relationship with that person. 丢弃；抛弃
	n. A ditch is a long narrow channel cut into the ground at the side of a road or field. 沟渠

双语例句

Surprisingly, Americans are ditching their U.S. passports in record numbers.（令人惊讶的是，空前数量的美国人正放弃本国国籍。）

They were seeking cover in a dry irrigation ditch when the bomb exploded.（当炸弹爆炸时，他们在一条干涸的灌溉水渠里寻求掩护。）

联想记忆

groove *n.* 凹槽；槽线 *v.* 开槽

pitch *v.* （棒球中）投球；（船或飞机）上下颠簸 *n.* 球场；投掷；沥青；音高

10. Often *associated* with warmer months, these wines are really year-round *options* when it comes to cuisine.

单词	释义
associate	*v.* If you associate someone or something with another thing, the two are connected in your mind. 使联系起来；有关联
	adj. Associate is used before a rank or title to indicate a lower level. 副的
	n. Your associates are the people you are closely connected with, especially at work. 同事，伙伴

双语例句

Like most Middle Eastern deserts, the Negev Desert is usually associated with sand, rock and the camel.（像大多数中东沙漠一样，内盖夫沙漠通常与沙地、岩石和骆驼联系在一起。）

The study was headed by Helen Blackwell, an associate professor of chemistry at the University of Wisconsin.（这项研究是由威斯康星大学化学副教授海伦·布莱克威尔牵头完成的。）

Special phone-order centers were set up in the beauty department for sales associates to contact customers.（美容部设立了专门的电话订购中心，以便销售人员与顾客联系。）

联想记忆

association *n.* 协会，社团；联想

单词	释义
option	*n.* An option is something that you can choose to do in preference to one or more alternatives. 供选择的东西；选择

双语例句

Students are exploring employment options long before they see a diploma.（学生早在拿到文凭之前就已经开始寻求就业去向。）

In recent years, the gap year option seems to be gaining greater acceptance in the academic community.（近年来，间隔年在学术界似乎越来越为人们所接受。）

联想记忆

optional *adj.* 可选择的 *n.* 选修科目
opt *v.* 选择

单元练习 1

使用本单元核心词汇的适当形式填空，并将句子译为中文。

1. After the match Henman told of his disappointment but was _____ about the future.
2. The team focused on nanotechnology research and its _____ for commercial application.
3. She is currently _____ editor for the magazine, where she covers the photography industry.
4. On the other hand, _____ in business programs, engineering and computer science is way up.
5. These senior executives have been clocking in long hours in _____ of the company's goal to expand.
6. Busy working and a complex interpersonal environment tend to make people mentally and physically _____.
7. Some of the best women left teaching as a career _____, bringing about a gradual decline in the quality of schooling.
8. Miami International Airport had only 15 _____ and three arrivals between 8 and 10 in the morning.
9. Many shops and restaurants, who are having their busiest period, are _____ at the software problems.
10. Facebook is uniquely positioned to give brands what they need: an _____ relationship with their target audience.

Unit 2

★ 本单元核心词汇 ★

cautious	retailer	brochure	outlook	disposal
underline	accidentally	adversity	ambition	arrest
metropolis	revenue	occupation	spectator	suicide
encounter	renovation	conscientious	longevity	usher

★ 本单元拓展词汇 ★

counsel	receptionist	articulate	vista	legalize
budget	leaflet	executive	promotional	onlooker
parachuting	fulfill	incidentally	mounting	initial
outskirts	hardware	commitment	euthanasia	dump
reputational	convention	discount	aspiration	booklet
pamphlet	prudent	panorama	escort	durability
ambitious	bump			

11. Travelers will *encounter* some construction headaches at Paris' Charles de Gaulle Airport, as it continues major *renovations*.

单词	释义
encounter	*v.* If you encounter something or someone, you meet them, usually unexpectedly. 遇到；邂逅
	n. An encounter is a particular type of experience. 偶遇；经历

双语例句

She works in counseling and understands, as I do, the challenges women veterans encounter.（她从事咨询工作，和我一样理解女性退伍军人面临的挑战。）

The 33-year-old Husheer still has a horrified look on his face when recalling the encounter.（当33岁的哈希尔回忆起他的遭遇时，仍面露恐惧。）

联想记忆

bump *v.* 碰上，撞上 *n.* 肿块；隆起；碰撞

单词	释义
renovation	*n.* Renovation means people repair and improve a building and get it back into good condition. 翻新，整修

双语例句

Renovation work is underway on a plane which used to carry in excess of 350 passengers.（这个曾经载客超过350人的飞机正在整修。）

The budget for stadium construction and renovation has risen by over 60% from the initial estimate.（场馆建设与装修的开支比最初预计的高出了60%以上。）

联想记忆

renovator *n.* 革新者；更新者；修理者
renovate *v.* 修复；革新

12. *Retailers* are sending increased numbers of *brochures* to customers in an attempt to draw their attention to the new products.

单词	释义
retailer	*n.* A retailer is a person or business that sells goods to the public. 零售商

双语例句

Target, the second largest discount retailer, blamed cold weather for weaker than expected figures.（第二大折扣零售商塔吉特将业绩低于预期归咎于寒冷的天气。）

The retailer increased its international store count from 37 in 2017 to 335 in 2022. （该零售商不断拓展全球店面，从2017年的37家增加到了2022年的335家。）

联想记忆

retail *n.* 零售 *adj.* 零售的 *adv.* 以零售方式

单词	释义
brochure	*n.* A brochure is a thin magazine with pictures that gives you information about a product or service. 小册子；资料（或广告）手册

双语例句

For more information about the Curriculum please consult the promotional brochure.（若想了解更多关于本课程的信息，请查阅宣传手册。）

The brochure details all the hotels, scenic spots, local food and facilities in the area.（这本小册子详细介绍了该地区所有的酒店、景点、当地美食和休闲设施。）

联想记忆

pamphlet *n.* 小册子
leaflet *n.* 传单
booklet *n.* 小册子

13. A man could be very *conscientious* in the duties of his *occupation* and still fail terribly in his calling as a father.

单词	释义
conscientious	*adj.* Someone who is conscientious is very careful to do their work properly. 认真的；自觉的

双语例句

We found ambition present in kids who were really conscientious and intelligent.（我们发现，非常认真且聪颖的孩子都有远大的理想。）

He was conscientious, and he was especially articulate, both verbally and in writing ability.（他工作认真，无论是口头上还是书面上都特别善于表达。）

联想记忆

conscience *n.* 道德心，良心
industrious *adj.* 勤奋的，勤勉的

单词	释义
occupation	*n.* Your occupation is your job or profession. 职业，工作
	n. An occupation is something that you spend time doing, either for pleasure or because it needs to be done. 消遣，业余活动
	n. The occupation of a country happens when it is entered and controlled by a foreign army. 占领

双语例句

Airplane pilots have the third most dangerous occupation, with a death rate of 101 per 100, 000. （飞行员是第三危险的职业，死亡率为十万分之一百零一。）

This young lady's main occupation seems to be parachuting and rock climbing. （这位年轻女士的主要消遣活动似乎是跳伞和攀岩。）

The history of the harsh occupation during the 1930s and 1940s is neither forgotten nor forgiven. （20世纪30年代至40年代被残酷占领的这段历史不能忘记，也不可以饶恕。）

联想记忆

occupational *adj.* 职业的；占领的

14. Until more visible progress can be seen, ordinary Vietnamese maintain their ***cautious outlook*** of the economy.

单词	释义
cautious	*adj.* Someone who is cautious acts very carefully in order to avoid possible danger. 谨慎的，小心的

双语例句

Mr. Blair, a cautious man, is unlikely to take a decision before he needs to. （布莱尔先生是一个谨慎的人，不到必要时他不太可能做出决定。）

He remains cautious about housing-related sectors such as furnishings, hardware and building materials. （他对家具、五金和建材等房地产相关行业仍持谨慎态度。）

联想记忆

caution *n.* 小心，谨慎 *v.* 警告；提醒
prudent *adj.* 谨慎的，慎重的

单词	释义
outlook	*n.* The outlook for something is what people think will happen in relation to it. 前景，展望
	n. Your outlook is your general attitude toward life. 态度；人生观

双语例句

The investment outlook might be affected unless the government is able to restore confidence quickly.（除非政府能够迅速恢复信心，否则投资前景可能会受到影响。）

In a broadcast address, the president called on people to adopt a more positive outlook on life.（在电视讲话中，总统呼吁人们采取更积极的生活态度。）

联想记忆

panorama *n.* 全景，全景图
vista *n.* 远景，展望

15. The fire was believed to have been started ***accidentally*** due to "careless ***disposal*** of smoking materials".

单词	释义
accidentally	*adv.* If something happens accidentally, it occurs by chance or as the result of an accident, and is not deliberately intended. 意外地，偶然地

双语例句

Mr. Peretz ended his short army career as a captain when he was accidentally wounded.（佩雷兹先生意外受伤，在上尉任职上结束了他短暂的军旅生涯。）

The turtles feed on jellyfish, and some have accidentally swallowed plastic bags dumped into the ocean.（这些海龟以水母为食，有的不小心还吞食了扔进海里的塑料袋。）

联想记忆

accidental *adj.* 意外的；偶然的
incidentally *adv.* 顺便说一句；附带地

单词	释义
disposal	*n.* Disposal is the act of getting rid of something that is no longer wanted or needed. 清除；处理
	n. If you have something at your disposal, you are able to use it whenever you want, and for whatever purpose you like. 任某人支配

双语例句

The farmers may have turned to a time-honored waste disposal method: dump it in the river.（农民们可能采用了一种由来已久的废物处理方法：倒进河里。）

Information technology is at our disposal in a way it never was 10 years ago.（我

们使用信息技术的方式绝不是十年前那样。）

联想记忆

dispose *v.* 处理，处置
disposable *adj.* 可自由支配的；一次性的 *n.* 一次性用品

16. The Greek Cabinet ***ushered*** in fresh measures to raise ***revenues*** in order to meet sky-high savings targets.

单词	释义
usher	*v.* If you usher someone somewhere, you show them where they should go by going with them. 引领；开创
	n. An usher is a person who shows people where to sit, for example at a wedding or at a concert. （婚礼、音乐会等的）引座员

双语例句

The 2020-2021 school year is certain to usher in new digital tools and different teaching approaches. （2020—2021学年必定会引入新型的数字工具和不同的教学模式。）

Graduated from high school, he did part-time work as an usher in a theatre. （高中毕业后，他在一家剧院兼职当引座员。）

联想记忆

receptionist *n.* 接待员
escort *n.* 护送；护卫队 *v.* 护送；护卫

单词	释义
revenue	*n.* Revenue is money that a company, organization, or government receives from people. （公司、组织或政府的）收入

双语例句

Led by the growth of the Chinese market, international box office revenues experienced continued growth. （在中国强劲市场的带动下，国际票房收入持续增长。）

As consumers spend more time on their mobile devices, revenue from broadcast advertising has suffered. （由于消费者在移动设备上花费的时间越来越多，广播的广告收入影响颇大。）

联想记忆

proceeds *n.* 收入，收益

17. The U.S. star is *underlining* what a threat he will be to England's *ambitions* at the World Cup in South Africa this summer.

单词	释义
underline	*v.* If one thing, for example an action or an event, underlines another, it draws attention to it and emphasizes its importance. 突出显示；强调
	v. If you underline something such as a word or a sentence, you draw a line underneath it in order to give it extra importance. 在……下面画线

双语例句

Nissan's chief executive Carlos underlined the company's commitment to its electric cars program.（日产汽车首席执行官卡洛斯强调，公司将致力于电动汽车的研发。）

The girl organized her neatly underlined notes in college into 15 different colored notebooks.（这个女孩把上大学时工工整整的笔记整理进了15本不同颜色的笔记本。）

联想记忆

underlie *v.* 支撑；是……的起因

单词	释义
ambition	*n.* If you have an ambition to do or achieve something, you want very much to do it or achieve it. 理想；雄心

双语例句

Complicating these negotiations is the fact that Visa also has its own mobile wallet ambitions.（让这些谈判更复杂的是，Visa也有自己的移动钱包野心。）

Morgan was born in Wales, but his ambition took him to Jamaica as a young man to seek fame and fortune.（摩根出生于威尔士，年少时便怀着雄心壮志去了牙买加追名逐利。）

联想记忆

ambitious *adj.* 雄心勃勃的，有雄心的
aspiration *n.* 渴望；抱负

18. Violence, poverty, or some other *adversity* in childhood could affect both IQ and the risk of *suicide*.

单词	释义
adversity	*n.* Adversity is a very difficult or unfavorable situation. 困境；逆境

双语例句

In the months ahead, Fred Wilpon must exhibit great resolve in the midst of adversity.（在未来几个月，弗雷德·威尔朋必须在逆境中表现出极大的决心。）

The Ministry of Trade and Industry was satisfied with the companies gaining strength through adversity.（贸易工业部对这些企业在逆境中成长感到满意。）

联想记忆

adverse *adj.* 不利的，有害的

单词	释义
suicide	*n.* People who commit suicide deliberately kill themselves because they do not want to continue living. 自杀

双语例句

The Netherlands was the first European country to legalize euthanasia and assisted suicide.（荷兰是将安乐死和辅助自杀合法化的第一个欧洲国家。）

The psychological burden is such that South Korea suffers from high student suicide rates.（由于心理负担过重，韩国学生的自杀率很高。）

联想记忆

suicidal *adj.* 自杀的，自杀性的

19. Four ***spectators*** were ***arrested*** at the game and the Football Association will investigate the crowd trouble.

单词	释义
spectator	*n.* A spectator is a person who watches something, especially a sports event. （体育赛事的）观众

双语例句

Hundreds of thousands of spectators usually turn out to support those taking part in the race.（成千上万的观众通常会来到现场支持那些参赛者。）

The most recent event attracted a record 20,000 spectators to the Anaheim Convention Center.（最近的一次比赛吸引了两万名观众到阿纳海姆会议中心，这一人数创下了纪录。）

联想记忆

onlooker *n.* 旁观者，观众

单词	释义
arrest	*v.* If the police arrest you, they take charge of you and take you to a police station, because they believe you may have committed a crime. 逮捕
	n. Arrest is also a NOUN. 逮捕

双语例句

Six people have been arrested across the country following several incidents of public disorder.（全国范围内发生了几起公共骚乱事件，目前已经有六人被逮捕。）

He was eventually placed under arrest at his heavily guarded house on the outskirts of Islamabad.（最终，他在伊斯兰堡郊区戒备森严的房子里被捕。）

联想记忆

seize *v.* 逮捕；抓住；占领；吸引

20. ***Longevity*** in Japan is more pronounced in the countryside and in small towns, where the pace of life is less stressful than in the ***metropolis***.

单词	释义
longevity	*n.* Longevity is a long duration of individual life. 长寿

双语例句

There is mounting evidence between increased sitting time and reduced longevity.（越来越多的证据表明，久坐时间增加和寿命降低之间有关联。）

Still more remarkable is that Mark Twain's reputational longevity is based on so few books.（更值得称道的是，马克·吐温声誉长存依赖于他寥寥可数的几本书。）

联想记忆

durability *n.* 持久性；耐用性

单词	释义
metropolis	*n.* A metropolis is the largest, busiest, and most important city in a country or region. 大都会

双语例句

The street runs far in both directions and connects the unique sections of the great metropolis.（街道向两个方向延伸很远，将这个大都市的独特景观连接在一起。）

New Orleans could once again become a prosperous metropolis, something it hasn't been for decades.（新奥尔良可能会再次成为繁荣的大都市，这样的景象已经几十年没有过了。）

联想记忆
metropolitan *adj.* 大都会的

单元练习 2

使用本单元核心词汇的适当形式填空，并将句子译为中文。

1. There are plans to _____ an extensive railway network that reaches Congo and Zambia.
2. Soccer games can now draw crowds of over 70,000 in cities where baseball attracts a mere 20,000 _____.
3. The importance of intercultural competence in a fast-changing world cannot be _____ too much.
4. While some people push forward through _____, many will give up at the first signs of failure.
5. Hundreds of _____ surnames are familiar to us: Archer, Carter, Fisher, Taylor, to name but a few.
6. J.P. Morgan has a reputation for being one of the better managed and more _____ of the world's huge banks.
7. A law in Massachusetts bans the _____ of medical sharps (needles and lancets) in household trash.
8. After the general was _____ into the area where the King sat on his throne, he got down on his knee to show respect.
9. Her Mediterranean island home is known for the _____ of its residents, claiming to have 370 centenarians.
10. Edward Shils, professor of sociology, recalls a teacher he _____ at the University of Pennsylvania in his youth.

Unit 3

★ 本单元核心词汇 ★

coma	minor	identify	brutal	innocent
launch	lethal	diverse	portion	comical
symptom	inverse	depiction	uncover	profession
ensure	controversy	accessible	comedy	sour

★ 本单元拓展词汇 ★

vocation	minority	trivial	ascertain	slice
barbarian	guilty	legislation	comic	mortal
unveil	ruthless	comma	distinguish	swirl
inaugurate	reverse	pungent	influenza	rumor
animation	overdose	autism	ballistic	landslip
suspend	dessert	voluntarily	fatal	stab
ethnically	caption			

21. The movie has been at the center of much ***controversy*** since its release, especially over its ***depiction*** of torture.

单词	释义
controversy	*n.* Controversy is a lot of discussion and argument about something, often involving strong feelings of anger or disapproval. 争论；论战

双语例句

In recent years, controversy has swirled around energy drinks, which also contain caffeine.（近年来，关于功能饮料有诸多争议，因为它们也含有咖啡因。）

Proposals to legalize or expand commercial gambling are never without controversy.（让赌博合法化或将其放开的提议一直饱受争议。）

联想记忆

controversial *adj.* 有争议的；有争论的

单词	释义
depiction	*n.* A depiction of something is a written description of it. 描述；描绘

双语例句

The agency reported that the images included "highly aggressive" depictions of very young children.（据该机构报道，这些图片包含对低幼儿童"极具攻击性"的描述。）

For years, public health groups have encouraged the movie industry to voluntarily reduce depictions of smoking.（多年来，公共卫生组织一直鼓励电影业主动减少对吸烟的描述。）

联想记忆

depict *v.* 描述；描绘
caption *n.*（图片的）说明文字 *v.* 加文字说明

22. One of the Founding Fathers and a scientist by ***profession***, Franklin set up the club to allow people from ***diverse*** backgrounds to share knowledge and propose ideas.

单词	释义
profession	*n.* A profession is a type of job that requires advanced education or training. 职业
	n. Profession is a declaration of belief or religion. 声明；宣布

双语例句

Most nurses are women, but in the higher ranks of the medical profession women are in the minority.（大多数护士是女性，但在医疗行业的高层中女性占少数。）

In the professions, he claimed that he had faced unfair treatment in the workplace.（在声明中，他声称自己在工作中受到了不公正的待遇。）

联想记忆

expertise *n.* 专业知识；专长
vocation *n.* 职业；使命

单词	释义
diverse	*adj.* Diverse people or things are very different from each other. 不同的；各种各样的

双语例句

Americans have diverse views on gun control, depending on where they grew up.（美国人对枪支管控意见不一，这取决于他们是在哪儿长大的。）

This region is the most ethnically diverse community in Cambodia — up to nine different ethnic groups are present.（这里是柬埔寨民族最多样化的地区，目前有九个不同的民族聚居在这里。）

联想记忆

diversity *n.* 多样性；差异
diversify *v.* 使多样化

23. All countries considered the exercise to be successful although some ***minor*** problems have been ***identified.***

单词	释义
minor	*adj.* You use minor when describing something that is less important, serious, or significant than other things in a group or situation. 次要的
	adj. A minor illness or operation is not likely to be dangerous to someone's life or health. 不严重的

双语例句

A British teenager playing a minor role in the film *Harry Potter* was stabbed to death in London on Saturday.（在电影《哈利·波特》中饰演配角的一位英国少年星期六在伦敦被刺身亡。）

Thanks to its elevated location above the valley, the hotel itself suffered relatively minor damage.（由于其位置高于山谷，酒店本身受到的损害相对较小。）

联想记忆

minority *n.* 少数 *adj.* 少数的
trivial *adj.* 琐碎的；不重要的

单词	释义
identify	*v.* If you can identify someone or something, you are able to recognize them or distinguish them from others. 识别，发现；确认

双语例句

There are a number of distinguishing characteristics by which you can identify a Hollywood epic.（通过诸多与众不同的特点，你可以识别出好莱坞的史诗影片。）

In May 2012, researchers identified some of the oldest-known musical instruments in the world.（2012年5月，研究人员发现了一些世界上最古老的乐器。）

联想记忆

identification *n.* 鉴定，识别；身份证明
identity *n.* 身份；同一性
ascertain *v.* 查明；确定

24. Some ***portions*** of the path are wheelchair-***accessible***, while others are intended for practiced long-distance hikers.

单词	释义
portion	*n.* A portion of something is a part of it. 部分
	n. A portion is the amount of food that is given to one person at a meal.（食物的）一份

双语例句

This portion of the park includes a water play area, rollercoaster and giftshop.（公园的这一部分包括水上游乐区、过山车和一家礼品店。）

For people who are on diet, desserts can be substituted by a portion of fresh fruit.（对于正在节食的人来说，甜点可以用一份新鲜水果代替。）

联想记忆

potion *n.* 药剂；一剂
slice *n.* 部分；（食物）薄片，（蛋糕）小块 *v.* 切成薄片

单词	释义
accessible	*adj.* If a place or building is accessible to people, it is easy for them to reach it or get into it. If an object is accessible, it is easy to obtain or use. 易于接近的；易使用的

双语例句

Most sites and programs in the park are accessible to persons with disabilities. （公园内的大多数场地和设施都可供残障人士使用。）

This book should be readily accessible to anyone with even a basic understanding of world history. （这本书对于了解一点世界历史的人都很容易理解。）

联想记忆

access *n.* 进入；通路；使用权 *v.* 接近；使用
accessibility *n.* 易接近；可以得到

25. There is no such thing as war without the ***brutal***, violent death of ***innocents***, including children.

单词	释义
brutal	*adj.* A brutal act or person is cruel and violent. 残暴的，野蛮的

双语例句

Unfortunately this case is neither isolated, nor the most brutal the nation has seen. （不幸的是，这一案件既不是孤立的，也不是该国发生最残忍的事件。）

While rumors had circulated for years, few expected such brutal truth to come fully to light. （虽然已谣传多年，但很少有人会想到这么残酷的事居然是真的。）

联想记忆

barbarian *adj.* 野蛮的，未开化的 *n.* 野蛮人
ruthless *adj.* 无情的，冷酷的

单词	释义
innocent	*n.* An innocent is someone who is not guilty. 无辜者；天真的人
	adj. If someone is innocent, they did not commit a crime that they have been accused of. 无辜的
	adj. If someone is innocent, they have no experience or knowledge of the more complex or unpleasant aspects of life. 阅历浅的；天真的

双语例句

In 2004, Dominique Perben, then justice minister, had apologized to the first group of innocents.（2004年，时任司法部长多米尼克·佩尔本向第一批无辜者道了歉。）

The murder of 20 innocent children in Newtown, Connecticut horrifies all Americans.（发生在康涅狄格州纽镇针对20个无辜孩子的谋杀事件令所有美国人感到恐惧。）

There are smiles everywhere, especially the kids with their incredibly bright, innocent, hopeful eyes.（到处都洋溢着微笑，尤其是孩子们那异常明亮又天真、满怀希望的眼睛。）

联想记忆

innocence *n.* 无罪；天真无邪
guilty *adj.* 有罪的；内疚的

26. **Symptoms** of an overdose include rapid heartbeat, heart failure, shortness of breath, unconsciousness and **coma**.

单词	释义
symptom	*n.* A symptom of an illness is something wrong with your body or mind that is a sign of the illness. 症状
	n. A symptom of a bad situation is something that happens which is considered to be a sign of this situation. 征兆

双语例句

Even though the symptoms may disappear in a few days, medical treatment is always important.（即使症状在几天后可能会消失，治疗还是非常重要的。）

The City Council said the recent landslip was a "symptom of the prolonged wet weather".（市议会表示，近期的塌方是"天气长期潮湿的表现"。）

联想记忆

symptomatic *adj.* 有症状的；症候的
indication *n.* 表示，暗示；迹象

单词	释义
coma	*n.* Someone who is in a coma is in a state of deep unconsciousness, usually caused by serious illness or injury. 昏迷

双语例句

When Portillo arrived at the hospital, he slipped into a coma with swelling in his brain.（当波蒂略被送到医院时，他因脑部肿胀而陷入昏迷。）

The 84-year-old has been in a coma since 2006, when he suffered a massive stroke.（这位84岁的老人自2006年严重中风以来一直处于昏迷状态。）

联想记忆

comma *n.* 逗号

27. Multiple investigations have been *launched* by the Federal Trade Commission to *uncover* the source of the problem.

单词	释义
launch	*v.* To launch a large and important activity means to start it; to launch a new product means to make it available to the public. 发起；推出（新产品）
	v. To launch a rocket, missile, or satellite means to send it into space. 发射
	n. Launch is also a NOUN. 发射；发起；推出（新产品）

双语例句

Officially launched in 2007, the bike-sharing program today is nearing 50 million unique rides annually.（共享单车项目于2007年正式启动，如今每年骑行近5 000万人次。）

The UN suspended a food aid deal after the nation launched a rocket as part of a ballistic missile program.（该国发射了一枚火箭，这是弹道导弹计划的一部分，此后联合国便暂停了一项粮食援助协议。）

They use willpower and a supportive press to push through a project from launch to completion.（他们凭借意志力和支持性的压力推动项目从启动直到完成。）

联想记忆

inaugurate *v.* 开创；举行就职典礼

单词	释义
uncover	*v.* If you uncover something, especially something that has been kept secret, you discover or find out about it. 发现，揭示

双语例句

When the vehicle was searched, police uncovered a loaded revolver in the front passenger footwell.（在对车辆进行搜查时，警方在前排乘客的脚底处发现了一把

上膛的左轮手枪。）

The study aimed to uncover what factors during pregnancy may have an impact on the risk of autism in children.（这项研究旨在揭示母亲怀孕期间的哪些因素会影响孩子患上自闭症。）

联想记忆

uncovered *adj.* 无盖的；未保险的
unveil *v.* 公开；揭示

28. Scientists observed a strong *inverse* association between coffee consumption and risk of *lethal* prostate cancer.

单词	释义
inverse	*adj.* If there is an inverse relationship between two things, one of them becomes larger as the other becomes smaller. 相反的
	n. The inverse of something is its exact opposite. 颠倒；相反的事物

双语例句

There is often an inverse relationship between the power of the tool and how easy it is to use.（工具的功能越强大，操作起来往往越费事。）

The inverse is true in sub-Saharan Africa, where 75% saw climate change as a threat last year.（撒哈拉以南非洲的情况正好相反，去年75%的人认为气候变化是一种威胁。）

联想记忆

inversion *n.* 倒置；反向；倒转
reverse *v.* 逆转；颠倒；倒车 *adj.* 相反的 *n.* 相反；背面

单词	释义
lethal	*adj.* A substance that is lethal can kill people or animals. 致命的
	adj. If you describe something as lethal, you mean that it is capable of causing a lot of damage. 危害极大的

双语例句

Grimsson had AIDS and tuberculosis, an especially lethal combination that has killed millions across Africa.（格里姆森患有艾滋病和肺结核，这是一种特别致命的情况，在非洲各地已造成数百万人死亡。）

"This is definitely one of the most lethal influenza viruses we have seen so far," WHO flu expert said at a news conference.（世界卫生组织流感专家在新闻发布会

上表示:"这无疑是迄今为止我们见过危害最大的流感病毒之一。")

联想记忆

fatal *adj.* 致命的;灾难性的
mortal *adj.* 致命的

29. The goalkeeper was wearing rather large *comical* gloves to *ensure* that the ball does not go past him.

单词	释义
comical	*adj.* If you describe something as comical, you mean that it makes you laugh because it is funny or silly. 滑稽的

双语例句

He falls off his chair and stumbles around in a comical manner to amuse us all.(他从椅子上摔下来,跌跌撞撞地走来走去,滑稽可笑,逗得我们大家都很开心。)

When we look back at those events from the current perspective, it almost seems comical.(我们从现在的角度回顾这些事件时,感到似乎很滑稽。)

联想记忆

comic *adj.* 喜剧的;滑稽的 *n.* 连环漫画;喜剧演员

单词	释义
ensure	*v.* To ensure something, or to ensure that something happens, means to make certain that it happens. 确保

双语例句

These standards, when introduced into national legislation, will help ensure food security.(这些标准一旦纳入国家法规,将有助于确保食品安全。)

The ship is still undergoing renovations to ensure it offers an authentic 1930s experience.(这艘船仍在进行翻修,确保让人感受到20世纪30年代的真实体验。)

联想记忆

insure *v.* 确保,保证;给……保险
assure *v.* 保证;担保;使确信

30. It is an enjoyable *comedy* with action, suspense and a love story thrown in — even if a horribly Hollywood ending may leave a *sour* taste.

单词	释义
comedy	*n.* Comedy consists of types of entertainment, such as plays and films, or particular scenes in them, that are intended to make people laugh. 喜剧

双语例句

Eight adult comedies and six children's animation series will be put to the public vote.（8部成人喜剧和6部儿童动画片将接受公众投票。）

Concerts, theater, comedy, and other social activities are best enjoyed with company.（演奏会、电影、喜剧以及其他一些社交活动都适合和他人一起分享。）

联想记忆

comedian *n.* 喜剧演员
clown *n.* 小丑，滑稽的人

单词	释义
sour	*adj.* Something that is sour has a sharp, unpleasant taste like the taste of a lemon. 酸的，酸味的
	adj. Sour milk has an unpleasant taste because it is no longer fresh. 馊的
	v. If a friendship, situation, or attitude sours or if something sours it, it becomes less friendly, enjoyable, or hopeful. 使变糟，变糟

双语例句

In Northern Thai, pungent fish sauce and plenty of lime juice keep the dressing pleasantly sour and sharp.（在泰国北部，辛辣的鱼酱和大量的青柠汁使调料酸爽可口。）

The minivan that took the Smiths to Disneyland had 95,000 miles on it and smelled like sour milk.（把史密斯一家载到迪斯尼乐园的面包车已行驶9.5万英里，车里有股馊牛奶的味道。）

More recently, the souring economy has begun to slow growth and damp the commercial real-estate market.（最近，经济增长开始放缓，抑制了商业房地产市场。）

联想记忆

acid *n.* 酸；尖刻的言语 *adj.* 酸的；酸性的；刻薄的
acrid *adj.* （气味）辛辣的；刻薄的

单元练习 3

使用本单元核心词汇的适当形式填空，并将句子译为中文。

1. The instruments may be able to _____ what Mars was like when those minerals formed.
2. On Monday, an act of terror wounded dozens and killed three _____ people at the Boston Marathon.
3. Bolt said he was looking forward to seeing Kenya's _____ wildlife, but was scared of meeting lions.
4. Abortion remains a sensitive issue everywhere, and is significantly more _____ in Northern Ireland.
5. It's the responsibility of everyone working in the NHS to _____ that private information is protected.
6. There is an _____ correlation between the number of words you say and your success at sales or persuasion.
7. With the use of electronic instruments, enormous gains have taken place in _____ and tracking storms.
8. Easily _____ by subway, the 7,500-seat park overlooks the Atlantic Ocean and Coney Island amusement park.
9. About 43 percent of the volunteers had infection plus cold _____, such as a stuffy nose, cough, and sore throat.
10. People then were eager to be part of Zuckerberg's network, which _____ at first only for Harvard students.

Unit 4

★ 本单元核心词汇 ★

grim	nourish	barrier	urgent	resort
abundant	induce	displace	recession	complex
contract	entitle	spouse	scarce	competent
adjacent	devastating	dynamic	ruin	tremor

★ 本单元拓展词汇 ★

herd	obstacle	assort	recede	pressing
exploit	vibrant	wreck	forbidding	hurdle
proximity	deduce	shiver	clearance	infectious
spreadsheet	refugee	intractable	primary	mammal
ghetto	revision	skyscraper	partition	rail
consultation	evolutionary	blockade		

31. Although land can be relatively ***abundant***, suburbs present other social and economic ***barriers*** that limit competition.

单词	释义
abundant	*adj.* Something that is abundant is present in large quantities. 丰富的

双语例句

Hendrick had abundant stocks of tinned food, fuel, and water with which to survive the winter.（亨德里克储备了充足的罐头食品、燃料和水，足以过冬。）

Despite its abundant resources there are 48 states with lower unemployment rates than California.（尽管加利福尼亚资源丰富，但是全美却有48个州的失业率都比它的低。）

联想记忆

abound *v.* 大量存在；盛产
abundance *n.* 充裕；丰富

单词	释义
barrier	*n.* A barrier is something such as a rule, law, or policy that makes it difficult or impossible for something to happen or be achieved. 障碍；隔阂
	n. A barrier is something such as a fence or wall that is put in place to prevent people from moving easily from one area to another. 栅栏；围墙

双语例句

Donation is generally safe and painless, and the chief barriers are psychological and cultural.（献血通常安全无痛，其主要障碍是心理和文化方面的。）

Last year a consultation showed residents' main concerns were noise and the appearance of the barrier.（去年的一次商讨表明，居民主要担心的是噪音和栅栏的外观。）

联想记忆

blockade *n.* 障碍物；屏障 *v.* 封锁；包围
obstacle *n.* 障碍；阻碍
hurdle *n.* 障碍；跨栏 *v.* 跨越（障碍物）；克服（困难）

32. The British economy ***contracted*** late last year, raising doubts about its recovery from the ***recession***.

单词	释义
contract	*v.* When something contracts or when something contracts it, it becomes smaller or shorter. 缩小，萎缩
	v. If you contract a serious illness, you become ill with it. 感染
	n. A contract is a legal agreement, usually between two companies or between an employer and employee, which involves doing work for a stated sum of money. 合同

双语例句

The decade saw the Ford plant contract and ultimately the company announced it was closing down.（十年间，福特汽车的这家工厂不断萎缩，最终公司宣布将其关闭。）

He is believed to have contracted the infectious virus while working in Sierra Leone in Africa.（人们认为，他是在非洲塞拉利昂工作时感染了这种传染性病毒。）

His five-year contract with the Rockets, valued at $70 million, will come to an end this summer.（他与火箭队五年7 000万美元的合同今年夏天将到期。）

联想记忆

contractor *n.* 承包商；立契约者
contraction *n.* 收缩，紧缩；（单词的）缩写形式

单词	释义
recession	*n.* A recession is a period when the economy of a country is doing badly.（经济）衰退，萧条

双语例句

The manufacturing figures increased the chances of the UK falling back into recession.（制造业数据增加了英国再度陷入衰退的可能性。）

The G20 have come up with a package of plans that add up to a trillion dollars to tackle the recession.（20国集团已经提出总计达万亿美元的一揽子计划，以应对经济衰退。）

联想记忆

recede *v.* 后退；减弱；撤回
recess *v.* 休息；休假 *n.* 休息；休会

33. Producing enough food to ***nourish*** populations of the future is among the most ***urgent*** problems facing mankind today.

单词	释义
nourish	*v.* To nourish a person, animal, or plant means to provide them with the food that is necessary for life, growth, and good health. 提供营养，滋养

双语例句

South American women use the fruit to nourish their skin and hair.（南美洲的妇女都用这种水果来滋养她们的皮肤和头发。）

The agricultural productivity has been falling and 30% of the population is permanently under-nourished.（农业生产力一直在下降，30%的人口长期营养不良。）

联想记忆

nourishment *n.* 营养品，滋养品

单词	释义
urgent	*adj.* If something is urgent, it needs to be dealt with as soon as possible. 紧急的，迫切的

双语例句

The coming food crisis is as intractable as global warming, and no less urgent.（未来的粮食危机和全球变暖一样棘手，也同样紧迫。）

There is an urgent need for a massive international effort to train more health care workers.（迫切需要国际上做出巨大努力，培养更多的医护人员。）

联想记忆

urgency *n.* 紧急；紧急的事
pressing *adj.* 紧迫的，迫切的

34. The country also faces the ***grim*** challenge of ***scarce*** resources and deteriorating environment.

单词	释义
grim	*adj.* A situation or piece of information that is grim is unpleasant, depressing, and difficult to accept. 严酷的；令人沮丧的
	adj. A place that is grim is unattractive and depressing in appearance. 阴沉的

双语例句

Accurate information about the oil spill is hard to come by, but what we know of the picture is pretty grim.（原油泄漏的准确信息很难获取，但我们了解到的情况是相当严峻的。）

The road to the school cuts across dusty fields and through grim industrial zones in southeast Phoenix.（去这所学校的路上要穿过尘土飞扬的田地，还要通过凤凰城东南部破旧的工业园区。）

联想记忆

forbidding *adj.* 冷峻的；令人生畏的

单词	释义
scarce	*adj.* If something is scarce, there is not enough of it. 缺乏的，稀少的

双语例句

Green energy may have its day, but only when coal, oil and gas become truly scarce.（只有煤炭、石油和天然气真正短缺的时候，绿色能源也许才会真正受欢迎。）

The refugees were herded into a ghetto in the city's northeast, where food was scarce and disease rampant.（难民被赶到城市东北部的一个贫民窟，那里食物匮乏，疾病肆虐。）

联想记忆

scarcity *n.* 不足，缺乏
scant *adj.* 少量的，不足的
devoid *adj.* 缺乏的；完全没有

35. In 2005, the southern African nation suffered ***devastating*** floods that killed at least 700 people and ***displaced*** millions.

单词	释义
devastating	*adj.* If you describe something as devastating, you are emphasizing that it is very harmful or damaging. 毁灭性的

双语例句

Due to the devastating floods, a record number of people have been thrown out of their homes.（由于洪水肆虐，空前数量的人被迫离开他们的家园。）

Doctors have long railed against black carbon for its devastating health effects in poor countries.（长期以来，医生们一直指责烟尘对贫困国家人们的健康造成了巨大影响。）

联想记忆

devastate *v.* 摧毁，毁坏
devastation *n.* 毁坏

单词	释义
displace	*v.* If a person or group of people is displaced, they are forced to move away from the area where they live. 使背井离乡
	v. If one thing displaces another, it forces the other thing out of its place, position, or role, and then occupies that place, position, or role itself. 取代

双语例句

In addition to shortages of water and medical care, the displaced also complain there is no freedom of movement.（除了缺乏水和医疗服务外，流离失所的人们还抱怨说，这里不允许他们自由活动。）

This year, India will displace the United States as the world's third largest beef exporter, behind Brazil and Australia.（今年，印度将取代美国成为世界第三大牛肉出口国，仅次于巴西和澳大利亚。）

联想记忆

displacement *n.* 取代；位移；（船的）排水量

36. She emphasized that Pakistan certainly need *competent* teachers, particularly *dynamic* teachers with global ideas.

单词	释义
competent	*adj.* Someone who is competent is efficient and effective. 有能力的

双语例句

Surveys show that men are also perceived as more competent than women in STEM fields.（调查显示，在工程技术领域，男性也被认为比女性更擅长。）

Like any CEO, a president must select competent people to place in positions of power.（就像首席执行官一样，总统必须选择有能力的人来担任各部门要职。）

联想记忆

competence *n.* 能力；权限

单词	释义
dynamic	*adj.* If you describe something as dynamic, you approve of it because it is very active and energetic. 有活力的
	adj. A dynamic process is one that constantly changes. 动态的
	n. The dynamic of a system or process is the force that causes it to change or progress. 动力，活力

双语例句

Chicago is a dynamic city with a strong cultural identity and a history of innovation.（芝加哥是一个充满活力的城市，有着浓郁的文化特色和创新历史。）

Scientists are now beginning to understand the dynamic evolutionary history of these Ice Age mammals.（科学家们现在开始了解这些冰河时期哺乳动物的动态进化史。）

Boutin has been involved in a number of projects to improve the cultural dynamic of the city.（布廷参与了多个项目来提升城市的文化活力。）

联想记忆

vibrant *adj.* 充满活力的；鲜亮的

37. As in most states, New Jersey courts ***entitle*** the surviving ***spouse*** to one-third of an estate, regardless of the will.

单词	释义
entitle	*v.* If you are entitled to something, you have the right to have it or do it. 使有权
	v. If the title of something such as a book, film, or painting is, for example, "Sunrise", you can say that it is entitled "Sunrise". 命名

双语例句

Everyone in Germany is entitled to and covered by health insurance, whether unemployed or retired.（在德国，每个人都可以享受健康保险，无论失业还是退休。）

Entitled *Fendi Baguette*, the book, which is published by Rizzoli, will hit bookstores on June 1.（这本名为《芬迪法棍》的书由里佐利出版社出版，将于6月1日在书店上架。）

联想记忆

entitlement *n.* 权利；津贴

单词	释义
spouse	*n.* Someone's spouse is the person they are married to. 配偶

双语例句

People often meet their spouses and their friends at school, through work or at bars.（人们通常在学校、单位或酒吧结识配偶和朋友。）

It is often helpful to have your spouse in the room when major news is expected.

（在等待重要消息时，另一半在场往往是很有好处的。）

联想记忆

spousal *adj.* 结婚的 *n.* 婚礼；结婚仪式
partner *n.* 同伴；合伙人；配偶

38. Record low snowfalls last winter ***ruined*** vacations and threatened to put some ***resorts*** out of business.

单词	释义
ruin	*v.* To ruin something means to severely harm, damage, or spoil it. 毁坏
	n. Ruin is also a NOUN. 毁坏；残存部分，废墟

双语例句

He refused to spend money repairing the roof, and now the rain has ruined half his furniture.（他不肯花钱维修屋顶，现在雨水毁坏了他的一半家具。）

Homes were in ruins after a tornado blew through Pratt City, a neighborhood in Birmingham, Alabama.（龙卷风袭击了位于阿拉巴马州伯明翰附近的普拉特城，房屋成了一片废墟。）

联想记忆

wreck *v.* 破坏；（船舶）失事 *n.* 沉船；残骸
spoil *v.* 破坏；溺爱；（食物）变质

单词	释义
resort	*n.* A resort is a place where a lot of people spend their holiday. 度假胜地
	v. If you resort to a course of action, you adopt it because you cannot see any other way of achieving what you want. 求助，诉诸

双语例句

A popular seaside resort in Maryland is urging tourists to book vacations now before the ocean disappears altogether.（位于马里兰州的一个著名海滨度假地呼吁人们在海洋消失前赶快去那里度假。）

Many people when traveling resort to emails to friends or spreadsheets to organize their trip plans.（在旅行时，许多人通过电子邮件和朋友联系，并使用电子表格来安排旅行计划。）

联想记忆

assort *v.* 分类；协调

39. Disney wanted a commercial *complex* of theaters, galleries, shopping centers and restaurants built *adjacent* to the school.

单词	释义
complex	*n.* A complex is a group or system of different things that are linked in a close or complicated way. 综合体；建筑群
	adj. Something that is complex has many different parts, and is therefore often difficult to understand. 复杂的

双语例句

Traders at Kansas City Wholesale Markets expressed fear over plans to close the complex.（堪萨斯城批发市场的商贩们对关闭该综合市场的计划表示担忧。）

She left the town with millions of dollars in debt from the building of a new sports complex.（因为修建一个新的体育综合设施，她离开小镇时欠下了数百万美元债务。）

The model needs revision, but this is a complex problem with many contributing factors.（该模式需要改变，但这是一个复杂的问题，涉及许多因素。）

联想记忆

complexity *n.* 复杂；复杂性
complexion *n.* 面色，面容
complication *n.* 复杂；并发症

单词	释义
adjacent	*adj.* If one thing is adjacent to another, the two things are next to each other. 相邻的，邻近的

双语例句

This explains why they keep building skyscrapers even though the adjacent ones are still vacant.（这就解释了为什么邻近的摩天大楼空置着，而他们却继续建造摩天大楼。）

Attached to the bedroom was a small washroom, and adjacent to the living room was a kitchen.（紧靠卧室是一个小的盥洗室，客厅旁边是厨房。）

联想记忆

proximity *n.* 接近，靠近

40. Some worry that the project might *induce* earthquakes, especially after it was linked to 50 tiny *tremors* in northern England last year.

Unit 4

单词	释义
induce	*v.* To induce a state or condition means to cause it. 引起
	v. If you induce someone to do something, you persuade or influence them to do it. 引诱；劝说

双语例句

Political pressures will induce politicians to open Medicaid to more uninsured people.（政治压力将促使政治家们向更多没有医疗保险的人开放医疗补助计划。）

The government is keen to induce foreign companies to take part in exploiting the region's oil reserves.（政府热衷于吸引外国公司参与开发该地区的石油储备。）

联想记忆

deduce *v.* 推断，演绎

单词	释义
tremor	*n.* A tremor is a small earthquake. 小地震
	n. A tremor is a shaking of your body or voice that you can't control. 颤抖
	n. If an event causes a tremor in a group or organization, it threatens to make the group or organization less strong or stable. 波动

双语例句

The tremor was felt as far away as Milan and Florence, Italian media say.（意大利媒体称，远在米兰和佛罗伦萨都有震感。）

He had a bad tremor, could not hold a cup of coffee and occasionally tripped.（他浑身颤抖得厉害，连一杯咖啡都拿不住，偶尔还会绊倒。）

The credit system in Europe may grind to a halt, which would send tremors throughout the world's financial system.（欧洲的信贷体系可能会陷入停滞，这将给全球金融体系带来震荡。）

联想记忆

tremble *v.* 发抖；用颤抖的声音说出
shiver *v.* （因寒冷或害怕）颤抖；打碎

单元练习 4

使用本单元核心词汇的适当形式填空，并将句子译为中文。

1. Trails link the Cameron Nature Preserve to the _____ Malibu Creek State Park.
2. Some patients were leaving hospital even more poorly _____ than they arrived.
3. Though Danish-born, he had never applied for the Danish citizenship to which he was _____.
4. The _____ natural resources in the country are what makes it a good place to set up a business.
5. Deep _____ usually generate a vicious circle between job losses and reduced economic activity.
6. The seaside _____ also became a cool summertime retreat for wealthy planters from the American South.
7. Boatloads of desperate Somalis still arriving illegally in Europe indicates the _____ of decent jobs.
8. General Motors has an extremely _____ management, supervised closely by a board of directors.
9. When Sandy hit the U.S. in October the storm caused floods which _____ thousands of homes in New Jersey.
10. An estimated 22 million people in America have _____ the virus, resulting in about 90,000 hospitalizations through Sept. 15.

Unit 5

★ 本单元核心词汇 ★

aggravate	intrusive	relocate	restriction	unaware
decline	indifferent	capture	reminder	savor
isolate	hinder	excessive	scornful	confront
shabby	premium	insurance	accusation	violate

★ 本单元拓展词汇 ★

disdain	contemptuous	restraint	heedless	vie
nonchalant	incline	notify	appeal	souvenir
solitude	quarantine	hamper	ailment	undue
worsen	cosmetic	documentation	ragged	dilapidated
infringe	sarcastic	sovereignty	intensify	attorney
probe	recline	aviation	passionate	digit
collapse	trafficking	bronchitis	impede	defy

41. The Afghan leaders are **scornful** of this kind of **intrusive** foreign help, and the large peace-keeping force that would need to go with it.

单词	释义
scornful	*adj.* If you are scornful of someone or something, you show contempt for them. 轻蔑的，嘲笑的

双语例句

The club appealed, claiming that Beckham's behavior had been neither "scornful nor sarcastic". （俱乐部提出上诉，声称贝克汉姆的行为既不是"蔑视也不是讽刺"。）

Some of the commentary on the presidential debate judged that Joe was too forceful, too scornful. （一些关于总统辩论的评论认为，乔过于强硬和轻蔑。）

联想记忆

scorn *v.* 轻蔑，鄙视 *n.* 蔑视
disdain *v.* 鄙视，不屑 *n.* 鄙视，蔑视
contemptuous *adj.* 轻蔑的，鄙视的

单词	释义
intrusive	*adj.* Something that is intrusive disturbs your mood or your life in a way you do not like. 侵入的；打扰的

双语例句

The small business owners don't want to be burdened by high taxes or intrusive regulations. （小企业主们不希望被高赋税或干扰性的监管所拖累。）

Mr. Hilton's classmates were concerned that the videos might cross the line from familiar to intrusive. （希尔顿的同学担心，这些视频可能会越过友好的界限，变成冒犯。）

联想记忆

intrude *v.* 闯入；侵入；打扰
intrusion *n.* 侵扰；闯入

42. The Arizona-based chemical factory planned to **relocate** to nearby Holbrook because of new **restrictions**.

单词	释义
relocate	*v.* If people or businesses relocate or if someone relocates them, they move to a different place. 迁移；重新安置

双语例句

The families affected have been relocated into social housing or are staying with relatives.(受灾的家庭已经搬迁到社会福利房,或住在亲戚家。)

When the others dropped out of Harvard to relocate to Seattle, Carol stayed behind.(当别人从哈佛大学辍学转到西雅图时,卡罗尔留下来了。)

联想记忆

relocation *n.* 重新安置

单词	释义
restriction	*n.* A restriction is an official rule that limits what you can do or that limits the amount or size of something. 限制,约束

双语例句

The majority were in favor of tighter restrictions on the advertising of cosmetic surgery.(大多数人赞成严格限制整容手术广告。)

The Federal Aviation Administration placed a flight restriction over the site of the explosion.(美国联邦航空管理局对爆炸地点实行了飞行管制。)

联想记忆

restrict *v.* 限制;约束;限定
restraint *n.* 克制;限制
limitation *n.* 限制;局限性

43. For the most part, the Malians interviewed were either ***unaware*** of or ***indifferent*** to the summit meeting in their capital.

单词	释义
unaware	*adj.* If you are unaware of something, you do not know about it. 不知道的;未察觉到的

双语例句

The spokesman for the Los Angeles city attorney's office said he was unaware of any probe.(洛杉矶市检察官办公室发言人表示,他对调查并不知情。)

Many people were unaware their smartphone apps would download data without notifying them.(许多人都不知道,智能手机应用程序会不通知他们就下载数据。)

联想记忆

heedless *adj.* 不注意的，不小心的

单词	释义
indifferent	*adj.* If you accuse someone of being indifferent to something, you mean that they have a complete lack of interest in it. 漠不关心的
	adj. If you describe something or someone as indifferent, you mean that their standard or quality is not very good, and often quite bad. 平庸的

双语例句

Few Mexicans are indifferent to the man who's vying to be Mexico's first leftist president.（很少有墨西哥人不关注这个想要成为墨西哥第一位左派总统的人。）

Despite an indifferent performance by us, he stood out as a very good player.（尽管我们的表现很平庸，但他仍然是一位非常出色的球员。）

联想记忆

nonchalant *adj.* 若无其事的，漠不关心的

44. The ***decline*** in moral standards — which has long concerned social analysts — has at last ***captured*** the attention of average Americans.

单词	释义
decline	*n.* If something experiences a decline, it becomes less in quantity, importance, or strength. Decline is also a VERB. 下降
	v. If you decline something or decline to do something, you politely refuse to accept it or do it. 谢绝

双语例句

Spotted owls are on the decline despite two decades of work to bring them back.（尽管在过去的20年人们为保护斑点猫头鹰做了很多工作，但它们的数量仍然在下降。）

Oil prices will decline until well into next year before recovering in the second half of 2021.（油价将在明年持续下跌，直到2021年下半年才会复苏。）

Mr. Davis declined to comment on the case, citing the police investigation that is under way.（戴维斯拒绝对此案发表评论，称警方调查正在进行中。）

联想记忆

incline *v.* 倾斜；倾向 *n.* 倾斜；斜面
recline *v.* 斜倚；使躺下

单词	释义
capture	*v.* If something captures your attention or imagination, you begin to be interested or excited by it. 吸引
	v. If you capture someone or something, you catch them. 捕获，俘虏
	v. If an event is captured in a photograph, it is photographed. 拍摄

双语例句

Stubbs was able to talk "passionately and openly", in a way that captured her attention.（斯塔布斯"热情奔放"的演讲吸引了她的注意力。）

The armed pirates forced the couple to sail toward Somalia after their boat was captured.（这对夫妇的船被捕获后，武装海盗胁迫他们驶向索马里。）

The photographer captured an extraordinary battle among zebras in Etosha National Park, Namibia.（摄影师在纳米比亚埃托沙国家公园拍摄到了非同寻常的斑马打斗画面。）

联想记忆

appeal *v.* 有吸引力；呼吁；申诉 *n.* 吸引力；呼吁

45. Most three-year degree programs have failed — a ***reminder*** that students still regard college as an experience to be ***savored***.

单词	释义
reminder	*n.* Something that serves as a reminder makes you think about another thing. 提醒；暗示

双语例句

Old instructional and safety posters still hang on the walls, a reminder that this was once a school.（旧的教学海报和安全告示仍然挂在墙上，提醒着人们这里曾经是一所学校。）

Such studies are a reminder that John Donne was right: No man is an island.（这些研究提醒人们，约翰·多恩是对的：没有人是一座孤岛。）

联想记忆

cue *n.* 暗示，提示 *v.* 暗示
hint *n.* 提示；迹象 *v.* 示意

单词	释义
savor	*v.* If you savor an experience, you enjoy it as much as you can. 尽情享受
	v. If you savor food or drink, you eat or drink it slowly in order to taste its full flavor. 品尝

双语例句

The Knicks will have to savor this victory in Minnesota a little longer than they initially expected.（尼克斯队将会在明尼苏达州庆祝这场胜利，庆祝时间比他们最初预期的长一些。）

We stopped at a pub and savored smoked Connemara salmon, brown bread, and fish chowder.（我们在一个酒吧停了下来，品尝了康尼马拉熏鲑鱼、黑面包和鱼片浓汤。）

联想记忆

savory *adj.* 可口的，风味极佳的 *n.* 开胃菜

46. Studies of children who are *isolated* from others reveal that their mental and psychological development is severely *hindered* by lack of language.

单词	释义
isolate	*v.* To isolate a person or organization means to cause them to lose their friends or supporters. 孤立；隔绝
	v. To isolate a sick person or animal means to keep them apart from other people or animals, so that their illness does not spread. 隔离

双语例句

Some children with a conduct disorder are socially isolated from their peer group.（有行为障碍的孩子在社会上会被同龄人孤立。）

The CDC finds it almost impossible to monitor, let alone isolate, so many sources of infection.（美国疾病控制中心发现监测如此多的感染源几乎不可能，更不用说单独隔离了。）

联想记忆

isolation *n.* 隔离；孤立
quarantine *n.* 隔离 *v.* 对……进行隔离
solitude *n.* 孤独；独处

单词	释义
hinder	*v.* If something hinders you, it makes it more difficult for you to do something or make progress. 阻碍，妨碍

双语例句

Further investigation was hindered by the loss of all documentation on the case.（由于有关此案的卷宗全部丢失，进一步的调查受到了阻碍。）

To make experiment easier, researchers attached a weight to the leg of the animal to hinder its movement.（为了让实验更顺利，研究人员将重物系在动物的腿上，避免其乱动。）

联想记忆

hamper *v.* 阻碍，妨碍
impede *v.* 阻碍，妨碍

47. The *excessive* heat continued to *aggravate* drought conditions in the southern part of the country.

单词	释义
excessive	*adj.* If the amount or level of something is excessive, it is more or higher than is necessary or reasonable. 过多的，过度的

双语例句

Littering and excessive use of plastic bags is one of the most visible environmental problems.（乱扔垃圾和过度使用塑料袋是最明显的环境问题。）

Unlike excessive drinking, eating junk food does not directly damage the well-being of people.（和酗酒不同，吃垃圾食品并不会立刻损害人们的健康。）

联想记忆

excess *n.* 超额，过量 *adj.* 过量的，额外的
undue *adj.* 不适当的；过度的；未到期的

单词	释义
aggravate	*v.* If someone or something aggravates a situation, they make it worse. 使恶化

双语例句

The collapse of Zimbabwe's agriculture has aggravated food shortages in neighboring countries.（津巴布韦农业的崩溃加剧了邻国的粮食短缺问题。）

Asthma, bronchitis and other lung ailments can be aggravated by exposure to second hand smoke.（哮喘、支气管炎和其他肺病可能会由于接触到二手烟而加重。）

联想记忆

aggravation *n.* 加剧，加重；恶化
worsen *v.* 恶化
intensify *v.* 加剧；增强

48. When *confronted* with the reality of a *shabby* England unlike the England of her dreams, she is utterly horrified.

单词	释义
confront	*v.* If you are confronted with a problem, task, or difficulty, you have to deal with it. 面临（问题、任务、困难等）
	v. If you confront a difficult situation or issue, you accept the fact that it exists and try to deal with it. 正视，面对；对峙

双语例句

Young people on campus are spending beyond their means, a problem now confronting the nation as a whole.（校园里的年轻人花钱大手大脚，这是整个国家都面临的问题。）

Taking daily steps to confront fears is one way to practice and develop confidence.（每天采取措施正视恐惧是锻炼和提升自信的一种方式。）

联想记忆

confrontation *n.* 对抗，对峙；面对
defy *v.* 违抗，不服从；挑战

单词	释义
shabby	*adj.* Shabby things or places look old and in bad condition. 破旧的，破烂的

双语例句

The general divided his time between his shabby offices and his home in Hampstead.（将军的时间一部分在他那破旧的办公室里度过，另一部分在汉普斯特德的家里度过。）

The first day I made it as far as Flagstaff, Arizona, where I found a shabby hotel.（第一天我到了很远的亚利桑那州弗拉格斯塔夫，找了一家破旧的旅馆。）

联想记忆

ragged *adj.* （衣服）破旧的；高低不平的
dilapidated *adj.* 破旧的，坍塌的
wornout *adj.* 穿旧的，磨损的

49. Sadly, many people pay far more money in *premiums* than is necessary because they don't know the secrets to getting cheap auto *insurance*.

单词	释义
premium	*n.* A premium is a sum of money that you pay regularly to an insurance company for an insurance policy. 保险费
	adj. Premium products are of a higher than usual quality and are often expensive. 高端的

双语例句

The Colorado mechanic feared that he and his wife won't be able to afford the monthly health insurance premium.（这位科罗拉多州的修理工担心，他和妻子无法支付每月的医疗保险费。）

The company charges a fee for premium services such as analysis of heart-rate data.（该公司对心率数据分析等高端服务收取一定的费用。）

联想记忆

bonus *n.* 奖金，津贴
dividend *n.* 股息，红利；被除数

单词	释义
insurance	*n.* Insurance is an arrangement in which you pay money to a company, and they pay you if something unpleasant happens to you, for example, if your property is stolen or damaged, or if you get a serious illness. 保险；保险业

双语例句

Since the legislation was introduced in 2015, health insurance costs have continued to rise by double digits.（自2015年颁布这项法律后，健康保险费用以两位数的速度持续增长。）

The couple had insurance, but their medical bills still landed them tens of thousands of dollars worth of debt.（这对夫妇都有保险，但医疗费仍然使他们背负数万美元的债务。）

联想记忆

insure *v.* 确保，保证；投保
insured *n.* 被保险人　*adj.* 已投保的
insurer *n.* 保险公司；承保人

50. He was removed from office amid ***accusations*** that he ***violated*** the constitution on eight accounts.

单词	释义
accusation	*n.* An accusation is a statement or claim that a particular person has committed a crime, although this has not yet been proved. 指控

双语例句

The exact details of the accusations against the CFO have not been made public.（针对首席财务官指控的具体细节尚未公布。）

During his campaign, Mr. Cartes had to confront accusations of fraud and links with drug trafficking.（在竞选期间，卡特斯不得不面对欺诈和参与毒品交易的指控。）

联想记忆

accuse *v.* 指责；控告
charge *v.* 指控；充电；收费 *n.* 电量；费用
sue *v.* 起诉，控告

单词	释义
violate	*v.* If someone violates an agreement, law, or promise, they break it. If a person violates someone's privacy or peace, they disturb it. 违反；侵犯

双语例句

Most disturbing is that the new Delaware bill would require physicians to violate medical ethics.（最令人感到不安的是，特拉华州的新法案会让医生违反医德。）

The ministry claimed that such attacks violate Pakistan's sovereignty and should be stopped immediately.（国防部称，袭击事件侵犯了巴基斯坦的主权，应立即停止。）

联想记忆

violation *n.* 违反；侵权行为
infringe *v.* 违反；侵犯

单元练习 5

使用本单元核心词汇的适当形式填空，并将句子译为中文。

1. James was astonished by the sudden _____ of a loud noise and quickly stood up.
2. When Mrs. Black introduced me to her husband, he gave me a rather _____ hand to shake.
3. Native tribes will not have to _____, but could face a change of lifestyle once water levels drop.
4. There's growing evidence that social _____ is connected with an increased risk of physical ill health.
5. Teachers have enjoyed a rise in their salaries, with the result that the practice of private tutoring is on the _____.
6. Like all branches of American industry, insurers are being _____ with an increasing number of lawsuits.
7. The museum is a _____ of the island's rich maritime history, housing quite a few 20th century lifeboats.
8. The government's failure to provide textbooks to state school pupils _____ their constitutional right to an education.
9. California's problems will be _____, the report said, by extreme drought conditions in the Pacific Northwest.
10. Adults around New Zealand submitted 350 photographs that _____ different elements of the country's biodiversity.

Unit 6

★ 本单元核心词汇 ★

syllabus	respond	permanent	dispute	halt
stuffy	breeze	compulsory	diagnosis	tackle
deteriorate	transfer	maiden	altitude	deficit
autonomous	accent	descent	elaborate	confirm

★ 本单元拓展词汇 ★

gust	venue	perpetual	destination	jury
degrade	straddle	compatible	longitude	defect
aptitude	ventilate	verify	intricate	ascent
sophisticated	clash	sway	obligatory	assess
tuition	transport	rover	latitude	waltz
comply	therapy	scream	curriculum	scar
grove	clarify	resolution		

51. As Derek quickly entered my room, I felt the cool *breeze* enter behind him, bringing with it welcome fresh air into my *stuffy* room.

单词	释义
breeze	*n.* A breeze is a gentle wind. 微风
	v. If you breeze into a place or a position, you enter it in a very casual or relaxed manner. 轻而易举

双语例句

Bamboo groves sway in the breeze, and persimmons hang bright orange on the trees.（竹林在微风中摇曳，树上挂着鲜艳的橙色柿子。）

Murray breezed through Iowa State University's electrical engineering program in six semesters.（墨里用六个学期轻松地完成了爱荷华州立大学电子工程专业的学习。）

联想记忆

gust *n.* 阵风，一阵狂风

单词	释义
stuffy	*adj.* If it is stuffy in a place, it is unpleasantly warm and there is not enough fresh air. 不通风的，闷热的

双语例句

It was hot and stuffy in the classroom even though two of the windows at the back had been opened.（尽管后面的两个窗户都已打开，但教室里还是很闷热。）

The stuffy hall of a private golf club in Smithville, Mo. is hardly a venue for creative ideas.（密苏里州史密斯维尔一家私人高尔夫俱乐部闷热的大厅很难成为创意的场所。）

联想记忆

stale *adj.* 不新鲜的；（空气）不清新的
ventilated *adj.* 通风的

52. The crowd *responded* enthusiastically when the governor said he would make the tax cut *permanent*.

单词	释义
respond	*v.* When you respond to something, you react to it by doing or saying something yourself. 回应，回答
	v. If a patient or their injury or illness is responding to treatment, the treatment is working and they are getting better. 做出反应

双语例句

Posts on social channels, such as Twitter and Facebook, would be responded to within one hour.（推特和脸书等社交渠道上的帖子会在一小时内得到回复。）

Both have responded so well to treatment that there is a chance they could figure against the Lakers on Saturday.（两人的治疗效果都很好，这样他们就有机会在周六对阵湖人队。）

联想记忆

response *n.* 响应；反应；回答
respondent *n.* 应答者，回答者

单词	释义
permanent	*adj.* Something that is permanent last forever. 永久的，固定的
	adj. A permanent employee is one who is employed for an unlimited length of time. 终身的

双语例句

That puts Cyprus at a permanent disadvantage as a holiday destination to nearby countries.（这使得塞浦路斯作为度假目的地，与周边国家相比长期处于劣势。）

Banks are unwilling to lend money to people without credit histories or proof of permanent residence.（银行不愿意贷款给没有信用记录或永久居住证明的人。）

联想记忆

perpetual *adj.* 永久的，永远的

53. Sudan has restarted oil production, more than a year after it was **halted** by **disputes** with its neighbor.

单词	释义
halt	*v.* When a person, vehicle, or activity halts or when something halts them, they stop moving in the direction they were going and stand still. 停住
	n. Halt is an interruption or end to activity, movement, or progress.（活动、运动或进展的）中止；终止

双语例句

The media group said it has been pressured to halt radio and TV broadcasts of political news.（这家媒体集团表示，迫于压力已停止在广播和电视上播放政治新闻。）

The airport almost ground to a halt for days in December 2020 due to heavy snowfall.（2020年12月，由于大雪，机场连续多天几乎处于停止运营的状态。）

联想记忆

halting *adj.* 犹豫的；蹒跚的

单词	释义
dispute	*n.* A dispute is an argument or disagreement between people or groups. 争论；纠纷
	v. If you dispute a fact, statement, or theory, you say that it is incorrect or untrue. 反驳；质疑

双语例句

There is little dispute that milk production has fallen to surprisingly low levels.（毫无疑问，牛奶产量已降至令人惊讶的极低水平。）

In the countryside, property and land disputes have become a leading cause of social unrest.（在农村，财产和土地纠纷已经成为社会动荡的主要因素。）

Peace talks over the disputed election are dragging on without any resolution.（关于饱受争议的选举，和平谈判仍在继续，没有任何解决方案。）

联想记忆

clash *n.* 冲突；争论；交锋 *v.* 发生冲突；迥然不同

54. All are taught together, covering the same *syllabus* at the same rate until they finish *compulsory* schooling.

单词	释义
syllabus	*n.* You can refer to the subjects that are studied in a particular course as the syllabus. 课程
	n. A syllabus is an outline or summary of the subjects to be covered in a course. 教学大纲

双语例句

An online syllabus could reach more students, and reduce tuition charges and eliminate room and board.（在线课程可以让更多的学生参与，还可以降低学费，免除食宿费用。）

This year a number of new syllabuses, including ICT, are being assessed for the first time.（今年，包括信息通信技术在内的一系列全新教学大纲将进行首轮评估。）

联想记忆

curriculum *n.* 课程；课程体系

单词	释义
compulsory	*adj.* If something is compulsory, you must do it or accept it, because it is the law. 强制性的；必修的

双语例句

The number of papers opposing compulsory health insurance has jumped from about 100 to 432.（反对强制医疗保险的论文数量从100篇猛增至432篇。）

Complying with nutritional standards of school food was compulsory for all local authority-run schools.（所有地方政府开办的学校都必须遵守校园食品营养标准。）

联想记忆

compulsive *adj.* 强制的；引人入胜的
obligatory *adj.* 有义务的，强制的

55. Seventeen years after the doctor's ***diagnosis***, Samra took the determination to ***tackle*** the world's tallest peak.

单词	释义
diagnosis	*n.* Diagnosis is the discovery and naming of what is wrong with someone who is ill. 诊断

双语例句

A diagnosis of depression does not necessarily imply some sort of drug therapy to treat it.（确诊为抑郁症并不一定意味着要使用药物治疗。）

They drew attention to the role played by ads in helping early diagnosis of serious conditions.（他们提醒人们注意广告在帮助早期诊断严重疾病方面所起的作用。）

联想记忆

diagnose *v.* 诊断，确诊
diagnostic *adj.* 诊断的；判断的 *n.* 诊断程序

单词	释义
tackle	*v.* If you tackle a difficult problem or task, you deal with it in a very determined or efficient way. 处理，应对

双语例句

The money raised could help ease traffic, fight poverty and tackle climate change.（筹集的资金将有助于缓解交通拥堵、消除贫困和应对气候变化。）

Tackling youth crime effectively involves police officers, social workers and education staff working together.（有效解决青少年犯罪问题需要警察、社会工作人员和教育工作者们共同合作。）

联想记忆

handle *v.* 应对；处理 *n.* 把手；（解决问题的）途径

56. Within hours, his condition ***deteriorated*** and he was ***transferred*** to Great Ormond Street Hospital for Children.

单词	释义
deteriorate	*v.* If something deteriorates, it becomes worse in some way. 恶化，变坏

双语例句

The check-out lines are painfully long and the overall shopping experience continues to deteriorate.（收银台前排着令人痛苦的长队，整体购物体验越来越差。）

The National Health Service has obviously deteriorated, despite increased spending.（尽管支出在增加，但国民医疗保健服务的质量却明显下降了。）

联想记忆

deterioration *n.* 恶化，退化
degrade *v.* 恶化；降解；贬低

单词	释义
transfer	*v.* If you transfer something or someone from one place to another, or they transfer from one place to another, they go from the first place to the second. 转移，移交；调动
	n. Transfer is also a NOUN. 移交；调动；转账

双语例句

He had transferred from one division to another, never finding a department that suited him.（他从一个部门调到另一个部门，从没找到适合他的部门。）

The jury heard millions of pounds were transferred from the UK to bank accounts in Spain.（陪审团听说数百万英镑从英国转移到了在西班牙的银行账户。）

In cases like the U.S. and Mexico, banks are competing with lower rates to handle transfers.（在美国和墨西哥等国家，银行以较低的转账费率相互竞争。）

联想记忆

mobilize *v.* 动员；调动；移动

57. On our *maiden* voyage, about three hours into the flight, the plane began to slow down and reduce *altitude* so that it could land in a small airport to refuel.

单词	释义
maiden	*adj.* The maiden voyage or flight of a ship or aircraft is the first official journey that it makes.（航行、飞行）首次的
	n. A maiden is a young girl or woman. 少女

双语例句

Transport Minister Harrison Mwakyembe boarded a train, along with passengers, for the maiden journey.（交通部长哈里森·穆瓦克耶贝登上列车，和乘客们一起开始体验其首次旅程。）

One by one the maidens waltzed with the young prince, hoping to win his heart.（这些少女一个接一个和年轻的王子跳着华尔兹，希望能俘获他的心。）

联想记忆

maid *n.* 女仆，女佣

单词	释义
altitude	*n.* If something is at a particular altitude, it is at that height above sea level. 海拔，高度

双语例句

Straddling Nepal and China, the world's highest mountain has an altitude of 8,848m.（世界上最高的山峰跨越尼泊尔和中国，海拔为8 848米。）

The team is also focusing on why climbers at high altitude experience poor sleep.（该团队也专注于研究为什么登山者在高海拔地区睡眠质量差。）

联想记忆

latitude *n.* 纬度
longitude *n.* 经度
aptitude *n.* 天赋；才能

58. The 2018 budget *deficit* was 8.5% of GDP, not the goal of 6%, in large part because of overspending by Spain's *autonomous* regions.

单词	释义
deficit	*n.* A deficit is the amount by which something is less than what is required or expected, especially the amount by which the total money received is less than the total money spent. 亏损；赤字

双语例句

In some countries, such as Indonesia, currencies remain weak because of trade deficits.（在印度尼西亚等国家，由于贸易赤字，货币仍然疲软。）

The Congress and the president are still locked in disagreement over proposals to reduce the massive budget deficit.（对于如何减少巨额预算赤字，国会和总统各持己见。）

联想记忆

deficient *adj.* 不足的；有缺陷的
defect *n.* 缺点，缺陷

单词	释义
autonomous	*adj.* An autonomous country, organization, or group governs or controls itself rather than being controlled by anyone else. 自治的，有自治权的
	adj. An autonomous person makes their own decisions rather than being influenced by someone else. 自主的

双语例句

Five of the six provinces are to become autonomous regions in a new federal system of government.（在新的联邦政府体制下，六个省份中的五个将成为自治区。）

Private schools and autonomous colleges have the authority to make and implement curriculum decisions.（私立学校和独立办学的高校可以制定和执行自己的课程。）

联想记忆

autonomy *n.* 自治，自治权

59. Charlie had a father who was born and raised in Memphis and who had a southern *accent*, and his mother was of Colombian *descent*.

单词	释义
accent	*n.* Someone who speaks with a particular accent pronounces the words in a distinctive way that shows which country, region, or background they come from. 口音；腔调

双语例句

He has a two-inch scar on his right arm, and speaks with a Scottish accent.（他右臂上有一个两英寸的疤痕，说话带有苏格兰口音。）

Safety instructions are screamed at passengers in four languages, each spoken with a terrible accent.（他们用四种语言向乘客大声发出安全指令，每种语言的口音都很难听。）

联想记忆

ascent *n.* 上升；攀登

单词	释义
descent	*n.* You use descent to talk about a person's family background, for example, their nationality or social status. 出身，血统
	n. A descent is a movement from a higher to a lower level or position. 下降

双语例句

Unemployment among young men of African descent runs much higher than the national average.（非洲裔年轻人的失业率远高于全国平均水平。）

Within about a minute the plane had reached 18,000 feet and then began an uncontrolled descent.（大约一分钟后，飞机就升到了18 000英尺，然后开始失控下降。）

联想记忆

descend *v.* 下降；遗传；屈尊
descendant *n.* 后裔，子孙

60. Rangers have ***confirmed*** that an incident took place but would not ***elaborate*** on the extent of McGregor's injuries.

单词	释义
confirm	*v.* If something confirms what you believe, suspect, or fear, it shows that it is definitely true. 证实，确认

双语例句

Downing Street has refused to confirm whether the prime minister pays the top rate of tax.（唐宁街拒绝证实首相是否支付最高税率的税款。）

Scientists have confirmed that each of the many intricate instruments on board the rover are working.（科学家们已经证实，火星车上各个复杂的仪器都在正常工作。）

联想记忆

verify *v.* 证实；证明
clarify *v.* 澄清；阐明

单词	释义
elaborate	*v.* If you elaborate on something that has been said, you say more about it, or give more details. 详细阐述
	v. If you elaborate a plan or theory, you develop it by making it more complicated and more effective. 周密制定
	adj. Elaborate clothing or material is made with a lot of detailed artistic designs. 精心制作的，复杂的

双语例句

A spokesman declined to elaborate on a statement released late yesterday.（发言人拒绝对昨天晚些时候发表的一份声明作出更多说明。）

Her task was to elaborate policies that would make a market economy compatible with a clean environment.（她的任务是制定与风清气正的环境相适应的市场经济政策。）

At nightfall visitors can watch an elaborate firework display over the Italian garden.（夜幕降临时，游客可以在这座意大利花园上空观看到绚丽的烟花表演。）

联想记忆

intricate *adj.* 复杂的，难理解的
sophisticated *adj.* 复杂的；精密的；老练的

单元练习 6

使用本单元核心词汇的适当形式填空，并将句子译为中文。

1. There was absolutely no room in their kitchen to support such _____ baked goods.
2. Today computers are moving into everything from medical _____ to self-driving cars.
3. He was kept in a Moscow jail, in conditions so poor that his health _____ rapidly.
4. In a _____ low-ceilinged room, the NFL and GE announced the launch of a new program.
5. More than 200 MPs signed a motion calling for financial education to be made _____ in schools.
6. Few will _____ that educating women has great social benefits, and it has enormous economic advantages as well.
7. Before 1977, the immigration system generally permitted the _____ residence of foreign-born physicians.
8. After two years at Wharton, Buffett _____ to the University of Nebraska in Lincoln, for his final year of college.
9. The author recalls the scene on May 27, 1936, when the cruise left Southampton on her _____ voyage to New York.
10. Nevada has passed a law allowing _____ vehicles to operate on its roads, and Oregon is considering similar legislation.

Unit 7

★ 本单元核心词汇 ★

circulation	exceed	distinct	stimulus	frugal
equivalent	boost	reassure	cartoonist	quote
bloom	varied	coax	pension	tragedy
deter	ease	notorious	undergo	discharge

★ 本单元拓展词汇 ★

surmount	distinctive	thrifty	soothe	quotation
variant	seduce	transcend	allowance	detergent
charter	infamous	undertake	expel	graphics
oust	devise	startling	subsidy	lure
judicial	substantial	graphene	erase	patrol
disrupt	shaky	confrontation	sewage	grant
volcano	vessel	distinction	brim	

61. The Canadian penny is being withdrawn from *circulation* because production costs have *exceeded* its monetary value.

单词	释义
circulation	*n.* If something is in circulation, it is being used by the public; if something is out of circulation, it is no longer available for use by the public. 流通
	n. Circulation is the movement of blood through your body or the movement of liquid, air in a system. （血液、空气等）循环
	n. The circulation of a newspaper or magazine is the number of copies that are sold each time it is produced. 发行量

双语例句

The Bank issues nearly a billion banknotes each year, and withdraws almost as many from circulation.（银行每年发行大约十亿英镑的纸币，回收几乎等量的货币，使之退出流通。）

Anyone with heart, lung, or circulation problems should seek medical advice before flying.（任何有心、肺或血液循环问题的人都应该在乘飞机前咨询医生。）

While other newspapers are losing circulation, we are bucking the trend.（其他报纸发行量在下降，而我们却逆势而上。）

联想记忆

circular *adj.* 循环的；环形的 *n.* 印刷品，传单
circulate *v.* 传播；流传

单词	释义
exceed	*v.* If something exceeds a particular amount or number, it is greater or larger than that amount or number. 超过（某数量）
	v. If you exceed a limit or rule, you go beyond it, even though you are not supposed to or it is against law. 超越（限制、规定）

双语例句

Parliament agreed that income from subsidies should not exceed 300,000 euros for any individual farm.（国会同意，对于任何单个农场其补助不得超过30万欧元。）

When demand for a charter school exceeds supply, the random drawing is required by law.（当特许公立学校的需求超过供给时，法律规定随机抽签。）

联想记忆

surmount *v.* 超越；克服（问题或困难）

transcend *v.* 超出，超越

62. Astonishingly, it has been found that babies display a ***distinct*** set of facial expressions in response to different ***stimuli***.

单词	释义
distinct	*adj.* If something is distinct from something else of the same type, it is different or separate from it. 不同的，有区别的
	adj. If something is distinct, you can hear, see, or taste it clearly. 清楚的

双语例句

Each of London's districts had a distinct character that marked it off from its neighbors. （伦敦的每个区都有鲜明的特征，使之与邻近地区区别开来。）

The 108-acre city-state has its own judicial system, distinct from the Italian system. （这个占地108英亩的城邦拥有自己的司法系统，与意大利的截然不同。）

联想记忆

distinctive *adj.* 有特色的，与众不同的
distinction *n.* 区别，差别

单词	释义
stimulus	*n.* A stimulus is something that encourages activity in people or things. 刺激，刺激物

双语例句

These stimulus programs did little to put the economy on a stronger, more sustainable trajectory. （这些刺激计划对推动经济走上更强劲、更可持续的轨道没有起到什么作用。）

According to the Mayor, scores of jobs are coming to Tucson because of stimulus and innovation. （根据市长的说法，由于经济刺激和创新，图森出现了许多就业机会。）

联想记忆

stimulate *v.* 鼓励；刺激
stimulant *n.* 兴奋剂；刺激物

63. ***Frugal*** engineers at private companies are devising technologies that are cheaper and sometimes better than their rich-world ***equivalents***.

单词	释义
frugal	*adj.* People who are frugal or who live a frugal life do not spend much money on themselves. 俭朴的，节俭的
	adj. A frugal meal is small and not expensive. （膳食）简单的；省钱的

双语例句

Frugal by reputation, Scott apparently lived in the same house for more than three decades.（斯科特以节俭著称，显然他在这栋房子里住了30多年。）

The elders were carried out to the lunch room, where they were served a frugal meal of rice and vegetables.（这些老人被带到午餐室吃了一顿简餐，有米饭和蔬菜。）

联想记忆

economical *adj.* 节俭的；经济实惠的
thrifty *adj.* 节俭的，节约的

单词	释义
equivalent	*n.* If one amount or value is the equivalent of another, they are the same. 等量物；等价物
	adj. Equivalent is also an ADJECTIVE. 等量的，等值的

双语例句

Both mechanical systems are said to be lighter and faster than their electrical equivalents.（据说，这两种机械系统均比电力系统更轻、更快。）

For most Portuguese workers, the annual tax rises are equivalent to more than a month's wages.（对大多数葡萄牙工人来说，每年的增税相当于一个多月的工资。）

联想记忆

equivalence *n.* 等价；相等

64. Several countries have already introduced price controls or ***boosted*** food supplies to ***reassure*** consumers.

单词	释义
boost	*v.* If one thing boosts another, it causes it to increase, improve, or be more successful. 促进，增强
	n. Boost is also a NOUN. 推动力，增强

双语例句

Starbucks plans to boost sales by expanding its food menu of its traditional coffee stores.（星巴克计划通过丰富其传统咖啡门店的菜单来提高销售额。）

More than one million Iranians visit every year, providing a huge boost for Syria's economy.（每年超过一百万伊朗人到叙利亚旅行，给该国经济注入强大动力。）

联想记忆

booster *n.* 助推器；起提振作用的事物；加强针

单词	释义
reassure	*v.* If you reassure someone, you say or do things to make them stop worrying about something. 使安心，消除顾虑

双语例句

School children have been reassured about exams that may be disrupted by the weather.（对于可能因天气而取消的考试，学生们的顾虑已经消除了。）

The Federal Reserve took extraordinary action over the weekend to reassure shaky financial markets.（美国联邦储备委员会周末采取了特别行动，来稳定动荡的金融市场。）

联想记忆

soothe *v.* 安慰，安抚；减轻

65. In 1957, writer and *cartoonist* Allen Saunders offered the *quote*: "Life is what happens to us while we are making other plans."

单词	释义
cartoonist	*n.* A cartoonist is a person whose job is to draw cartoons for newspapers and magazines. 漫画家

双语例句

During the 1990s, *Guardian* cartoonist Steve Bell depicted the Prime Minister as a cat.（20世纪90年代，《卫报》漫画家史蒂夫·贝尔把首相描绘成一只猫。）

Born into a wealthy family in 1928, he studied to be a doctor, but chose instead the less respectable life of a cartoonist.（1928年他出生于一个富裕的家庭，曾经学过医，最终却选择了漫画家这样不受尊崇的职业。）

联想记忆

cartoon *n*. 卡通片；连环漫画
caricature *n*. 漫画；夸张的描述 *v*. 将……画成漫画
miniature *n*. 缩微模型；微型画 *adj*. 微型的

单词	释义
quote	*n*. A quote is a group of words or a short piece of writing taken from a book, play, speech, etc. 引语，引文
	v. If you quote someone as saying something, you repeat what they have written or said. 引用
	v. If someone quotes a price, they say how much money they would charge you for a service. Quote is also a NOUN. 报价

双语例句

Below is a quote by Hemingway on how exercise helped him with his work and depression.（下面是引用海明威的一句话，关于运动是如何帮助他促进工作和缓解抑郁的。）

"People in Norway have a spiritual relationship with fire," Mr. Moeklebust was quoted as saying.（报道援引默克勒巴斯特先生称，"挪威人在精神上与火有关联。"）

Customers have the opportunity to shop around for a cheaper quote if they wish.（如果愿意的话，顾客们可以到附近逛逛，有机会得到更便宜的报价。）

联想记忆

quotation *n*. 引用；印证；报价单
cite *v*. 引用；引证

66. Summer vacation planning is in full ***bloom***, and money-saving travel options are as ***varied*** as June flowers.

单词	释义
bloom	*n*. A bloom is the flower on a plant. 花朵
	v. When a plant or tree blooms, it produces flowers. When a flower blooms, it opens. 开花
	v. If someone or something blooms, they develop good, attractive, or successful qualities. 蓬勃发展

双语例句

It is a good spot for horse riding when the summer wild flowers are in bloom.（夏

天野花盛开时，这个地方很适合骑马。）

Its creator was inspired by his own garden, which blooms with white and blue irises in spring.（创作者从自己的花园获得了灵感，春日里白色和蓝色的鸢尾花竞相绽放。）

With profits and new products blooming, few investors see a need for further confrontation.（由于利润扩大，新产品不断推出，投资者认为没有必要进一步对抗。）

联想记忆

blossom *n.* 花；花期；兴旺期 *v.* 开花；兴旺

单词	释义
varied	*adj.* Something that is varied consists of things of different types, sizes, or qualities. 各式各样的

双语例句

The food he serves is as varied in flavors and weights as Thanksgiving dinner itself.（他端上来的食物和感恩节晚宴一样，味道各式各样，份量不尽相同。）

Rajasthan is the must-see state of India, brimming with varied and startling attractions.（拉贾斯坦邦是印度之行必去的地方，那里有各种各样令人惊叹的景点。）

联想记忆

variable *adj.* 可变的，易变的 *n.* 变量
variant *adj.* 不同的，多样的 *n.* 变体

67. Retired people could be *coaxed* back to work, especially if they could claim their *pensions* while working.

单词	释义
coax	*v.* If you coax someone into doing something, you gently try to persuade them to do it. 哄；劝诱

双语例句

There are some signs that the long-term jobless can be coaxed back into the working world.（有迹象表明，长期失业者可以被劝回到工作岗位。）

The research team run surveys designed to coax people to describe their lifestyles and health conditions.（研究小组进行了一些调查，目的是让人们谈谈他们的生活方式和健康状况。）

联想记忆

seduce *v.* 诱惑；勾引
lure *v.* 引诱，诱惑 *n.* 诱惑物；诱饵

单词	释义
pension	*n.* Someone who has a pension receives a regular sum of money from a former employer because they have retired or because they are widowed or disabled. 养老金；抚恤金
	v. When someone is pensioned off, he leaves employment and receives a regular sum of money, typically due to age or ill health. 给予养老金

双语例句

In 1983, with just over 18 years of service he was granted a disability pension.（1983年，服役超过18年的他获得了残疾抚恤金。）

Corporate "brain-drain" could lead to higher unemployment and a less "pensioned" population.（企业人才流失可能导致失业率上升和领取养老金者减少。）

联想记忆

pensioner *n.* 领取养老金（抚恤金）的人
allowance *n.* 津贴，补助；允许

68. In the days since the ***tragedy*** in Newtown, Americans from all over the country have called for action to ***deter*** mass shootings and reduce gun violence.

单词	释义
tragedy	*n.* A tragedy is an extremely sad event or situation. 灾难；悲剧

双语例句

The report says design faults in both the vessels contributed to the tragedy.（报道称，两艘船在设计上的缺陷是造成这起事故的原因。）

Mr. Pratt said tighter controls on gun sales would not put an end to similar tragedies in this country.（普拉特表示，对枪支销售进行更严格的管控也无法结束该国类似的悲剧。）

联想记忆

tragic *adj.* 悲剧的；悲痛的，不幸的

单词	释义
deter	*v.* To deter someone from doing something means to make them not want to do it or continue doing it. 阻止

双语例句

Authorities say the massive security operation is not intended to deter people from coming to Washington. （当局表示，大规模的安全行动并不是为了阻止人们前往华盛顿。）

A substantial number of mothers with young children are deterred from undertaking paid work because they lack access to childcare. （很多有小孩的母亲找不到人照顾孩子，因此无法上班挣钱。）

联想记忆

determent *n.* 制止；威慑
detergent *n.* 洗衣粉，洗涤剂

69. The plans will *ease* congestion around the Iron Bridge — which is a ***notorious*** accident blackspot.

单词	释义
ease	*v.* If something unpleasant eases or if you ease it, it is reduced in degree, speed, or intensity. 减轻，减缓
	n. Ease is the state of being very comfortable and able to live as you want, without any worries or problems. 舒适，悠闲
	n. If you talk about the ease of a particular activity, you are referring to the fact that it is easy to do. 简便，容易

双语例句

Freezing conditions are continuing to disrupt transport in northwest Europe, although heavy snow has eased. （尽管大雪有所缓解，但寒冷的天气继续影响着欧洲西北部的交通。）

The school organizes programs to help foreign students feel more at ease in their new surroundings. （学校组织一些活动，帮助外国学生适应新的环境。）

Electrons can flow through graphene with remarkable ease, making it an ideal material for transistors. （电子可以非常容易地通过石墨烯，这使其成为制作晶体管的理想材料。）

联想记忆

erase *v.* 擦掉，抹去；删除

单词	释义
notorious	*adj.* To be notorious means to be well known for something bad. 声名狼藉的

双语例句

At that time Japan was notorious in the western world for the shabby goods that it produced.（当时，日本因其生产的低劣商品而在西方世界声名狼藉。）

Graphics cards are notorious power hogs, and generate enough heat to warm a house.（显卡是出了名的耗电器件，产生的热量可以让一间房子变暖。）

联想记忆

infamous *adj.* 声名狼藉的；无耻的

70. Mr. Reid, who has **undergone** three operations for head and face injuries, was **discharged** from Demiford Hospital in Plymouth.

单词	释义
undergo	*v.* If you undergo something necessary or unpleasant, it happens to you. 经历；经受

双语例句

The 23-year-old boy will undergo surgery and is set to miss three-to-four months of action.（这名23岁的男子将进行手术，三四个月内将无法下床活动。）

The lens must undergo more testing before gaining approval from the Food and Drug Administration.（这种镜片必须经过更多测试，才能获得美国食品药品管理局的批准。）

联想记忆

undertake *v.* 承担；从事

单词	释义
discharge	*v.* When someone is discharged from a hospital, prison, or one of the armed services, they are officially allowed to leave. 批准离开
	v. If something is discharged from inside a place, it comes out. 排出

双语例句

Most of the rescued were transported to local hospitals for treatment, and some have been discharged.（大部分被解救的人员被送往当地医院治疗，一些已经出院了。）

Most cities in the developing world discharge their sewage untreated into rivers or the sea. （发展中国家大多数城市将未经处理的污水排入河流或大海。）

联想记忆

expel *v.* 开除；驱逐；排出
oust *v.* 罢免；驱逐

单元练习 7

使用本单元核心词汇的适当形式填空，并将句子译为中文。

1. In the current economic climate the Nexus 7 has a _____ advantage over any of the iPads.
2. We are facing a planetary emergency, which would _____ anything we've ever experienced in history.
3. News media _____ anonymous sources as saying Moscow could end its relations with the Island country.
4. I've been in a position of watching a lot of people _____ career transitions during the past several years.
5. Two hundred people move to Las Vegas every day, adding the _____ of a St Joseph, Missouri every year.
6. One University of Miami study found that a brief self-massage at work reduces stress and _____ job performance.
7. The school has become _____ in recent years for the association of a number of its faculty with terrorism.
8. More than 70% of the companies surveyed said they allowed executives to retire on a full _____ at the age of 60.
9. WSJ had a very small _____ as it was published for a special readership of people interested in business news.
10. President Reagan addressed the nation to _____ citizens that the tragedy would not stop American space exploration.

Unit 8

★ 本单元核心词汇 ★

gourmet	testify	advent	hermit	elevate
priority	myth	shatter	threshold	stereo
feat	transform	luxurious	toil	deserve
tournament	elegant	conceive	approve	grind

★ 本单元拓展词汇 ★

ballet	authorize	laborious	affirm	lavish
distraction	endorse	magnet	conserve	secluded
radiation	stroll	escalator	prioritize	mirage
watershed	onset	fable	outbreak	windshield
fragment	sprawl	rechargeable	wondrous	chic
pastime	stereoscope	debris	garbage	seclusion
luxuriant	formulate	almond	delicacy	

71. Anyone who has ***toiled*** through the Scholastic Assessment Test (SAT) will ***testify*** that test-taking skill also matters.

单词	释义
toil	*v.* When people toil, they work very hard doing unpleasant or tiring tasks. 辛苦工作
	n. Toil is also a NOUN. 辛苦的工作

双语例句

These workers toil with heavy machinery in the woods accessible by dirt roads. （这些工人在只有土路通到的树林里用重型机械辛勤劳作。）

The poor ballet dancer must devote years of toil to her task before she can shine in it. （可怜的芭蕾舞演员为了事业必须付出多年辛劳，才能在表演中脱颖而出。）

联想记忆

toilsome *adj.* 辛苦的，劳累的
laborious *adj.* 艰苦的，费力的

单词	释义
testify	*v.* When someone testifies in a court of law, they give a statement of what they know of a situation. 作证；证明

双语例句

An FBI agent testified that no evidence of arsenic was found in searches of Curtis' home. （联邦调查局一名特工证实说，在搜索柯蒂斯的住所时没有发现砒霜。）

Those who have worked with Delia Smith testify to her love of football. （曾与迪莉娅·史密斯共事过的人都证实，她的确热爱足球。）

联想记忆

testimony *n.* 证言；证据
affirm *v.* 断言；证实，确认

72. With the ***advent*** of the Internet and e-commerce, it's now possible to be a complete ***hermit*** and still shop.

单词	释义
advent	*n.* The advent of an important event, invention, or situation is the fact of it starting or coming into existence. 出现，到来

双语例句

With the advent of widespread online learning, we may be able to create more effective learning pathways.（随着在线学习的普及，我们便有了更高效的学习途径。）

So much has changed since the advent of technologies that enable employees to work remotely.（自从员工通过技术能远程办公以来，情况发生了巨大的变化。）

联想记忆

dawn *n.* 黎明，拂晓；开端
onset *n.* （尤指某种不好的事情）开始

单词	释义
hermit	*n.* A hermit is a person who lives alone, away from people and society. 隐士，隐居者

双语例句

One local hermit, Pietro del Morrone, was elected as the head of the Catholic Church in 1294.（1294年，当地的一位隐士彼得罗·德尔·莫罗内被推选为天主教会的领袖。）

In the Middle Ages the area was a magnet for hermits, who came there to devote themselves to prayer.（中世纪时，这个地区吸引了许多隐士，他们来到这里潜心祷告。）

联想记忆

recluse *n.* 隐居者 *adj.* 隐居的
secluded *adj.* 隐居的；僻静的

73. I joined the Secretary in February during her first trip to Kenya, where she *elevated* the climate change challenge to a top *priority*.

单词	释义
elevate	*v.* If you elevate something to a higher status, you consider it to be better or more important than it really is. 抬高（地位，重要性）
	v. To elevate something means to increase it in amount or intensity, or raise it higher. 提高；举起

双语例句

She later moved to San Diego Union Tribune, where she was elevated to publisher in 1989.（她后来加入圣地亚哥联合论坛报，于1989年荣升为发行人。）

Although elevated levels of radiation are being detected, they do not pose a risk to human health.（尽管已经检测到辐射水平升高，但是不会对人类健康造成危害。）

联想记忆

elevation *n.* 提高；高地；海拔
elevator *n.* 电梯，升降机
escalator *n.* 自动扶梯

单词	释义
priority	*n.* If something is a priority, it is the most important thing you have to deal with, or must be done before everything else. 优先处理的事

双语例句

The spokesman promised that his party would continue to give top priority to environmental concerns.（发言人承诺，其政党将继续优先解决环境问题。）

The school gives priority to educating the "whole child", with a strong emphasis on creativity.（这所学校将"教育孩子全面发展"作为首要任务，重点强调创造力。）

联想记忆

prior *adj.* 优先的；在前的
prioritize *v.* 区分优先次序，按优先顺序排列

74. The ***myth*** that buying a home is a good, safe investment since prices never fall has been absolutely ***shattered***.

单词	释义
myth	*n.* If you describe a belief or explanation as a myth, you mean that many people believe it but it is actually untrue. 谬见
	n. A myth is a well-known story which was made up in the past to explain natural events or to justify religious beliefs or social customs. 神话

双语例句

The idea that people need less sleep as they age is a myth, sleep experts say.（睡眠专家说，人们随着年龄的增长所需要的睡眠越来越少是错误的观念。）

This corner of southeast Turkey is coated under layers of history, myth and folklore.（土耳其东南部一隅有着厚重的历史、古老的神话和民间传说。）

联想记忆

fable *n.* 寓言；无稽之谈 *v.* 虚构
legend *n.* 传说；传奇

单词	释义
shatter	*v.* If something shatters your dreams, hopes, or beliefs, it completely destroys them. 粉碎（梦想、希望、信仰等）
	v. If something is shattered, it breaks into small pieces. 破坏，摧毁

双语例句

The experiences often shatter the confidence and ambition of talented women who could otherwise seize the career-transforming opportunities.（这些经历往往会击碎天资聪颖女性的信心和决心，她们本可以抓住改变职业生涯的机会。）

The bus had a shattered windshield from gunfire at the start of its journey.（这辆公共汽车刚准备出发时，挡风玻璃就被炮火击碎了。）

联想记忆

fragment *v.* 使破碎；分裂 *n.* 片段；碎片
debris *n.* 碎片；残骸

75. Ear health means little to those chasing the magic number: 194 decibels, thought to be a ***threshold*** beyond which ***stereos*** might explode.

单词	释义
threshold	*n.* An threshold is an amount, level, or limit on a scale. When the threshold is reached, something else happens or changes. 界限，临界点
	n. The threshold of a building or room is the floor in the doorway, or the doorway itself. 门口，门槛

双语例句

Germany and Britain have plans to raise the threshold of retirement age to 67 or beyond.（德国和英国计划将退休年龄提高到67岁或以上。）

My translator tripped over the threshold as we left the room, and went sprawling on the carpet.（我们离开房间时，翻译员被门槛绊了一下，摔倒在地毯上。）

联想记忆

watershed *n.* 分水岭，转折点

单词	释义
stereo	*n.* A stereo is a CD player with two speakers. 立体音响
	adj. Stereo is used to describe a sound system in which the sound is played through two speakers. 立体声的

双语例句

Hillary packed her books, stereo, and clothes into her Volkswagen and headed south.（希拉里把她的书本、音响和衣服装进大众汽车里，然后向南驶去。）

It's the first stereo speaker to offer 360-degree sound and features a 15-hour rechargeable battery.（这是第一个能提供360度环绕声的立体扬声器，并配有续航15小时的充电电池。）

联想记忆

stereoscopic *adj.* 立体的；体视镜的
high-fidelity *n.* 高保真

76. As technology evolves to meet the demands of our dreams, more and more wondrous *feats* of engineering will *transform* our world.

单词	释义
feat	*n.* If you refer to an action, or the result of an action, as a feat, you admire it because it is an impressive and difficult achievement. 功绩；壮举

双语例句

His feats will inspire young Africans to reach the top in their own life journeys.（他的成就将激励非洲年轻人在人生旅途中勇攀高峰。）

Wales arrived seeking a third successive away victory, a feat they had not managed for 26 years.（威尔士队在客场取得三连胜，这是他们26年来从未取得过的成绩。）

联想记忆

fete *n.* 庆祝；节日 *v.* 宴请，招待

单词	释义
transform	*v.* To transform something or someone means to change them completely so that they are much better or more attractive. 彻底改变；转换

双语例句

Garbage can be transformed into various sources of energy and then sold for a profit.（垃圾可以转变为各种能源，然后出售获利。）

Dell and his wife have given more than $700 million in grants to help transform the lives of African children.（戴尔和妻子已经捐赠了7亿多美元来帮助改变非洲儿童的生活。）

联想记忆

transformation *n.*（彻底或重大的）转变，变革；变换
transformer *n.* 变压器；转换器；促使改变的人（或物）

77. Food is another focus of the *luxurious* journey, with *gourmet* dishes emphasizing regional ingredients.

单词	释义
luxurious	*adj.* If you describe something as luxurious, you mean it is very comfortable and expensive. 豪华的；奢侈的

双语例句

Our honeymoon was three days in Las Vegas at a luxurious hotel called Le Mirage.（我们的蜜月为期三天，是在拉斯维加斯一家名为"幻影"的豪华酒店度过的。）

Today, she lives in seclusion in a luxurious home in Tokyo with her musician husband.（如今，她和音乐人丈夫隐居在东京一处豪华的住宅里。）

联想记忆

luxury *n.* 奢华；奢侈品；享受
luxuriant *adj.* 繁茂的，丰富的
lavish *adj.* 奢侈的，大方的

单词	释义
gourmet	*adj.* Gourmet food is nicer or more unusual or sophisticated than ordinary food, and is often more expensive. 精美的；美味的
	n. Gourmet is good food, or a person who knows a lot about food and wine. 美食；美食家

双语例句

The home features a gourmet kitchen, enormous great room with gas fireplace and pool.（该住宅有美食厨房，宽敞的房间，还有燃气壁炉和泳池。）

I stopped for some Tasmanian and local cheese, almonds and olives at one of the gourmet shops.（我在一家美食店停下来，买了一些塔斯马尼亚及当地的奶酪、

杏仁和橄榄。）

联想记忆

delicacy *n*. 美味，佳肴；精致；微妙

78. Nigeria ***deserved*** to win and put up their most convincing performance since the start of the ***tournament***.

单词	释义
deserve	*v*. If you say that a person or thing deserves something, you mean that they should have it or receive it because of their actions or good qualities. 值得；应得；应受

双语例句

He deserves respect for his career at United and for his hugely professional attitude.（他在曼联的职业生涯和异常专业的态度令人敬重。）

Anyone who thinks Lay deserved to spend the rest of his life in jail is either a fool or a politician.（任何认为雷应该在监狱里度过余生的人，要么是傻瓜，要么是政客。）

联想记忆

reserve *v*. 预留，预订
conserve *v*. 保护，保存；节约

单词	释义
tournament	*n*. A tournament is a sports competition in which players who win a match continue to play further matches in the competition until just one person or team is left. 联赛，锦标赛

双语例句

Wales has only ever qualified for one major tournament in its history, the World Cup back in 1958.（威尔士队历史上只参加过一次重要赛事，那就是1958年的世界杯。）

Walton pocketed more money from this tournament than in his entire three years as a professional.（沃尔顿在这次锦标赛中赚的钱比他作为一名职业运动员整整3年的还要多。）

联想记忆

championship *n*. 锦标赛；冠军称号，冠军地位

79. Housed in an *elegant* five-storey Art Deco building of glass and steel, the foundation was *conceived* by Mr. Cartier-Bresson and his wife to showcase his life's work.

单词	释义
elegant	*adj.* If you describe a person or thing as elegant, you mean that they are pleasing and graceful in appearance or style. 优雅的
	adj. If you describe a piece of writing, an idea, or a plan as elegant, you mean that it is simple, clear and clever. 精妙的

双语例句

The elegant study in this 4-bedroom home provides quiet privacy from the living room and kitchen.（这套四居室住宅的典雅书房远离客厅和厨房，既安静又私密。）

Both elegant and functional, the stand complements the screen without creating any visual distraction.（这个柜子精致又实用，它对屏幕起到补充作用，但不会分散注意力。）

联想记忆

elegance *n.* 典雅，高雅
chic *adj.* 时髦的，雅致的

单词	释义
conceive	*v.* If you conceive a plan or idea, you think of it and work out how it can be done. 构想出
	v. If you conceive something as a particular thing, you consider it to be that thing. 认为；想象

双语例句

Leah had conceived the idea of a series of novels, each of which would reveal some aspect of rural life.（莉亚构思了一系列小说，每一部都反映农村生活的某个方面。）

The ancients conceived the earth as afloat in water and also believed that the earth was the center of the universe.（古人想象地球是漂浮在水上的，还认为地球是宇宙的中心。）

联想记忆

formulate *v.* 制定，规划；用公式表示
devise *v.* 设计；发明

80. The U.S. Department of Agriculture (USDA) last year *approved* the use of irradiated *ground* beef in the National School Lunch Program.

单词	释义
approve	*v.* When something is approved, it is accepted or allowed officially. 批准
	v. If you approve of something or someone, you like them. 赞成；喜欢

双语例句

The City Council is set to approve proposals for a major irrigation project.（市议会将批准关于一项重要灌溉工程的提案。）

In a recent survey, 50% approved of gay marriage, while 48% said they opposed it.（在最近的一次调查中，50%的受访者赞成同性婚姻，而48%的人表示反对。）

联想记忆

endorse *v.* 赞同，认可；背书
authorize *v.* 批准；授权

单词	释义
grind	*v.* If you grind a substance such as corn, you crush it between two hard surfaces or with a machine. 磨碎，碾碎

双语例句

Cargill Inc. recalled 36 million pounds of ground turkey on Aug. 3 in response to the outbreak.（由于疫情暴发，嘉吉公司8月3日召回了3 600万磅碎火鸡肉。）

The satellite will collect, grind and analyze around 70 samples of rock and soil from Mars.（卫星将收集、研磨并分析近70个来自火星的岩石和土壤样本。）

联想记忆

ground *adj.* 磨碎的，绞碎的
flour *n.* 面粉；粉状物 *v.* 撒粉于；磨成粉

单元练习 8

使用本单元核心词汇的适当形式填空,并将句子译为中文。

1. Health and education are top _____ of the government of President Jacob Zuma.
2. The Norwegian Cruise Line decided to make them the most _____ ships on the water.
3. Soccer is, now more than ever, a global game and _____ to be shared across the world.
4. The explosions, near the marathon's finish line, _____ windows and sent smoke into the air.
5. After centuries of expansion, the Palace was finally _____ into a museum of the imperial era.
6. With the _____ of digital photography, the industrial demand for silver has dropped dramatically.
7. As time passes such novelties become popular, and eventually some of them are _____ into art forms.
8. A high-risk warning has been issued by the Agriculture Department over _____ beef produced by an Illinois company.
9. There is a funny _____ that you have to go to big places such as New York or California to make your fame and fortune.
10. Drug development is a time-consuming process, requiring multiple rounds of FDA trials before a drug can be _____.

Unit 9

★ 本单元核心词汇 ★

insight	soar	infant	muffle	deprive
destined	clutch	vain	landmark	steadily
commemorate	shrink	fervent	embrace	abandon
impose	wither	portray	capacity	contagious

★ 本单元拓展词汇 ★

transmission	wane	capacitance	sore	premature
toddler	scarf	discard	portrayal	gallery
zinc	grip	grab	zeal	vanity
journalist	stifle	idyllic	harbor	steadfast
noticeable	tug	attenuate	dwindle	cling
hallmark	numerous	disrepair	carol	clue
comprehension	enact			

Unit 9

81. In northwestern Nebraska, tobacco crops have *withered* due to a lack of rainfall and *soaring* temperatures.

单词	释义
wither	*v.* If a flower or plant withers, it dries up and dies.（花朵或植物）枯萎
	v. If someone or something withers, they become very weak. 变虚弱

双语例句

An exceptionally hot, dry summer has withered nearly three-quarters of this year's crops.（异常炎热干燥的夏季使今年近四分之三的农作物枯萎。）

The company's U.S. market share has continued to wither, falling to less than 25% today.（该公司在美国的市场份额仍在持续萎缩，如今已下降至不到25%。）

联想记忆

wane *v.* 月亏；衰落 *n.* 减弱；衰退
wilt *v.* 枯萎，凋谢；萎靡不振

单词	释义
soar	*v.* If the amount, value, level, or volume of something soars, it quickly increases by a great deal. 急剧增加
	v. If something such as a bird soars into the air, it goes quickly up into the air. 高飞

双语例句

The pay of such people from executives to investment bankers and software engineers in Silicon Valley is soaring.（在硅谷，从高管到投资银行家和软件工程师，薪酬都大幅提升。）

If the time is right, a splendid golden eagle may soar into view.（如果时机合适，美丽的金色雄鹰可能会跃入视线。）

联想记忆

sore *adj.* 疼痛的；痛苦的；恼怒的

82. Orphaned *infants* left in a hospital in the central Russian city of Yekaterinburg had their mouths taped in order to *muffle* their cries.

单词	释义
infant	*n.* An infant is a baby or very young child. 婴儿；幼儿

双语例句

Previous studies have suggested that underweight or premature infants have a higher risk of autism.（先前的研究表明，体重不足或早产婴儿患自闭症的风险更高。）

Strong emotional bonds between mothers and infants increase children's willingness to explore the world.（母亲和婴儿之间强烈的情感纽带增加了儿童探索世界的意愿。）

联想记忆

infancy *n.* 初期；婴儿期
infantry *n.* 步兵；步兵团
toddler *n.* 学步的儿童

单词	释义
muffle	*v.* If something muffles a sound, it makes it quieter and more difficult to hear. 压低（声音）
	v. Muffle also means to wrap up (the head) in a scarf, cloak, etc, especially for warmth. 包住；裹起来

双语例句

In such bad weather, we have to wrap scarves around our faces and speak in muffled voices.（在这样恶劣的天气里，我们不得不用围巾捂住脸，说话时声音低沉。）

Many of us, well muffled up, have carried lanterns around our local area to sing carols to neighbors.（我们许多人都裹得严严实实，提着灯笼在附近的地方给邻居们唱颂歌。）

联想记忆

muffled *adj.* 听不清的；蒙住的
stifle *v.* 抑制；强忍住；使窒息

83. Many girls and women, ***deprived*** of an education and health care, are ***destined*** to a life of poverty, generation after generation.

单词	释义
deprive	*v.* If you deprive someone of something that they want or need, you take it away from them, or you prevent them from having it. 剥夺，使丧失

双语例句

An individual who is constantly sleep deprived during weekdays might try to catch up during weekends.（工作日连续睡眠不足的人会在周末努力补觉。）

Coming from one of the UK's economically deprived areas, Grant has never visited an art gallery before.（格兰特来自英国的经济贫困地区，他以前从未参观过艺术馆。）

联想记忆

deprivation *n.* 剥夺，丧失；贫困

单词	释义
destined	*adj.* If something is destined to happen, it is certain to happen or be done. 注定的
	adj. If someone or goods are destined for a particular place, they are traveling toward that place or will be sent to that place. 去往某地的

双语例句

Contrary to what many people believe, highly intelligent children are not necessarily destined for academic success.（与很多人的想法相反，高智商儿童不一定会在学术上有所成就。）

The Titanic was destined for New York and carried hundreds of Americans on board.（泰坦尼克号当时准备前往纽约，上面载有数百名美国人。）

联想记忆

destiny *n.* 命运，天命

84. Photographs were widely available of Kurdish women ***clutching*** their children to their breasts in the ***vain*** attempt to protect them against the gas.

单词	释义
clutch	*v.* If you clutch at something or clutch something, you hold it tightly, usually because you are afraid or anxious. （因为害怕或焦虑而）抓牢
	n. In a vehicle, the clutch is the pedal that you press before you change gear. 离合器踏板

双语例句

Scott clutched his daughter on the floor of their hallway as the tornado tugged at the home's foundation.（龙卷风撕扯房屋的地基时，斯科特在他们家走廊的地板上紧紧抱住女儿。）

The dual-clutch transmission works via buttons in the center console that change the car from park to drive.（双离合变速器通过中控台上的按钮控制，可将汽车从驻车挡切换到前进挡。）

联想记忆

grab *v.* 抓住；利用（机会）；（匆忙地）取，吃
grip *v.* 握紧，抱住 *n.* 紧握；控制
cling *v.* 抓住，抱紧；依附；坚信

单词	释义
vain	*adj.* A vain attempt or action is one that fails to achieve what was intended. 徒劳的
	adj. If you describe someone as vain, you are critical of their extreme pride in their own beauty, intelligence, or other good qualities. 自负的

双语例句

Due to the severe weather conditions, the plane circled twice, trying in vain to line up with the runway.（由于天气恶劣，飞机盘旋了两圈，试图在跑道上降落却没能成功。）

Hans was a man of good and kindly nature, a little vain and self-important, but earnest and upright.（汉斯是个善良的人，有点虚荣自大，但为人真诚率直。）

联想记忆

vanity *n.* 虚荣，虚荣心
futile *adj.* 徒劳的，无用的

85. Throughout much of history the ***landmarks*** of life — birth, love, marriage and death — have been ***commemorated*** with jewelry.

单词	释义
landmark	*n.* A landmark is an event or discovery marking an important stage or turning point in something. 里程碑；划时代的事
	n. A landmark is a building or feature easily recognized from a distance, especially one that enables someone to establish their location. 地标

双语例句

In 1960 he helped organize the first exhibition, an important landmark in British abstract art.（1960年，他帮助组织了首次展览，这是英国抽象艺术的一个重要里程碑。）

The Norumbega Castle in the coastal town of Camden, Maine, has become a landmark in the area.（诺兰伯加城堡位于缅因州的滨海小镇卡姆登，已经成为这里的一个地标。）

联想记忆

milestone *n.* 里程碑，转折点
breakthrough *n.* 突破，重大进展

单词	释义
commemorate	*v.* To commemorate an important event or person means to remember them by means of a special action, ceremony, or specially created object. 纪念

双语例句

The room contained a gallery of paintings commemorating great moments in baseball history.（这个房间里有一个画廊，陈列着纪念棒球史上伟大时刻的绘画作品。）

The president put aside politics Thursday to commemorate the September 11 terrorist attacks.（总统周四暂停了政治活动，来纪念9·11恐怖袭击事件。）

联想记忆

commemorative *adj.* 纪念的
commemoration *n.* 纪念；纪念活动

86. While nuclear energy production has *steadily* increased, its piece of the global electricity pie is *shrinking* compared to traditional sources.

单词	释义
steadily	*adv.* If something happens steadily, it goes in a regular and even manner. 稳定地，持续地

双语例句

After the 2003 invasion by the U.S. and British forces, their lives got steadily worse.（2003年被美英军队入侵后，他们的生活越来越糟糕。）

Over the past 15 years the number of exam boards has steadily decreased, from over 20 to only 5 in Scotland now.（在过去的十五年间，苏格兰的考试委员会数量逐步下降，从20多个降到现在只有5个。）

联想记忆

steady *adj.* 稳定的；平稳的；可靠的 *v.* 使平稳；使镇定
steadfast *adj.* 坚定的；不变的

单词	释义
shrink	*v.* If something shrinks or something else shrinks it, it becomes smaller. 缩小；使缩小
	v. If clothing shrinks, it becomes smaller in size, usually as a result of being washed. 缩水

双语例句

The price advantage of natural gas over gasoline shrinks as cars become more fuel efficient.（随着汽车变得越来越节能，天然气较之汽油的价格优势也变小了。）

Amazingly, when he did, the clothes shrank before his eyes to form a perfect fit.（令人惊讶的是，他照着做了以后，衣服在他眼前缩水，于是变得特别合身。）

联想记忆

attenuate *v.* 衰减，减弱
dwindle *v.* 逐渐减少；缩小

87. My *fervent* hope is that both the president and Gov. Mitt Romney will *embrace* these proposals.

单词	释义
fervent	*adj.* A fervent person has or shows strong feelings about something, and is very enthusiastic about it. 热情的；热烈的；强烈的

双语例句

These choices may disappoint his own party as well as some of his most fervent supporters.（这些选择可能会让他所在的党派和一些热切的支持者们感到失望。）

We watched as the fervent and enthusiastic Christians prayed on the interstate's shoulder in Dallas.（我们看着这些狂热的基督徒在达拉斯境内的州际公路边做祷告。）

联想记忆

passion *n.* 热情，激情
zeal *n.* 热情，热忱

单词	释义
embrace	*v.* If you embrace a change, political system, or idea, you accept it and start supporting it or believing in it. 欣然接受；信奉
	v. If you embrace someone, you put your arms around them and hold them tightly, usually to show your love for them. 拥抱
	v. If something embraces a group of people, things, or ideas, it includes them in a larger group or category. 包括

双语例句

We should embrace these challenges as an opportunity to innovate and approach social issues.（我们应该欣然接受这些挑战，以此为契机来创新解决社会问题。）

In perfect silence, he embraced each of his players and sent them off.（在一片沉默中，他拥抱每个队员，然后目送他们离开。）

His career embraces a number of activities — composing, playing, and acting.（他的职业生涯包括诸多方面——作曲、演奏和表演。）

联想记忆

hug *v.* 拥抱；紧靠 *n.* 拥抱

88. When faced with increasing opposition, the country ***abandoned*** its plan to ***impose*** large taxes on housing.

单词	释义
abandon	*v.* If you abandon a place, thing, or person, you leave the place, thing, or person permanently or for a long time. 抛弃
	v. If you abandon an activity or piece of work, you stop doing it before it is finished. 中途放弃
	v. If you abandon yourself to something, you allow yourself to indulge in it. 放纵，放任

双语例句

Over the years, the market fell into disrepair and was abandoned as shopping malls grew.（这个市场已年久失修，随着购物中心越来越多，市场便被废弃了。）

He then abandoned his music career to devote himself to promoting Islam.（然后，他放弃了音乐生涯，致力于宣扬伊斯兰教。）

Every year the city abandons itself to the heady allure of the world's largest arts festival.（这座城市每年都会沉浸在世界上最大的艺术节狂欢中。）

联想记忆

discard *v.* 扔掉，弃置
desert *v.* 抛弃，遗弃 *n.* 沙漠

单词	释义
impose	*v.* If you impose something on people, you force them to accept it. 强制实行
	v. If you impose your opinions or beliefs on other people, you try to make people accept them. 把（观点、信仰等）强加于

双语例句

In 1971 President Nixon imposed wage and price controls in an attempt to stop inflation.（1971年，尼克松总统对工资和物价实行管制，以避免通货膨胀。）

The Costa Ricans hold to a strict view of personal morality; they do not impose their views on others.（哥斯达黎加人坚守严格的道德观念，他们不会将自己的观点强加于他人。）

联想记忆

imposition *n.* 强加；征税；（规章、制度）实施
enact *v.* 制定；颁布；扮演

89. The photographs give an *insight* into the team's Antarctic journey and *portray* the harsh conditions Scott's team faced.

单词	释义
insight	*n.* If you gain insight or an insight into a complex situation or problem, you gain an accurate and deep understanding of it. 深刻见解；洞察力

双语例句

The data provide insights into their culture and, upon reflection, clues about our own.（这些数据让人们深入了解他们的文化，也为我们了解自己的文化提供了线索。）

This information should give scientists fresh insight into the internal structure of Earth's satellite.（这一信息会让科学家对地球卫星的内部结构产生新的认识。）

联想记忆

insightful *adj.* 有深刻见解的；富有洞察力的
comprehension *n.* 理解；领悟力

单词	释义
portray	*v.* When a writer or artist portrays something, he or she writes a description or produces a painting of it. 描绘（事物）
	v. When an actor or actress portrays someone, he or she plays that person in a play or movie. 扮演

双语例句

Portrayed as idyllic in tourist brochures, they in fact harbor an independence movement.（在旅游宣传册上，这里被描绘成世外桃源，但实际上正孕育着一场独立运动。）

When an actress portrays a character, viewers see her emotions physically, on her face and in her body.（当演员扮演一个角色时，观众可以从她的面部和身体上看到她的内心情感。）

联想记忆

portrayal *n.* 画像；肖像

90. There is no doubt that hospitals filled to *capacity* are more likely to have outbreaks of *contagious* diseases.

单词	释义
capacity	*n.* The capacity of a container or room is the maximum amount that something can contain. 容量；负载量
	n. The capacity of something such as a factory, industry, or region is the quantity of things that it can produce. 产量

双语例句

On the premier's last press conference the hall was filled to capacity by journalists.（总理召开最后一次记者招待会的时候，记者们把大厅挤得水泄不通。）

The project at full capacity is designed to produce 15,000 tons of zinc per month.（根据设计，该项目满负荷运行每月可生产15 000吨锌。）

联想记忆

capability *n.* 能力；容量
capacitance *n.* 电容

单词	释义
contagious	*adj.* A disease that is contagious can be caught by touching people or things that are infected with it. 传染的，传染性的
	adj. A feeling or attitude that is contagious spreads quickly among a group of people. 有感染力的

双语例句

Polio is highly contagious and affects the nervous system, sometimes resulting in paralysis.（小儿麻痹症传染性极强，它会影响神经系统，有时甚至导致瘫痪。）

His energy, enthusiasm and contagious smile have become hallmarks for the four-year all star.（他的精力、热情和极具感染力的微笑已经成为这位四年全明星的标志。）

联想记忆

infectious *adj.* 传染的；有感染力的

单元练习 9

使用本单元核心词汇的适当形式填空，并将句子译为中文。

1. A new study found that obesity may be socially _____ among family and friends.
2. The Post Office issued three stamps to _____ the 2014 World Cup held in Brazil.
3. Many European governments have _____ policies that used to encourage people to retire early.
4. Although many local dramas have _____ or even become extinct, *Wanbang* is surprisingly popular.
5. Nationally, gun sales have _____ since the Sandy Hook elementary school shootings that killed 20 children.
6. The 2009 coup has left Madagascar isolated by the international community and _____ of foreign aid.
7. It comprises 66 giant radio telescopes _____ to observe the sky in millimeter and sub-millimeters wavelengths.
8. Chipmakers can cut costs by _____ the size of their semiconductors and fitting more on a single silicon wafer.
9. Many teachers would love to be given more educational freedom and _____ changes to the lecture-listen model of schooling.
10. The plant generally runs at full _____ from December through May and then undergoes two weeks of maintenance.

Unit 10

★ 本单元核心词汇 ★

courteous	exclusively	initiate	evaluate	fluid
entrepreneur	virtually	trigger	eliminate	congestion
victim	commensurate	torture	aggressive	friction
traverse	profound	qualification	vigorous	frail

★ 本单元拓展词汇 ★

palette	courtesy	cyclist	appraise	coach
proportionate	polio	flick	vaccination	burglar
arouse	intensive	retiree	obsolete	lane
advisable	militant	captive	divergence	stir
afflict	initiative	jam	torment	rapport
fiction	occasionally	feeble		

91. Those tax increases were aimed almost *exclusively* at the *entrepreneurs*, risk takers and small businesses.

单词	释义
exclusively	*adv.* Exclusively is used to refer to situations or activities that involve only the thing or things mentioned, and nothing else. 排他地；独占地

双语例句

Susan paints from a palette consisting almost exclusively of grey and mud brown.（苏珊画画几乎只用灰色和土褐色的色调。）

Business travelers used to work almost exclusively on their BlackBerrys or their big laptops.（过去，商务旅行者几乎只在黑莓手机或大屏笔记本电脑上工作。）

联想记忆

exclusive *adj.* 独有的；排外的；专一的 *n.* 独家新闻；独家经营的项目
exclude *v.* 排除；拒绝接纳；逐出

单词	释义
entrepreneur	*n.* An entrepreneur is a person who sets up businesses and business deals. 创业者

双语例句

James Hill, founder of the Great Northern Railway, is a classic example of a commercial entrepreneur.（大北部铁路公司的创始人詹姆斯·希尔是商业企业家的典型代表。）

The Internet is making it easier for small-scale African entrepreneurs to sell farm goods in Europe.（互联网让部分非洲企业家更容易在欧洲销售农产品。）

联想记忆

entrepreneurial *adj.* 企业家的；与企业有关的

92. Derek was always *courteous* but all seven members of his family agreed that he never once *initiated* conversation.

单词	释义
courteous	*adj.* Someone who is courteous is polite and respectful to other people. 彬彬有礼的

双语例句

Anyone who has dealt with Tom knows that he is a courteous, mild-mannered country man.（凡是和汤姆打过交道的人都知道，他是一个彬彬有礼、温文尔雅的乡下人。）

There are some speedy cyclists, but the vast majority are reasonable and courteous to others along the trail.（有些骑行者速度很快，但绝大多数人比较理性，对沿途的其他人很有礼貌。）

联想记忆

courtesy *n.* 礼貌；好意；恩惠　*adj.* 殷勤的；被承认的；出于礼节的
courteously *adv.* 有礼貌地；亲切地

单词	释义
initiate	*v.* If you initiate something, you start it or cause it to happen. 开始，发起
	v. If you initiate someone into something, you introduce them to a particular skill or type of knowledge and teach them about it. 使初步了解；传授

双语例句

It is in this context that the Silk Roads Project, initiated by UNESCO, assumes its significance.（在这种背景下，教科文组织发起的丝绸之路项目才体现出其重要意义。）

In small groups, people have a better chance to initiate contact and establish rapport with them.（在小的群体中，人们更容易了解他人，并建立融洽的关系。）

联想记忆

initiative *n.* 倡议；主动性
initially *adv.* 开始，最初

93. The health of each pet is *evaluated*, and *fluids* and medical treatment are provided as needed.

单词	释义
evaluate	*v.* If you evaluate something or someone, you consider them in order to make a judgment about them. 评估，评价

双语例句

The FDA evaluated the drug on May 15, and approval could come as soon as June.（5月15日食品药品管理局对该药品进行了评估，最快将在6月予以批准。）

They appeared to be in good health and were taken to a hospital to be evaluated. （他们的身体状况似乎都不错，之后被送往医院进行检查。）

联想记忆

evaluation *n.* 评估；评价；估价
assess *v.* 评估，评价
appraise *v.* 评价；鉴定

单词	释义
fluid	*n.* A fluid is a liquid. 液体，流体
	adj. Fluid movements or lines or designs are smooth and graceful. 流动的；流畅的

双语例句

He went home with advice to get some rest and drink plenty of fluids.（他回家了，医生的建议是注意休息并多喝水。）

The costume, staging and music are all original, and the performances are fluid and graceful.（服装、舞台和音乐都很新颖，表演也优雅流畅。）

联想记忆

fluidity *n.* 流动性

94. Graduates struggling to get jobs **commensurate** with their **qualifications** are becoming sadly familiar.

单词	释义
commensurate	*adj.* If the level of one thing is commensurate with another, the first level is in proportion to the second. 成比例的；相称的

双语例句

Throwing money at education has not produced results commensurate with the cost.（在教育上投资并没有产出与成本相应的结果。）

Genuine ads typically target applicants with specific experience and pay salaries commensurate with their backgrounds.（真正的招聘广告通常针对有特定经验的求职者，并根据他们的背景支付相应的薪酬。）

联想记忆

proportionate *adj.* 成比例的，相称的 *v.* 使成比例

单词	释义
qualification	*n.* Your qualifications are the official documents or titles you have that show your level of education and training. 资格；学历
	n. Qualification is the action or fact of being eligible for something. 资格取得，获得资格

双语例句

He graduated in law from the University of Chicago and later obtained numerous other qualifications.（他毕业于芝加哥大学获得法律学位，后来又拿到了一些其他文凭。）

The coach remained determined to guide his team to World Cup qualification in 2022.（教练仍然决定带领球队取得2022年世界杯预选赛资格。）

联想记忆

qualify *v.* 取得资格；使具有资格
qualified *adj.* 合格的，有资格的
certificate *n.* 证明，证书；文凭

95. He was especially excited about new software his team created that would *eliminate* network *congestion*.

单词	释义
eliminate	*v.* To eliminate something means to remove it or get rid of it completely. 根除；消灭
	v. When a person or team is eliminated from a competition, they are defeated and so stop participating in the competition. 淘汰

双语例句

The company will eliminate health insurance for salaried retirees starting next year.（该公司从明年起将取消受薪退休人员的医疗保险。）

It is reported that Italy has been defeated by Slovakia and is eliminated from the tournament after the group stage.（据报导，意大利队不敌斯洛伐克队，在小组赛阶段被淘汰出局。）

联想记忆

elimination *n.* 消除；淘汰
obsolete *adj.* 淘汰的；过时的

单词	释义
congestion	*n.* If there is congestion in a place, the place is extremely crowded and blocked with traffic or people. 拥挤，拥塞
	n. Congestion in a part of the body is a medical condition in which the part becomes blocked. （身体部位的）堵塞

双语例句

The bus lanes are designed to ease traffic congestion but they remain controversial. （设计公交车道是为了缓解交通拥堵，但人们对此仍有争议。）

The swimmers frequently suffered from lung congestion, breathing difficulties, and sneezing. （这些游泳选手经常出现肺部淤血、呼吸困难以及打喷嚏等症状。）

联想记忆

jam *n.* 堵塞，拥挤；果酱 *v.* 挤满；卡住

96. As the agency has discovered, ***virtually*** anything from loss of a job to family breakup can ***trigger*** poverty.

单词	释义
virtually	*adv.* You can use virtually to indicate that something is so nearly true that for most purposes it can be regarded as true. 几乎；实际上
	adv. If something exists virtually, it is created by means of virtual reality techniques. 虚拟地

双语例句

By the 1960s, widespread vaccination campaigns had virtually eliminated polio from Europe. （到20世纪60年代，由于疫苗接种广泛，欧洲几乎根除了小儿麻痹症。）

On the other hand, the community is only virtually there, and disappears with the flick of a button. （另一方面，这个社区只是虚拟的，轻轻点一下按钮就会消失。）

联想记忆

virtual *adj.* 虚拟的；实际的

单词	释义
trigger	*v.* If something triggers an event or situation, it causes it to happen. To trigger a bomb or system means to cause it to function. 引起，导致；引爆
	n. The trigger of a gun is a small lever which you pull to fire it. 扳机

双语例句

The move triggered protests around the country, with some calling for the king to step down.（此举引发了全国各地的抗议活动，一些人要求国王下台。）

Burglars broke into his house and fled empty-handed after triggering the alarm.（窃贼闯入他的房子，触发报警器后空手而逃。）

The youngster is said to have admitted to pulling the trigger in the shootings.（据说，这个年轻人承认在枪击事件中扣动了扳机。）

联想记忆

arouse *v.* 引起，激起；唤醒
provoke *v.* 引起；激怒，挑衅
stir *v.* 搅拌；激发；爆炒 *n.* 搅拌；激动

97. The *victim* volunteered at the Redress Charity, a human rights organization which supports survivors of *torture*.

单词	释义
victim	*n.* A victim is someone who has been hurt or killed, or someone who has suffered as a result of unpleasant circumstances. 受害者；牺牲品

双语例句

The elder victim was seriously injured when rocks were dropped on his head.（当石头掉落砸到他头上时，这位高龄受害者受了重伤。）

The victim is described as white, 5ft, slim, with shoulder length brown hair and glasses.（据描述，受害者是白人，身高五英尺，身材纤瘦，有着齐肩棕发并戴着眼镜。）

联想记忆

victimize *v.* 使受害；使牺牲

单词	释义
torture	*v.* If someone is tortured, another person deliberately causes them terrible pain over a period of time, in order to punish them or to make them reveal information. 折磨；拷打
	n. Torture is also a NOUN. 折磨；拷打

双语例句

The soldiers have been kidnapped by Iraqi militants, often tortured, sometimes killed.（这些士兵被伊拉克武装分子绑架，经常受到折磨，有的人被杀害了。）

They were treated well but being held captive had been "psychological torture". （他们受到了很好的待遇，但被关押是一种"心理折磨"。）

联想记忆

torment *v.* 折磨；使痛苦 *n.* 折磨；痛苦
afflict *v.* 折磨，使痛苦

98. The dog's barking and *aggressive* behavior was a frequent source of *friction* between the two neighbors.

单词	释义
aggressive	*adj.* An aggressive person or animal has a quality of anger and determination that makes them ready to attack other people. 好斗的；侵略性的
	adj. People who are aggressive in their work or other activities behave in a forceful way because they are very eager to succeed. 好强的

双语例句

Brain injury is likely to increase the risk of violent and aggressive behavior.（大脑损伤可能会增加暴力和攻击性行为的风险。）

Taro finally came to the conclusion that he should be aggressive in order to survive in a free society.（塔罗最后得出结论，要在一个自由的社会生存下去就必须奋力拼搏。）

联想记忆

aggression *n.* 侵略；侵犯；进攻

单词	释义
friction	*n.* If there is friction between people, there is disagreement and argument between them. 摩擦，分歧
	n. Friction is the force that makes it difficult for things to move freely when they are touching each other. 摩擦力

双语例句

Signs of friction between Citi and Wells Fargo popped up this week, though without much notice.（花旗银行和富国银行之间本周出现了摩擦的迹象，不过没有引起太多注意。）

These substances reduce friction between the moving parts of equipment.（这些物质能减少设备运动部件之间的摩擦。）

联想记忆

divergence *n.* 差异，不同；分歧

fiction *n.* 小说；虚构的事

99. ***Traversing*** the mountains on a summer holiday had a ***profound*** effect on the 19-year-old author-to-be.

单词	释义
traverse	*v.* If someone or something traverses an area of land or water, they go across it. 穿过，穿越

双语例句

At the age of 72 he began fitness preparations traversing Nepal east to west on foot.（他在72岁时开始健身，准备由东至西徒步穿越尼泊尔。）

As we turned inland and traversed through Nevada and Arizona, I noticed an interesting phenomenon.（当我们转向内陆地区穿越内华达州和亚利桑那州时，我发现了一个有趣的现象。）

联想记忆

traverser *n.* 穿越者；（铁路的）转盘

单词	释义
profound	*adj.* You use profound to emphasize that something is very great or intense. 深刻的；极大的

双语例句

It is widely accepted that environment has a profound influence on one's personality.（人们普遍认为，环境对人的性格有深远影响。）

Over the next several months, Mr. Hilton's career would undergo profound changes in multiple aspects.（在接下来的几个月里，希尔顿先生的职业生涯将在多方面发生深刻变化。）

联想记忆

intensive *adj.* 加强的；集中的

100. The pope kept up his full, ***vigorous*** schedule this Christmas Eve, despite his ***frail*** health.

单词	释义
vigorous	*adj.* A vigorous person does things with great energy and enthusiasm. 精力充沛的
	adj. A vigorous physical activity involves using lots of energy, usually to do short and repeated actions. 用力的；有力的

双语例句

The oldest of the four candidates, Gary leaves no doubt he is vigorous and healthy.（盖瑞在四位候选人中年龄最大，但毫无疑问他精力充沛，身体健康。）

It's often advisable to see a physical therapist before starting a vigorous jogging training program.（在开始剧烈的慢跑训练计划之前，通常建议去咨询理疗师。）

联想记忆

vigor *n.* 精力；活力

单词	释义
frail	*adj.* Someone who is frail is not very strong or healthy. 虚弱的
	adj. Something that is frail is easily broken or damaged. 易碎的；脆弱的

双语例句

He looks somewhat frail, relying on a cane and using a wheelchair occasionally.（他看起来有些虚弱，拄着拐杖，偶尔还需要使用轮椅。）

Companies in the agricultural sector face opportunities, despite a frail global economy.（尽管全球经济疲软，农业领域的公司却迎来发展机遇。）

联想记忆

feeble *adj.* 虚弱的；微弱的

单元练习 10

使用本单元核心词汇的适当形式填空，并将句子译为中文。

1. The CAW has seen some 15,000 auto industry jobs _____ in Canada since 2009.
2. Early life exposures may have a _____ influence on health in childhood and beyond.
3. Despite their dedication, the pay they receive is not _____ with their time and effort.
4. It is currently the world's only online guitar shop catering _____ for left-handed people.
5. The celebration of Labor Day, in honor of the working class, was _____ in the United States in 1882.
6. Poor eating habits and irregular sleeping patterns may play a role in _____ mental problems.
7. While college enrollment is at an all-time high, completion rates have remained _____ flat over the past 30 years.
8. The President hoped the _____ of this tragedy would get the medical and psychological support they need.
9. There is a body of research suggesting that violent games can lead to _____ thoughts, if not to violence itself.
10. Portland residents are among the most road rage-free in the nation, followed by the _____ drivers in Cleveland and Baltimore.

Unit 11

★ 本单元核心词汇 ★

arduous	temporary	imminent	diminish	vanish
immigration	ravage	occurrence	frustrate	emerge
destructive	authentic	horizon	flourish	disclose
confidential	tempting	tremendous	adventure	supervise

★ 本单元拓展词汇 ★

strenuous	plate	activist	charity	radial
raze	champagne	incur	oxygen	calendar
bustling	dim	thrive	colossal	bother
diversity	genuine	festival	perception	vertical
arise	venture	route	precaution	enclose
transcription	recur	whisper	folksong	gigantic

Unit 11

101. After an ***arduous*** journey across the mountains, she and her family found ***temporary*** shelter in the home of an Albanian man.

单词	释义
arduous	*adj.* Something that is arduous is difficult and tiring, and involves a lot of effort. 艰难的；费力的

双语例句

After an arduous 22-hour train journey, the brothers were dropped off in Glasgow. （经过22个小时艰辛的火车之旅后，兄弟俩在格拉斯哥下车了。）

The worst outcome would be arduous rules that do little to improve food safety. （最坏的结果可能是，费劲制定的规则对改善食品安全作用微乎其微。）

联想记忆

strenuous *adj.* 费力的；艰苦的

单词	释义
temporary	*adj.* Something that is temporary lasts for a limited time. 暂时的，临时的

双语例句

About 1,000 temporary jobs would be created during the construction period of the farm. （在农场建设期间将会产生大约1 000个临时工作岗位。）

Students on the farm, supervised by an instructor, are paid on a temporary basis for their assistance. （农场的实习学生在师傅的指导下工作，因其协助而获得临时报酬。）

联想记忆

temporarily *adv.* 临时地；暂时地
temporal *adj.* 暂时的；时间的

102. Despite facing an ***imminent*** labor shortage as its population ages, Japan has done little to open itself up to ***immigration***.

单词	释义
imminent	*adj.* If you say something is imminent, especially something unpleasant, you mean it is almost certain to happen very soon. 即将发生的

双语例句

More explosions could be imminent from bombs planted in unknown locations. （放置在不明地点的炸弹可能会引起更多爆炸。）

One out of ten surveyed charities said they were in imminent danger of folding due to financial reasons.（十分之一被调研的慈善机构表示，由于经济原因，它们面临即将关闭的风险。）

联想记忆

forthcoming *adj.* 即将到来的
pending *adj.* 即将发生的

单词	释义
immigration	*n.* Immigration is the coming of people into a country in order to live and work there. 移居；移民

双语例句

The economy and illegal immigration are the biggest problems facing the United States.（经济低迷和非法移民是美国面临的两个最大问题。）

Activist marched through the city center, promoting worker rights and immigration reform.（活动人士在市中心游行，呼吁改善工人权益，并改革移民制度。）

联想记忆

immigrant *n.* 移民 *adj.* 移民的；迁入的
immigrate *v.* 移民；移居入境
migrate *v.* （候鸟或动物）迁徙；移居；迁移

103. Frequent floods *ravage* cities in the south and east, and droughts are a regular *occurrence* in the north and west.

单词	释义
ravage	*v.* A town, country, or economy that has been ravaged is one that has been damaged so much that it is almost completely destroyed. 摧毁，破坏

双语例句

Irene had ravaged the Bahamas and struck North Carolina early Saturday with winds over 75 mph.（艾琳肆虐巴哈马群岛，于周六早些时候袭击了北卡罗莱纳州，风速超过每小时75英里。）

Efforts to make it a national park began in the 1970s but were held up by decades of war that ravaged the country.（20世纪70年代曾着手把它建成国家公园，但数十年的内战使国家满目疮痍，该计划也被搁置下来。）

联想记忆

raze *v.* 破坏；拆毁；夷为平地

单词	释义
occurrence	*n.* An occurrence is something that happens, or the fact that something happens. 发生的事情；发生

双语例句

Working through lunch breaks is a common occurrence for many office workers in Britain.（对英国的许多上班族来说，午休时间进行工作是很常见的。）

The destructive and deadly wind gust on Saturday evening in Indianapolis was no chance occurrence.（周六晚上印第安纳波利斯的破坏性致命阵风绝不是偶然发生的。）

联想记忆

occur *v.* 发生；出现；存在
recur *v.* 反复出现；复发
incur *v.* 引发；招致

104. Known sometimes as the "birthdate effect", this generally ***diminishes*** as children get older but does not ***vanish***.

单词	释义
diminish	*v.* When something diminishes or when something diminishes it, it becomes reduced in size, importance or intensity. 变少；使减少

双语例句

His need for oxygen and fluids diminished, and his blood pressure returned to normal.（他需要的氧气和输液减少，血压恢复了正常。）

To compare Jobs to da Vinci is an absurd idea that diminishes the value of true innovators.（将乔布斯与达·芬奇相提并论是荒谬的，这样贬低了真正创新者的价值。）

联想记忆

dim *adj.* 暗淡的，昏暗的；模糊的；悲观的 *v.* 变暗淡；使暗淡

单词	释义
vanish	*v.* If something such as a species of animal or a tradition vanishes, it stops existing. 消失；消亡
	v. If someone vanishes, they disappear suddenly or in a way that cannot be explained. 失踪

双语例句

Bald eagles had vanished from all but the remote corners of the country.（除了偏远的角落，秃鹰已经从全国各地消失了。）

The business of journalism is changing, and many newspapers will vanish in the coming years.（新闻报刊业正悄然发生变化，许多报纸将在未来几年内消失。）

Miss McNicol from Essex vanished on the way home from a music festival in Hampshire.（来自艾塞克斯的麦克尼科尔小姐参加完汉普郡音乐节后，在回家的路上失踪了。）

联想记忆

fade *v.* 逐渐消失；褪色

105. People with conduct disorders can become *frustrated* and angry, which can contribute to their *destructive* behaviors.

单词	释义
frustrate	*v.* If something frustrates you, it upsets or angers you because you are unable to do anything about the problems it creates. 使沮丧，使感到灰心
	v. If someone or something frustrates a plan or attempt to do something, they prevent it from happening. 挫败

双语例句

Long lines around the country frustrated voters in the election's early hours.（选举最初的几个小时，全国上下长长的队伍让选民感到很沮丧。）

Environmentalists got four of seven plans passed, though the most ambitious was frustrated.（环保主义者七项计划中有四项获得通过，不过最为看好的一项却受挫。）

联想记忆

frustration *n.* 挫折；挫败
bother *v.* 费心；烦扰

单词	释义
destructive	*adj.* Something that is destructive causes or is capable of causing great damage or harm. 破坏的；毁灭性的

双语例句

A destructive storm hit North Carolina last week, its winds reaching 145 mph.（一场破坏性风暴上周袭击了北卡罗莱纳州，风速高达每小时145英里。）

The virus is so destructive that it can even infect unborn children.（该病毒具有很强的破坏性，甚至可以感染未出生的胎儿。）

联想记忆

destruction *n.* 破坏；摧毁
destruct *v.* 破坏；自毁

106. Out of the darkness of the bushes, we see the soaring of an ***authentic*** American eagle on the ***horizon***.

单词	释义
authentic	*adj.* An authentic person, object, or emotion is genuine. An authentic piece of information or account of something is reliable. 真正的；真实可靠的
	adj. If you describe something as authentic, you mean that it is such a good imitation that it is almost the same as the original. 逼真的

双语例句

After quite a few hamburgers, a friend persuaded me to try an authentic Italian dinner.（吃过几次汉堡后，一个朋友劝我尝试一下正宗的意大利餐。）

Viewing movies with this type of glasses provides listeners with an authentic theater experience.（戴这种眼镜看电影可以让观众体验逼真的影院效果。）

联想记忆

genuine *adj.* 真实的；真正的

单词	释义
horizon	*n.* The horizon is the line in the far distance where the sky seems to meet the land or the sea. 地平线
	n. Your horizons are the limits of what you want to do or of what you are interested or involved in. 眼界，阅历

双语例句

As the sky darkened and storm clouds gathered on the horizon, our jeep turned toward home.（天色变暗，乌云笼罩在地平线上，我们便开着吉普车掉头回家。）

The festival became a source of expanding the horizons for each participant of the event in his perception of cultural diversity.（这个庆典活动能让每位参与者感受文化多样性，拓宽视野。）

联想记忆

horizontal *adj.* 水平的；地平线的
vertical *adj.* 垂直的，竖直的

107. ***Emerging*** from the main buildings, outdoor gardens ***flourish*** with more than 30,000 plants.

单词	释义
emerge	*v.* To emerge means to move out of or away from something and become visible. 出现；显现
	v. If you emerge from a difficult or bad experience, you come to the end of it. 摆脱；恢复过来

双语例句

The committees is working on reform proposals, but so far no one plan has emerged for consideration.（委员会正在研究改革方案，但至今还没有提出一项可以供讨论的计划。）

Then it emerged that the temperature had begun rising centuries earlier than carbon dioxide.（后来发现，在二氧化碳出现前几个世纪气温就已经开始上升了。）

Mixed economic signals call into question how long it will take for the country to emerge from recession.（喜忧参半的经济信号让人困惑，这个国家需要多长时间才能走出衰退。）

联想记忆

emergence *n.* 出现；发生
arise *v.* 产生，出现；起身

单词	释义
flourish	*v.* If a plant or animal flourishes, it grows well or is healthy because the conditions are right for it.（动植物因环境适宜而）旺盛
	v. If something flourishes, it is successful, active, or common, and developing quickly and strongly. 繁荣，兴旺

双语例句

Some 3,000 species of flowering plants flourish in Jamaica, 800 of them unique to the island.（牙买加繁茂的开花植物约有3 000种，其中800种是这个岛国的独

有品种。)

Private radio stations and newspapers have flourished in Pakistan over the past few years.（在过去几年，巴基斯坦的私营广播电台和报纸行业蓬勃发展。）

联想记忆

thrive *v.* 兴旺，繁荣；茁壮成长

108. The venture firm doesn't *disclose* much detail about its investments, which it says should be kept *confidential*.

单词	释义
disclose	*v.* If you disclose new or secret information, you tell people about it. 透露；揭露；公开

双语例句

Military officials will not disclose the actual route of the flight as a precaution.（为了防患未然，军方官员不会透露飞机的实际飞行路线。）

Additional details will be disclosed when the company reports full financial results next week.（更多细节将在公司下周公布完整的财务报告时披露。）

联想记忆

disclosure *n.* 披露；公开
enclose *v.* 包围，围住；随信附上

单词	释义
confidential	*adj.* Information that is confidential is meant to be kept secret. 保密的
	adj. If you talk to someone in a confidential way, you talk to them quietly because what you are saying is secret or private. 悄悄的

双语例句

The spokesman added that interview transcriptions could not be published as the details were confidential.（发言人补充道，访谈内容不能公开，因为很多细节都是保密的。）

They held champagne glasses and leaned together, talking in confidential whispers.（他们举着香槟酒杯，倚靠在一起，说着悄悄话。）

联想记忆

confidentiality *n.* 机密，保密性

109. The *tremendous* growth of drugs markets in the developing world proved too *tempting* to ignore.

单词	释义
tremendous	*adj.* You use tremendous to emphasize how strong a feeling or quality is, or how large an amount is. 非常的；巨大的
	adj. You can describe someone or something as tremendous when you think they are very good or very impressive. 极好的，精彩的

双语例句

These data clearly show the majority of consumers had tremendous confidence in the Toyota brand.（这些数据清楚地表明，大多数消费者都对丰田品牌抱有巨大信心。）

Overall her songs are really tremendous folksongs and she's a great performer.（总的来说，她的歌都是非常精彩的民歌，她也是一位优秀的歌手。）

联想记忆

gigantic *adj.* 巨大的；不可思议的
colossal *adj.* 巨大的，庞大的

单词	释义
tempting	*adj.* If something is tempting, it is attractive and makes you want to do it or have it. 诱人的；有吸引力的

双语例句

It is tempting to dig deeper into his past to find the roots of his success.（人们特别想了解他的过去，探寻他成功的根源。）

These days, the city is musically bustling, its concert listings packed with tempting choices.（近些天，这个城市音乐活动丰富，演奏会的曲目都非常吸引人。）

联想记忆

temptation *n.* 引诱；诱惑物
tempt *v.* 诱惑；引起；冒……的风险
enticing *adj.* 诱人的；有吸引力的

110. The *adventure* park includes a climbing wall and employed three full-time staff members to *supervise* children.

Unit 11

单词	释义
adventure	*n.* If someone has an adventure, they become involved in an unusual, exciting, and somewhat dangerous trip or series of events. 冒险经历
	v. Adventure means engage in a risky activity or put one's money or life at risk. 冒险干；冒……的风险

双语例句

The 13,400-acre private resort in Montana targets the super-rich with a taste for adventure.（这个位于蒙大拿州的私人度假村占地13 400英亩，主要面向喜欢冒险的超级富豪。）

The document contains lists of the men and women who adventured money to the electric company.（文件列出了冒险向这家电力公司投资的人员名单。）

联想记忆

adventurous *adj.* 爱冒险的；大胆的；充满危险的
venture *n.* 风险；风险项目 *v.* 冒险去做

单词	释义
supervise	*v.* If you supervise an activity or a person, you make sure that the activity is done correctly or that the person is doing a task or behaving correctly. 监督

双语例句

The flights are operated by on-board systems supervised by a ground-based observer pilot.（飞机靠机载系统操作，由一名地面观察飞行员进行控制。）

Radial units allow nurses to visually supervise patients and spend more time on patient care.（放射状单元能让护士直观地管理病人，因此能有更多的时间对他们进行护理。）

联想记忆

supervision *n.* 监督，管理

单元练习 11

使用本单元核心词汇的适当形式填空，并将句子译为中文。

1. The government _____ the preparations for national elections taking place last week.
2. The increasing frequency of his injuries has led to wild rumors of an _____ retirement.
3. Brenda _____ in February 2012 after last being seen dropping off her children at school.
4. The quiet neighborhood has quite a few excellent restaurants serving _____ local cuisine.
5. The school district _____ this week that it opened an internal inquiry in November 2021.
6. Theft is rare _____ there because the punishment feels completely out of balance with the crime.
7. The vehicle ban coming into effect Friday applies to cars bearing _____ black license plates.
8. As the calendar approaches December 25th, inventory levels will continually _____ throughout the stores.
9. There are companies that have survived, and even _____, in this era of decline for headphone manufacturers.
10. Car dealerships will treat your _____ information with the utmost security, under the so-called Red Flags Rule.

Unit 12

★ 本单元核心词汇 ★

stunning	prescription	surplus	yield	enhance
limp	tolerant	abuse	dismal	promptly
axe	enforce	delivery	attain	mission
flexible	considerable	triumph	erupt	addicted

★ 本单元拓展词汇 ★

cocaine	wrestler	migraine	subscribe	elastic
intimidate	commodity	redundant	malaria	intervention
surrender	succumb	enclave	amplify	bid
hobble	assassination	fleet	breed	slash
maltreatment	gorgeous	dreary	miserable	explode
maintain	downsize	execute	humanitarian	colony
calcium	inscribe	vaccine	triumphant	seal

111. When his grandmother passed away, he started getting migraines and became ***addicted*** to ***prescription*** painkillers.

单词	释义
addicted	*adj.* Someone who is addicted to something cannot stop it. 上瘾的
	adj. If you say that someone is addicted to something, you mean that they like it very much and want to spend as much time doing it as possible. 入迷的

双语例句

The children of mothers who use cocaine are often born addicted to the drug.（吸食可卡因的母亲生下的孩子通常对这种毒品也上瘾。）

By the time I graduated from third grade I was already addicted to history.（三年级刚上完时，我就对历史着迷了。）

联想记忆

addict *v.* 使上瘾；使沉溺 *n.* 上瘾者
addictive *adj.* 上瘾的
addiction *n.* 上瘾；沉溺

单词	释义
prescription	*n.* A prescription is the piece of paper on which a doctor writes an order for medicine. 处方
	n. A prescription is a medicine that a doctor has told you to take. 处方药

双语例句

Some drugs have so few side effects that they are available without a prescription.（一些药物的副作用很小，无需处方便可购买。）

At the chemist picking up my prescription, I saw two young guys waving to me.（在药剂师处取药时，我看见两个年轻人向我挥手。）

联想记忆

prescribe *v.* 规定；开处方
subscribe *v.* 订阅，订购
inscribe *v.* 铭刻；书写

112. The finances are in better shape than they were a decade ago during a budget ***surplus***, when the comparable ***yield*** was 5.5%.

单词	释义
surplus	*n.* If there is a surplus of something, there is more than is needed. 过剩
	adj. Surplus is used to describe something that is extra or that is more than is needed. 过剩的，多余的
	n. If a country has a trade surplus, it exports more than it imports. （贸易）顺差

双语例句

Universities need an income surplus of 3% a year for reinvestment and to fund future developments. （大学每年需要3%的收入盈余用于再投资，为未来发展提供资金。）

The food aid plan may be expanded to other surplus commodities, Agriculture Secretary Dan said. （农业部长丹表示，粮食援助计划可能扩大到其他过剩商品。）

Spain, which is the eurozone's fourth-largest economy, has not recorded a monthly trade surplus since 1971. （作为欧元区第四大经济体，西班牙自1971年以来从未出现过月度贸易顺差。）

联想记忆

redundant *adj.* 多余的，冗余的

单词	释义
yield	*n.* A yield is the amount of profit produced by an investment, or the amount of food produced on an area of land or by a number of animals. 收益；产量
	v. If something yields a result or piece of information, it produces it. 产生
	v. If you yield to someone or something, you stop resisting them. 屈服

双语例句

Based on the current stock price, investors can expect a yield of about 2.3% going forward. （根据目前的股价，投资者可以预期未来的收益率约为2.3%。）

The students' opinions of distance learning versus traditional methods yielded mixed results. （学生对远程教学和传统教学的看法褒贬不一。）

It is reported that the company yielded to the toughest demand to avoid government intervention. （据说这家公司为了避免政府干预，对这些强硬的要求妥协了。）

联想记忆

surrender *v.* 投降；放弃 *n.* 投降；屈服
succumb *v.* （向诱惑、压力）屈服

113. Mr. Wellstone's image as a fighter has been ***enhanced*** by a ***limp***, which was the product of being a wrestler while at college.

单词	释义
enhance	*v.* To enhance something means to improve its value, quality or attractiveness. 提高，增强；改善

双语例句

In the corner of the El Paso supermarket, enhanced versions of bath tissue and paper towels are hitting shelves now.（在埃尔帕索这家超市的角落里，增强型厕纸和纸巾已经上架。）

The international community should take necessary steps to enhance cooperation to prevent and combat terrorism.（国际社会应采取必要措施加强合作，来预防和打击恐怖主义。）

联想记忆

heighten *v.* 提高；增强
amplify *v.* 放大；增强；详述

单词	释义
limp	*n.* If a person walks with a limp, they walk in an uneven way because one of their legs or feet is injured. 跛行
	v. Limp is also a VERB. 瘸着脚走，跛行

双语例句

He was left with a permanent limp from the accident, which was considered an assassination attempt.（那次意外导致他终生跛行，外界认为那是针对他的一次暗杀行动。）

Last year, Bryan limped across the finish line of the 10k race he entered.（去年，布莱恩参加了10 000米长跑比赛，最后一瘸一拐地穿过了终点线。）

联想记忆

hobble *v.* 跛行；蹒跚 *n.* 跛行步态

114. This has created an environment which is ***tolerant*** of or even favorable to drug ***abuse*** and spoils international drug prevention efforts currently under way.

单词	释义
tolerant	*adj.* Someone who is tolerant allows other people to say and do as they like and he is willing to accept different races, religions, and lifestyles. 宽容的；容忍的；忍受的
	adj. If a plant, animal, or machine is tolerant of particular conditions or types of treatment, it is able to bear them without being damaged. 有耐受性的

双语例句

The French seem extraordinarily tolerant about being spied on in their daily life. （法国人似乎对日常生活中被人监视格外宽容。）

Over the next year investigators will test the various strains of salt-tolerant rice they've bred.（在接下来的一年时间里，研究人员将测试他们培育的各种耐盐水稻品种。）

联想记忆

tolerance *n.* 宽容；容忍；公差
tolerate *v.* 忍受；默许；宽恕

单词	释义
abuse	*n.* Abuse of something is the use of it in a wrong way or for a bad purpose. 滥用
	n. Abuse of someone is cruel and violent treatment of them. 虐待
	v. Abuse is also a VERB. 虐待

双语例句

In recent years, the abuse of prescription drugs, particularly by children, has soared.（近年来，滥用处方药，特别是儿童滥用处方药的情况急剧上升。）

Young people are often unaware that domestic abuse included intimidating and controlling behavior.（年轻人往往不知道，家暴包括恐吓和控制行为。）

The doctor notices scars, burns, and slashes on the boy, and assumes the boy is being abused.（医生注意到男孩身上的疤痕、烧伤和刀伤，认为男孩受到了虐待。）

联想记忆

abusive *adj.* 滥用的；虐待的；辱骂的
maltreatment *n.* 虐待，粗暴对待

115. When the company recently announced *dismal* earnings, its shares *promptly* fell 10% and have not recovered.

单词	释义
dismal	*adj.* Something that is dismal is bad in a sad or depressing way. 惨淡的
	adj. Something that is dismal is sad and depressing, especially in appearance.（尤指外表）沉闷的，阴郁的

双语例句

The initial public offering market is reviving after a dismal period from 2007 to early 2010.（股票公开发行市场经历了2007年到2010年初的低迷时期后开始慢慢复苏。）

Nobody's mood was helped by the dismal weather outdoors; the sky was grey and the wind was blasting.（外面阴沉的天气无法让人心情好起来，天空灰暗，狂风怒作。）

联想记忆

dreary *adj.* 沉闷的；令人沮丧的
miserable *adj.* 悲惨的；痛苦的

单词	释义
promptly	*adv.* If you do something promptly, you do it immediately. 立即，迅速地
	adv. If you do something promptly at a particular time, you do it at exactly that time. 准点地

双语例句

When the Braves cut him last year, Sanchez promptly quit baseball and went back to school.（勇士队去年将他开除后，桑切斯立即退出棒球界，回到了学校。）

At the front of this big store are large double doors that open promptly at 9 a.m.（这家大商场的正门是超大双拉门，每早九点准时打开。）

联想记忆

prompt *adj.* 敏捷的，迅速的 *v.* 提示；促进；激起 *n.* 提词；提示

116. Thousands of jobs have been ***axed*** in the electricity supply sector since the price cuts were ***enforced*** last year.

单词	释义
axe	*v.* If someone's job or something such as a public service or a television program is axed, it is ended suddenly and without discussion. 削减
	n. An axe is a tool used for cutting wood. It consists of a heavy metal blade that is sharp at one edge and attached by its other edge to a handle. 斧子

双语例句

The firm slashed its dividend and announced that it will axe more than 11,000 jobs.（公司削减了股息，并宣称将裁减超过11 000个工作岗位。）

He maintained that he was protecting himself from Mr. Cox, who came at him with an axe.（他坚持认为他是正当防卫，因为考克斯手持斧头向他逼过来。）

联想记忆

downsize *v.* 使缩小规模

slash *v.* 削减；严厉批评 *n.* 砍伤；斜杠

单词	释义
enforce	*v.* If people in authority enforce a law or a rule, they make sure that it is obeyed, usually by punishing people who do not obey it. 实施，强制执行

双语例句

Gay relationships are still a crime in Burma, but the law is not strictly enforced.（同性恋在缅甸仍然是一种违法行为，但法律并没有严格执行。）

Kenya's elephant population fell from 40,000 in 1970 to 5,000 in 1988, and only began to rise when the trading ban was enforced.（肯尼亚的大象数量从1970年的40 000头下降到1988年的5 000头，直到贸易禁令实施后其数量才开始上升。）

联想记忆

enforcement *n.* 执行

execute *v.* 执行，实施；处决

117. He touched on areas from rebuilding water and electrical systems to mail *delivery* and simplified procedures to *attain* federal help.

单词	释义
delivery	*n.* Delivery is the bringing of letters, packages, or other goods to someone's house or to another place where they want them. 递送，交付
	n. You talk about someone's delivery when you are referring to the way in which they give a speech or lecture. 演讲方式
	n. Delivery is the process of giving birth to a baby. 分娩

双语例句

The uprising is threatening the delivery of humanitarian supplies of food and medicine.（这场暴乱影响着食品和药品等人道主义物资的运送。）

His speeches were magnificently written but his delivery was hopeless.（他的演讲词写得很好，但演讲却不敢恭维。）

Ms. Cadell said it is still "very important" for women to receive the vaccine after delivery.（卡德尔女士说，女性分娩后接种该疫苗仍然非常重要。）

联想记忆

deliver *v.* 交付；递送；给……接生

单词	释义
attain	*v.* If you attain something, you gain it or achieve it, often after a lot of effort. （经过努力）获得；达到

双语例句

His company may achieve the level of international success that Apple has attained.（他的公司可能会像苹果公司那样在国际上取得成功。）

In 1973, the Bahamas attained full independence within the Commonwealth, having been a British colony since 1783.（1973年，巴哈马群岛在英联邦内获得完全独立，该岛国自1783年以来一直是英属殖民地。）

联想记忆

attainment *n.* 达到；成就；造诣
accomplish *v.* 达到，实现

118. The colleges remain firmly focused on their *mission* of providing a *flexible* and quality education to nontraditional students.

单词	释义
mission	*n.* If you say that you have a mission, you mean that you have a strong commitment and sense of duty to do or achieve something. 使命，任务
	n. A mission is a group of people who have been sent to a foreign country to carry out an official task. 驻外使团

双语例句

He always thought that his main mission in life, and his greatest pleasure, was in teaching the deaf.（他一直认为，他人生的主要使命和最大乐趣就是教授聋哑人。）

Indonesia and Spain have agreed to send more trade missions in the future in a bid to further promote trade relations.（为了进一步促进贸易关系，印度尼西亚和西班牙同意将来互派更多贸易代表团。）

联想记忆

missionary *adj.* 传教的；传教士的 *n.* 传教士

单词	释义
flexible	*adj.* Something or someone that is flexible is able to change easily and adapt to different conditions and circumstances as they occur. 灵活的
	adj. A flexible object or material can be bent easily without breaking. 柔韧的

双语例句

Remote working technologies make it easy for her to have a flexible schedule.（远程办公技术让她可以灵活地安排时间。）

Those who come to Yoga learn ways to breathe, stretch and become more flexible.（来练瑜伽的人学会用各种方式呼吸、伸展，使身体变得更加柔韧。）

联想记忆

flexibility *n.* 灵活性
elastic *adj.* 灵活的；有弹性的

119. In the 1980s there was ***considerable*** debate over which of the two great tech enclaves, Boston's Rte. 128 and Silicon Valley, would ***triumph***.

单词	释义
considerable	*adj.* Considerable means great in amount or degree. 相当多的；相当大的

双语例句

Google has spent considerable effort building an electric car fleet at its headquarters.（谷歌已着手下功夫在总部建立一个电动汽车研发团队。）

Considerable evidence has accumulated that vitamin D and calcium help to treat bone loss.（大量证据表明，维生素D和钙有助于治疗骨质疏松。）

联想记忆

considerate *adj.* 体贴的；考虑周到的

单词	释义
triumph	*v.* If someone or something triumphs, they gain complete success, control, or victory, often after a long or difficult struggle. 获胜
	n. A triumph is a great success or achievement, often one that has been gained with a lot of skill or effort. 胜利；成功

读美句·学单词

双语例句

Ireland needed to win by six points to reach the semi-final qualifier but triumphed 34-16 to advance.（爱尔兰队需要赢6分才能进入半决赛预选赛，但最终以34-16获胜晋级。）

Though it looks like a modest dust mask, the N95 is a triumph of materials science.（虽然N95看起来像普通的防尘面罩，但它是材料学的巨大成功。）

联想记忆

triumphant *adj.* 胜利的；成功的；得意洋洋的

120. Frustration recently *erupted* into violence in the *stunning* wine-producing valleys of the Western Cape where I traveled.

单词	释义
erupt	*v.* You say that someone erupts when they suddenly have a change in mood; if violence or fighting erupts, it suddenly begins or gets worse in a violent way. 爆发，突然发生
	v. When a volcano erupts, it throws out a lot of hot, melted rock called lava, as well as ash and steam. 喷发

双语例句

Jordan has declared that, should war erupt, it would seal its borders to prevent more Iraqis flooding across.（约旦方面称，一旦爆发战争就会封锁边界，防止更多的伊拉克人涌入。）

Although these volcanoes do not erupt frequently, they threaten major populations and developments.（虽然这些火山不常喷发，但给主要人口聚集区和当地发展造成了威胁。）

联想记忆

eruption *n.* 爆发；喷发
explode *v.* 爆炸；爆发；激增

单词	释义
stunning	*adj.* A stunning person or thing or event is extremely beautiful or impressive. 极美的；令人震惊的

双语例句

There is nowhere better to experience stunning scenery, great country pubs and warm hospitality than the Yorkshire Dales. （没有什么地方比约克郡山谷更适合欣赏美丽的风景，体验非凡的乡村酒吧，感受当地人的热情好客了。）

Now we are seeing stunning progress, with many countries reporting dramatic reductions in malaria cases. （我们现在取得了巨大进展，许多国家的疟疾病例显著减少。）

联想记忆

stun *v.* 使震惊；给人以深刻印象
gorgeous *adj.* 绚丽的；令人愉快的
spectacular *adj.* 壮观的，令人惊叹的

单元练习 12

使用本单元核心词汇的适当形式填空，并将句子译为中文。

1. The victory is celebrated by firecrackers and lights to signify the _____ of good over evil.
2. Dias has claimed that the church policies are not _____ equally against men and women.
3. The country's long struggle with racism _____, with thousands of people taking to the streets.
4. People can be _____ to different things — alcohol, drug, certain foods, or even television.
5. In 2016, Fred landed in Laramie, Wyoming, where he _____ purchased his new residence.
6. For 20 plus years, Jamba Juice has been on a _____ to simplify and improve healthy living.
7. Despite the efforts to _____ rights for women and girls in Afghanistan, stories of abuse keep coming to light.
8. It is desired to build a _____ education system where children practice solving social challenges.
9. His initial response to Sunday's dramatic events _____ in the form of a written statement.
10. Miss Brown rose from the table _____ annoyed, and went straight home in a flood of tears and a sedan chair.

Unit 13

★ 本单元核心词汇 ★

shift	lessen	emission	highlight	cater
amateur	perceive	indulge	acquaintance	motive
inadequate	decent	sympathetic	instinctive	skepticism
hostility	partial	dimension	mutual	cordial

★ 本单元拓展词汇 ★

gravity	seismic	mitigate	confine	empathy
vegetarian	amicable	tailor	layman	hobbyist
marvelous	compensate	contact	prosecutor	sadden
observatory	aquarium	insufficient	jovial	stroke
intuitive	senator	resentment	infrastructure	breadth
proportional	swing	reciprocal	compassionate	session
conflict	emit			

121. Some companies have been ***shifting*** production outside of Japan to ***lessen*** the impact of the rising currency.

单词	释义
shift	*v.* If you shift something or if it shifts, it moves slightly. 转移，移动
	v. If someone's opinion, a situation, or a policy shifts or is shifted, it changes slightly. Shift is also a NOUN. 改变

双语例句

Like a human, the robot can quickly shift its center of gravity and change direction.（和人类一样，这个机器人能够迅速调整重心，改变方向。）

I have never seen such a seismic shift in public opinion in such a short period of time.（我从来没有见过公众舆论在这么短的时间内发生如此突然的逆转。）

联想记忆

swing *v.* 摆动；改变 *n.* 摇摆；秋千

单词	释义
lessen	*v.* If something lessens or you lessen it, it becomes smaller in size, amount, degree, or importance. 减少；降低；减轻

双语例句

If these reserves were developed, our dependence on overseas energy sources would considerably lessen.（如果这些矿藏能得以开发，我们对海外能源的依赖性将大大降低。）

Modern lifestyles have somehow lessened children's ability to deal with common infections.（现代生活方式在某种程度上削弱了儿童应对常见感染的能力。）

联想记忆

mitigate *v.* 减轻，缓和

122. The problem of rising CO_2 ***emissions*** was ***highlighted*** again recently with the publication of the Global Carbon Project 2015.

单词	释义
emission	*n.* An emission of something such as gas or radiation is the release of it into the atmosphere. 排放

双语例句

This latest technology lowers power usage and heat emission, and boosts battery life.（这项最新技术将降低功耗，减少散热，延长续航时间。）

Particle emissions can cause breathing problems and have also been linked to increased risk of developing cancer.（排放的微粒会导致呼吸问题，而且会增加罹患癌症的风险。）

联想记忆

emit *v.* 发出；发射
emitter *n.* 发射器；发射极

单词	释义
highlight	*v.* If someone or something highlights a point or problem, they emphasize it or make you think about it. 强调；使注意
	v. To highlight a piece of text means to mark it in a different color, either with a special type of pen or on a computer screen.（用不同颜色）标出；（在电脑屏幕上）突出显示
	n. The highlights of an event, activity, or period of time are the most interesting or exciting parts of it. 最精彩的部分

双语例句

Results of the survey highlight the fact that drug use is not confined to our major cities.（调查的结果显示，吸毒不仅仅发生在大城市。）

We identified four periods, highlighted in yellow, which experienced clear rate increases.（我们确定了四个时期，以黄色进行标注，其增长率明显增加了。）

This performance is a highlight of the events celebrating 40 years of diplomatic relations between China and France.（这个表演是中法邦交四十年庆典活动最精彩的环节。）

联想记忆

highlighter *n.* 荧光笔

123. The observatory *caters* for *amateur* astronomers and holds lectures, short talks, debates and observing sessions.

单词	释义
cater	*v.* To cater to a group of people means to provide all the things that they need or want. 满足……需要，迎合
	v. If a person or company caters an occasion such as a wedding or a party, they provide food and drink for all the people there.（在婚礼、派对等场合）提供餐饮服务，承办酒席

双语例句

The food caters well for vegetarians and the staff are really friendly and professional.（这些食物符合素食主义者的口味，而且服务员非常友好，也很专业。）

Currently the industry reporting the highest rate of unemployment is the hotel and catering sector.（目前，失业率最高的行业是酒店和餐饮业。）

联想记忆

tailor *v.* 迎合，适应；定做（衣服） *n.* 裁缝

单词	释义
amateur	*adj.* Amateur sports or activities are done by people as a hobby and not as a job. 业余的
	n. An amateur is someone who does something as a hobby and not as a job. 业余爱好者

双语例句

She developed a passion for acting, as a member of the local amateur dramatic society.（她对表演产生了浓厚的兴趣，于是加入当地的业余戏剧协会。）

Prior to 1968, tennis players were all considered "amateurs" and were not eligible to receive prize money.（1968年以前，一般认为网球运动员都是业余的，没有资格领取奖金。）

联想记忆

layman *n.* 外行
hobbyist *n.* 业余爱好者

124. Sadly, however, those who often seek office are ***perceived*** to be self-***indulged*** rather than have the public good in mind.

单词	释义
perceive	*v.* Perceive means to regard someone or something in a particular way. 认为；理解
	v. If you perceive something, you see, notice, or realize it, especially when it is not obvious. 感知到，注意到

双语例句

People often perceive that some illnesses only happen to older people; however, this isn't the case.（人们总是认为一些疾病只有老年人才会得，然而事实并非如此。）

Smokers clearly perceive benefits from smoking, otherwise they would not pay to do it.（显然，吸烟者可以从吸烟中感受到乐趣，否则他们就不会为此花钱了。）

联想记忆

perception *n.* 知觉；洞察力

单词	释义
indulge	*v.* If you indulge in something or if you indulge yourself, you allow yourself to have or do something that you know you will enjoy. 沉溺；使沉溺
	v. If you indulge someone, you let them have or do what they want, even if this is not good for them. 纵容，迁就

双语例句

Switzerland is a marvelous place to indulge in all your favorite winter sports.（瑞士是个好地方，在这里你可以纵情享受喜爱的冬季运动。）

To compensate for the harshness of his life, his mother indulged him.（为了补偿他在生活中受的苦，母亲非常娇惯他。）

联想记忆

indulgent *adj.* 放纵的；纵容的
indulgence *n.* 沉迷；放纵

125. After interviews with his family, friends and ***acquaintances***, investigators determined that there was no personal ***motive*** for the attack.

单词	释义
acquaintance	*n.* An acquaintance is someone who you have met and know slightly, but not well. 相识之人
	n. If you have an acquaintance with someone, you have met them and you know them. 结识；了解

双语例句

Most of my friends and acquaintances are anti-war or at least uncomfortable about it.（我大多数朋友和熟人都反对战争，至少对战争感到反感。）

His limited acquaintance with business was through his father's large holdings of property in Prague.（他父亲在布拉格拥有大量地产，由此他对商业略知一二。）

联想记忆

acquaint *v.* 使熟悉；使认识
contact *n.* 联系；联络人；熟人 *v.* 联系，联络

单词	释义
motive	*n.* Your motive for doing something is your reason for doing it. 动机

双语例句

During the trial, prosecutors indicated robbery might have been one possible motive for the attacks.（在审判期间，检察官表示劫财可能是袭击事件的一个动机。）

The book introduces the reader to some key concepts related to the profit motive in education.（这本书向读者介绍了一些在教育领域中与利润动机相关的核心概念。）

联想记忆

motivation *n.* 动机；积极性
motivate *v.* 刺激；使有动机

126. Large numbers of people received wages entirely *inadequate* to maintain a *decent* standard of living.

单词	释义
inadequate	*adj.* If something is inadequate, there is not enough of it or it is not good enough. 不足的；不够好的

双语例句

Bradford Community Primary School was marked as "inadequate" in a report published on Monday.（在周一发布的一份报告中，布拉德福德社区小学被评为"不合格"。）

Electric vehicles aren't popular in India due to lack of infrastructure and inadequate investment.（由于基础设施缺乏，投资不足，电动汽车在印度并不普及。）

联想记忆

inadequacy *n.* 不适当；不充分
insufficient *adj.* 不足的，不够的

单词	释义
decent	*adj.* Decent is used to describe something which is morally correct or acceptable. 合宜的；像样的
	adj. Decent people are honest and behave in a way that most people approve of. 正直的

双语例句

Even with a decent internet connection it can take hours to download a single game.（即使网络连接不错，下载一个游戏也要花费好几个小时。）

I suppose they're all decent, nice people, but we don't have much in common.（我认为他们都是正直善良的人，但是我们没什么共同点。）

联想记忆

decency *n.* 体面；庄重；合乎礼仪

127. After seeing the television pictures most people were ***sympathetic*** to the man's ***instinctive*** reaction.

单词	释义
sympathetic	*adj.* If you are sympathetic to someone who is in a bad situation, you are kind to them and show that you understand their feelings. 同情的
	adj. If you are sympathetic to a proposal or action, you approve of it and are willing to support it. 赞同的

双语例句

We were saddened and sympathetic when we learned of her battle with cancer.（得知她正与癌症做斗争时，我们非常难过并表示同情。）

The overwhelming majority of Muslims are not terrorists or sympathetic to terrorists.（绝大多数穆斯林都不是恐怖分子，也不赞同恐怖分子。）

联想记忆

sympathy *n.* 同情；赞同
empathy *n.* 同情，感同身受
compassionate *adj.* 有同情心的，怜悯的

单词	释义
instinctive	*adj.* An instinctive feeling, idea, or action is one that you have or do without thinking or reasoning. 本能的

双语例句

Some say only humans are conscious and animals are instinctive and machinelike.（有人认为只有人类才有意识，而动物是出于本能，行为非常机械。）

Samsung is giving consumers a more instinctive and intuitive way to control the Smart TVs.（三星为消费者提供了一种更本能、更直观的方式来控制智能电视。）

联想记忆

instinct *n.* 本能，直觉
intuitive *adj.* 直觉的；有直觉力的

128. The FDA should be encouraging such breakthroughs, not indulging its current ***skepticism***, which borders on ***hostility***.

单词	释义
skepticism	*n.* Skepticism is great doubt about whether something is true or useful. 怀疑

双语例句

There are clearly some good reasons why educators look at social media with skepticism.（显然，教育工作者对社交媒体持怀疑态度是有充分理由的。）

The former U.S. senator expressed deep skepticism that the North Korea could be trusted in negotiations.（这位美国前参议员对朝鲜在谈判中是否值得信任深表怀疑。）

联想记忆

skeptical *adj.* 怀疑的；怀疑论的
skeptic *n.* 怀疑者；怀疑论者

单词	释义
hostility	*n.* Hostility is unfriendly or aggressive behavior toward people or ideas. 敌意；敌对

双语例句

Yale Law School professor Stephen complained about the government hostility toward religious communities.（耶鲁大学法学院教授史蒂芬指出，政府对宗教团体不友好。）

Relations between Poland and Russia are marked by centuries of mutual hostility and military conflicts.（波兰和俄罗斯几个世纪以来相互敌对，军事冲突不断。）

联想记忆

hostile *adj.* 敌对的；敌方的
resentment *n.* 怨恨，愤恨

129. Published within one year of the war, the book offers only a ***partial*** view of the international ***dimension*** of the crisis.

单词	释义
partial	*adj.* You use partial to refer to something that is not complete or whole. 部分的，局部的
	adj. Someone who is partial supports a particular person or thing instead of being completely fair. 偏袒的；偏爱的

双语例句

He suffered a partial stroke that left the right side of his body without feeling.（他患上了局部中风，身体右半部分失去了知觉。）

They are particularly partial to restaurants displaying fully-stocked aquariums.（他们尤其喜欢那些鱼缸里装满鱼的饭店。）

联想记忆

partially *adv.* 部分地；偏袒地

单词	释义
dimension	*n.* A particular dimension of something is a particular aspect of it. 方面
	n. A dimension is a measurement such as length, width, or height. If you talk about the dimensions of an object or place, you are referring to its size and proportions. 尺寸，比例大小

双语例句

These gardens are one of the city's most distinctive features, and they add a special dimension to visitors' enjoyment.（这些园林是这座城市最鲜明的特点之一，游客们又多了一个游玩的好去处。）

Like the original Galaxy S, these successors are high-end devices with stylish dimensions and fast chips.（与最初的Galaxy S一样，这些后续推出的产品都是高端机，其尺寸时尚，运行速度快。）

联想记忆

dimensional *adj.* 空间的；尺寸的
breadth *n.* 宽度，幅度

130. The meeting provided a welcome opportunity to exchange the views on key issues of *mutual* interest in a *cordial* atmosphere.

单词	释义
mutual	*adj.* You use mutual to describe something such as an interest which two or more people share. 共同的
	adj. You use mutual to describe a situation, feeling, or action that is experienced, felt, or done by both of two people mentioned. 相互的

双语例句

Men preferred friends with mutual interests, while women valued honesty and trust.（男人更喜欢和有共同爱好的人交朋友，而女人更注重这个人是否诚实和值得信任。）

A family is not a business; it is a home that should be run out of mutual love and respect.（家庭不是生意场，而是一个需要相互关爱、相互尊重的港湾。）

联想记忆

reciprocal *adj.* 相互的，互惠的 *n.* 倒数

单词	释义
cordial	*adj.* Cordial means friendly. 友善的；热情的

双语例句

Both parents and teachers must try to create a friendly and cordial atmosphere for the children.（家长和老师都要尽量为孩子创造一个友好、亲切的氛围。）

Relations between the country's main ethnic groups have been cordial in recent years.（近年来，这个国家的主要少数民族群体之间关系一直非常融洽。）

联想记忆

jovial *adj.* 天性快活的
amicable *adj.* 友好的；亲切的

单元练习 13

使用本单元核心词汇的适当形式填空，并将句子译为中文。

1. He was an _____ bee keeper but now does it on a more commercial basis.
2. Standing in line to pay, he was spotted by an old _____ from his San Francisco days.
3. It is estimated that 880 million people worldwide have _____ access to safe drinking water.
4. The two companies will also explore other areas of _____ cooperation including sharing of networks.
5. He had _____ use of his hands enough to write two books and more than a dozen scientific articles.
6. Brandolini has come by her success without formal training, a fact which only _____ her genius.
7. The Asian country is moving quickly in reducing greenhouse gas _____ and promoting sustainability.
8. His strategy has been met with widespread _____, but it paid off during the final two months of last year.
9. At some point in the future, new energy technologies and conservation will _____ our dependence on oil.
10. Men are _____ as more competent than women in STEM (Science, Technology, Engineering and Mathematics) fields.

Unit 14

★ 本单元核心词汇 ★

proportion	coincide	prestigious	esteemed	inmate
stationary	dominate	stride	anticipate	vacant
unrest	scrutiny	inferior	pervasive	remedy
inflation	chaotic	disperse	conceal	prohibit

★ 本单元拓展词汇 ★

landfill	ratio	prose	renowned	revered
brake	convict	jailbird	stationery	cathedral
interconnect	principal	concourse	ovation	saunter
valid	scatter	aftermath	occupied	unease
scrutinize	drought	ubiquitous	herbal	redeem
tension	dominant	procession	steer	hectic
veto				

131. Numerous studies show that high ***proportions*** of women directors ***coincide*** with superior corporate performance.

单词	释义
proportion	*n.* The proportion of one kind of person or thing in a group is the number of people or things of that kind compared to the total number of people or things in the group. （某部分在总体中所占的）比例；部分

双语例句

Back then only a small proportion of the population enjoyed the comforts of life. （那时，只有少部分人能享受舒适的生活。）

In Andorra, the proportion of waste sent to landfill improved by five percentage points last year. （在安道尔，去年送往垃圾填埋场的垃圾比例提高了5个百分点。）

联想记忆

proportional *adj.* 成比例的；相称的；协调的
ratio *n.* 比例，比率

单词	释义
coincide	*v.* If one event coincides with another, they happen at the same time; if the ideas or interests of two or more people coincide, they are the same. 同时发生；（观点或兴趣）一致

双语例句

The event will coincide with Teachers' Day, and will feature poetry, prose, photography, and art. （该活动恰逢教师节，届时将进行诗歌、散文、摄影和艺术展演。）

Happily, these commercial interests may also coincide with the government's plans. （令人高兴的是，这些商业利益可能也符合政府的计划。）

联想记忆

coincident *adj.* 一致的；符合的
coincidence *n.* 巧合；一致

132. She is as famous and ***prestigious*** as her father, and very ***esteemed*** with her warm and sympathetic personality.

单词	释义
prestigious	*adj.* A prestigious institution, job, or activity is respected and admired by people. 有声望的

双语例句

Mantel is the first woman to win the prestigious literary prize twice.（曼特尔是第一位两次荣获该著名文学奖的女性。）

The brothers lived in the Massachusetts town of Cambridge, home of the prestigious Harvard University.（兄弟俩住在马萨诸塞州剑桥镇，这里是著名的哈佛大学所在地。）

联想记忆

prestige *n.* 声望；声誉
renowned *adj.* 著名的，有声望的

单词	释义
esteemed	*adj.* You use esteemed to describe someone who you greatly admire and respect. 受尊敬的

双语例句

The Booker Prize in literature is not much money, but it is widely esteemed.（布克文学奖的奖金不多，但是受到人们的广泛认可。）

Secretary of State Hillary Clinton treated Livni like the most esteemed politician in Israel.（美国国务卿希拉里·克林顿将利夫尼视为以色列最受人尊敬的政治家。）

联想记忆

esteem *v.* 尊敬；认为；考虑 *n.* 尊敬，敬重
revered *adj.* 受尊敬的

133. Female ***inmates*** at an Arizona jail take turns on a ***stationary*** bike to power their TV to watch their favorite soap operas.

单词	释义
inmate	*n.* The inmates of a prison or mental hospital are the prisoners or patients who are living there. 监犯；（精神病院的）住院者

双语例句

This jail has a reputation for overcrowding, poor management and brutal treatment of inmates.（这所监狱因过度拥挤、管理不善和虐待囚犯而臭名昭著。）

Several hours later the second inmate surrendered peacefully after being tracked down by police.（几小时后，第二名囚犯在被警方追捕后主动投降。）

联想记忆

convict *n.* 囚犯，犯人 *v.* 宣判……有罪
jailbird *n.* 囚犯；累犯

单词	释义
stationary	*adj.* Something that is stationary is not moving. 静止不动的；稳定的

双语例句

The average citizen spends 18% of his income on running a car that is usually stationary.（一般人将收入的18%花在一辆不常使用的汽车上。）

Curtis Granderson has been cleared to increase his workouts and is set to start riding a stationary bike.（医生允许柯蒂斯·格兰德森增加运动量，他准备开始骑健身自行车。）

联想记忆

static *adj.* 静态的；静电的 *n.* 静电
stationery *n.* 文具，文具用品

134. Nuclear energy is a very male ***dominated*** industry, but Anne has made great ***strides*** in getting women in management positions.

单词	释义
dominate	*v.* To dominate a situation means to be the most powerful or important person or thing in it. 占主要地位；支配

双语例句

In a series of interconnected moves, Microsoft is laying the groundwork to dominate the gaming industry.（通过一系列相互关联的举措，微软正在为主导游戏行业奠定基础。）

For as far as the eye could see, the filled-to-capacity cathedral was dominated by the color red.（放眼望去，座无虚席的大教堂里一片红色。）

联想记忆

dominant *adj.* 支配的；统治的
principal *adj.* 主要的，首要的 *n.* （中学）校长

单词	释义
stride	*n.* If you make strides in something you are doing, you make rapid progress in it. 进步，进展
	n. A stride is a long step when you are walking or running. 大步
	v. If you stride somewhere, you walk there with quick, long steps. 大步走

双语例句

Indonesia has made impressive strides in meeting the global Education for All (EFA) targets.（印度尼西亚在实现全球全民教育目标方面取得了巨大进展。）

The passengers took a few hundred quick strides through an airport concourse to catch a plane.（乘客们迈着大步，走了几百步穿过机场大厅赶飞机。）

Jobs strode onto stage as the event began and received a standing ovation.（发布会开始时，乔布斯大步走上舞台，全场起立鼓掌。）

联想记忆

stroll *v.* 散步，闲逛 *n.* 溜达
saunter *v.* 漫步，闲逛 *n.* 漫步

135. We *anticipate* a severe nursing shortage in the next few years and presently do not have enough techs to fill *vacant* positions.

单词	释义
anticipate	*v.* If you anticipate an event, you realize in advance that it may happen and you are prepared for it. 预期；预先准备

双语例句

It is crucial not to brake suddenly but anticipate the turn in advance, and make smooth steering inputs.（重要的是不能急刹车，而是提前预判转弯，并平稳地转向。）

Mobile operators are spending more to land customers than was anticipated in early 2021.（为了吸引客户，移动运营商的投入超过了2021年初的预期。）

联想记忆

anticipation *n.* 希望；预感；先发制人

单词	释义
vacant	*adj.* If something is vacant, it is not being used by anyone. 空着的
	adj. A vacant look or expression is one that suggests someone does not understand something. 茫然的

双语例句

Thousands of migrants simply ignored the law and settled illegally on vacant land of the country.（成千上万的移民无视法律，在这个国家的空地上非法定居。）

His eyes were open but vacant, staring at something that wasn't even there.（他虽然睁着眼睛却神情茫然，盯着根本不存在的东西。）

联想记忆

vacate *v.* 空出，腾出
vacancy *n.* 空缺；空位
occupied *adj.* 已占用的；使用中的；无空闲的

136. Under the new law, movies featuring social ***unrest***, religion, sex and violence are likely to face extra ***scrutiny***.

单词	释义
unrest	*n.* If there is unrest in a particular place or society, people are expressing anger and dissatisfaction, often by demonstrating. 骚乱；动荡的局面

双语例句

The Middle East market has been significantly affected by the political unrest throughout the region.（中东市场受到整个地区政治动荡的影响非常明显。）

Syria has been in the midst of nearly 16 months of unrest, resulting in thousands of deaths.（叙利亚在近16个月的时间里都处于动荡之中，导致数千人死亡。）

联想记忆

tension *n.* 紧张，不安；张力，拉力
unease *n.* 不安，焦虑

单词	释义
scrutiny	*n.* If a person or thing is under scrutiny, they are being studies or observed very carefully. 仔细研究；仔细观察

双语例句

Jefferson's business dealings with a telecommunications firm have been under scrutiny for some time.（杰弗逊与一家电信公司的商业交易受到关注有一段时间了。）

The company's records have come under new scrutiny since the recalls were announced earlier this month.（自从本月早些时候宣布召回其产品开始，这家公司的销售记录受到了新的严格审查。）

联想记忆

scrutinize *v.* 详细检查；细看

137. The *inferior* education they provided, then and now, helps explain the *pervasive* achievement gap between today's black and white students.

单词	释义
inferior	*adj.* If something is inferior, it's lower in rank, status, or quality. 较差的
	n. If a person is regarded as inferior, he is not as good as someone else, or is lower in rank or status. 不如别人的人；（级别或地位）较低的人

双语例句

Back in the 1970s, some in Congress argued foreign doctors were inferior to US-educated physicians.（在20世纪70年代，一些国会议员认为外国医生不如在美国接受教育的医生。）

Much of the oil is of inferior quality, selling for less than a third of average international prices.（这些石油大多质量低劣，售价不到国际平均价格的三分之一。）

联想记忆

superior *adj.* 更好的，更优的；上级的 *n.* 上级，上司

单词	释义
pervasive	*adj.* Something, especially something bad, that is pervasive is present or felt throughout a place or thing. （尤指不好的事物）无处不在的

双语例句

Global warming is happening and undoubtedly it has a pervasive influence on all aspects of weather.（全球变暖正在发生，毫无疑问，它对天气的各个方面都有广泛的影响。）

Drought conditions were most pervasive in the Plains states, including in top wheat producer Kansas.（旱情在平原地区最为普遍，包括在最大的小麦生产地堪萨斯州。）

联想记忆

pervade *v.* 遍及；弥漫
ubiquitous *adj.* 普遍存在的

138. For much of the 1970s neither Democrats nor Republicans had a sound explanation or *remedy* for widespread *inflation*.

单词	释义
remedy	*n.* A remedy is a successful way of dealing with a problem. 解决办法
	n. A remedy is something that is intended to cure you when you are ill or in pain. 治疗，疗法；药品
	v. If you remedy something that is wrong or harmful, you correct it or improve it. 补救；纠正；改善

双语例句

A fiscal remedy like a massive tax cut is unrealistic in the face of the current deficit.（面对当前的赤字，像大规模减税这样的财政补救措施是不现实的。）

Most of modern medicine's prescription drugs grew out of traditional herbal remedies.（大多数现代医学的处方药是由传统的草药疗法发展而来的。）

There is a fundamental imbalance in how schools are funded, which is nearly impossible to remedy.（学校的经费支持存在根本性的不平衡，这几乎是无法改变的。）

联想记忆

remedial *adj.* 治疗的；补救的
redeem *v.* 补救；挽回（声誉）；兑换（优惠券）；赎回（股票、债券）

单词	释义
inflation	*n.* Inflation is a general increase in the prices of goods and services in a country. 通货膨胀

双语例句

The country is fighting inflation, a problem that is causing social and political tension.（该国正在抵御通货膨胀，这是一个导致社会动荡和政局紧张的问题。）

Not until the summer of 2018 did official government figures begin to acknowledge the scope of inflation.（直到2018年夏季，政府的官方数据才开始承认通货膨胀的规模。）

联想记忆

inflate *v.* 膨胀；充气

139. He described the *chaotic* scene where security forces opened fire into the air upon arrival to *disperse* onlookers.

单词	释义
chaotic	*adj.* Something that is chaotic is in a state of complete disorder and confusion. 混乱的，无秩序的

双语例句

The processions of thousands of people created chaotic traffic situations in the city.（成千上万人的游行导致该城市交通混乱。）

In the immediate chaotic aftermath of the attack, exact figures were difficult to come by.（袭击发生后一片混乱，很难得到确切的伤亡数据。）

联想记忆

chaos *n.* 混乱；混沌
messy *adj.* 凌乱的；不整洁的

单词	释义
disperse	*v.* When a group of people disperses or when someone disperses them, the group splits up and the people leave in different directions. 驱散；散开
	v. When something disperses or when you disperse it, it spreads over a wide area. 使分散；扩散

双语例句

The police said it was an illegal gathering and fired tear gas to disperse the crowd.（警方称这是非法集会，并用催泪瓦斯驱散聚集人群。）

As the sun always rises, so do dust storms slowly disperse and surrender to blue skies.（正如太阳总会升起一样，沙尘暴终归会慢慢消散，重现蓝天。）

联想记忆

dispersion *n.* 分散；散布；（统计）离散度
scatter *v.* 散开；播撒；（物理）散射 *n.* 零星散布的东西
decentralize *v.* 分散；下放权力

140. Although she had a *concealed* weapons permit, university policies *prohibited* her from carrying a gun.

单词	释义
conceal	*v.* If you conceal something, you cover it or hide it carefully. 掩盖；隐藏
	v. If you conceal a piece of information or a feeling, you do not let other people know about it. 隐瞒（信息）；掩饰（情感）

双语例句

Mississippi allows concealed carry on campus only for those who complete a firearm safety course.（密西西比州只允许修完枪支安全课程的人在校园携带隐蔽武器。）

They went to extraordinary lengths to conceal preparations for and evidence of this underground test.（他们竭尽全力掩盖这次地下试验的准备工作和相关证据。）

Grown-ups learn to conceal their emotions, in the workplace, in social settings, and at home.（成年人学会了在工作场所、社交场合和家里掩饰自己的情绪。）

联想记忆

mask *v.* 隐瞒，掩饰；伪装 *n.* 口罩；面具

单词	释义
prohibit	*v.* If a law or someone in authority prohibits something, they forbid it or make it illegal. 禁止

双语例句

Today the vast majority of U.S. colleges and universities, public and private, prohibit guns.（现在绝大多数美国高校，不论是公立还是私立，都禁止携带枪支。）

A 1971 policy prohibited players from using any medication without a valid prescription.（1971年发布的一项政策禁止运动员在没有有效处方的情况下服用任何药物。）

联想记忆

prohibition *n.* 禁止；禁令
veto *v.* 否决；禁止 *n.* 否决权；拒绝认可

单元练习 14

使用本单元核心词汇的适当形式填空，并将句子译为中文。

1. The adverse health effects of car exhaust are _____ and difficult to measure.
2. The government should _____ people from rebuilding structures damaged by storms.
3. Some 90% of mobile phones sold in Africa are basic models in which Nokia still _____.
4. His career as a producer _____ with one of the most profound periods in pop music history.
5. These commodities lose a huge _____ of their value the moment they are taken off the shelf.
6. In some subjects, U.K. universities are world-beaters, ahead even of the most _____ U.S. universities.
7. Our customers, especially those on international flights, are often _____ for what may be several hours.
8. His arrival in Edinburgh last week was met with _____ scenes as scores of journalists attended his press launch.
9. The quality of medical care that Americans buy is often _____ to the treatment people get in other countries.
10. The street was dotted with discount stores and souvenir shops, as well as a number of locations that stayed _____ for years.

Unit 15

★ 本单元核心词汇 ★

fantasy	explicit	feasible	vulnerable	elite
pose	coverage	accelerate	statue	submit
identical	trough	spark	blaze	plausible
ridiculous	rotate	interval	detrimental	prospect

★ 本单元拓展词汇 ★

exeptional	provision	donate	transparent	crystal
implicit	prospective	athletic	elicit	asteroid
destruction	susceptible	haunt	penguin	stance
peak	hasten	crew	interim	bronze
statute	objection	nudge	burglary	trench
inconsistency	catalyst	illumination	absurd	iconic
adolescent				

141. The Western preference for *fantasy* over reality was given *explicit* expression by former US president Bill Clinton in September.

单词	释义
fantasy	*n.* A fantasy is a pleasant situation or event that you think about and that you want to happen, especially one that is unlikely to happen. 幻想
	n. You can refer to a story or situation that someone creates from their imagination as fantasy. 虚幻的故事；幻想的情境

双语例句

A Canadian company believes it could transform the fantasy into reality within the next decade.（加拿大一家公司认为能在未来十年把这个幻想变成现实。）

Nobody could have foreseen that they would fulfill the science-fiction fantasies of little boys and put a man on the moon.（没有人能预料到，他们居然把小孩子的幻想变为现实，将人类送上了月球。）

联想记忆

fantastic *adj.* 空想的；极好的；不可思议的

单词	释义
explicit	*adj.* Something that is explicit is expressed or shown clearly and openly, without any attempt to hide anything. 明确表达的；公开显露的

双语例句

The provisions require companies to obtain explicit permission from individuals before using their data.（这些条款要求，企业在使用个人数据之前必须得到他们的明确许可。）

To encourage people to donate, charities should be explicit about how and where they are applying these funds.（为了鼓励人们捐款，慈善机构应明确阐述这些资金是如何使用的，用于哪些方面。）

联想记忆

transparent *adj.* 透明的；一目了然的
crystal *adj.* 晶莹的；清澈透明的 *n.* 水晶；晶体
implicit *adj.* 含蓄的；暗含的

142. Technological advances have made it economically *feasible* for these *elite* institutions to compete in international markets.

Unit 15

单词	释义
feasible	*adj.* If something is feasible, it can be done, made, or achieved. 可行的

双语例句

Interest rates have already come down considerably but further cuts are quite feasible as well.（利率已经大幅下降，但进一步降低也是相当可行的。）

Wind farms on land are controversial but they do represent the cheapest feasible way of meeting CO_2 targets.（陆地上的风力发电场存有争议，但它们的确是实现二氧化碳减排目标最廉价可行的方式。）

联想记忆

feasibility *n.* 可行性；可能性

单词	释义
elite	*adj.* Elite people or organizations are the best. 精英的

双语例句

For most elite athletes, the key to success is exceptional talent and world-class athletic ability.（对大多数优秀运动员来说，成功的关键是非凡的天赋和一流的竞技能力。）

A growing number of elite institutions, including Stanford and New York University are beginning to offer online courses.（包括斯坦福大学和纽约大学在内的越来越多的名校也开始开设在线课程。）

联想记忆

elicit *v.* 引起；探得（信息）

143. Even with a well-designed protected ecosystem, animals remain *vulnerable* to the dangers *posed* by humans.

单词	释义
vulnerable	*adj.* Someone or something is vulnerable can be easily attacked or harmed, either physically or emotionally. 脆弱的，易受伤害的

双语例句

Young children are particularly vulnerable to the health impact of passive smoking.（儿童特别容易因被动吸烟受到健康危害。）

Estonia's defence looked extremely vulnerable, with Rooney and Joe Cole particularly dangerous.（爱沙尼亚队的后防看起来不堪一击，鲁尼和乔·科尔尤其危险。）

联想记忆

vulnerability *n.* 易损性；弱点
susceptible *adj.* 易受影响的

单词	释义
pose	*v.* If something poses a problem or a danger, it is the cause of that problem or danger. 造成（问题或危险）
	v. If you pose a question, you ask it. If you pose an issue that needs considering, you mention the issue. 提出（问题）
	v. If you pose for a photograph or painting, you stay in a particular position so that someone can photograph you or paint you. 摆姿势

双语例句

Malnutrition poses a challenge for all low-income developing countries, large or small.（营养不良对于所有低收入发展中国家（不论大小）都是一个挑战。）

When his father flies in for a visit he makes small talk, unable to pose the questions that haunt him.（当父亲飞过来探望时，他只是寒暄了几句，没有提出困扰他的问题。）

David found the penguin looking into his camera as two others appeared to pose for a photograph.（大卫发现这只企鹅正朝他的相机里看，另外两只企鹅似乎在摆姿势拍照。）

联想记忆

posture *n.* 姿势；态度，立场
stance *n.* 观点，态度；站立姿势

144. Employers are increasingly dropping their employees' health ***coverage*** — a trend that the new health care law will ***accelerate***.

单词	释义
coverage	*n.* The coverage is the amount of protection given by an insurance policy. 范围；保险范围
	n. The coverage of something in the news is the reporting of it. 报道

双语例句

They plan to increase the amount of permanent life insurance and reduce term coverage annually.（他们计划每年增加终身寿险的保额，减少定期保险。）

Adolescent coverage for whooping cough is about 41 percent nationally and 43 percent in California.（全国范围内，青少年百日咳的比例约为41%，加利福尼亚州为43%。）

He received a national news Emmy Award for his coverage of the 1988 Sudan famine.（他因对1988年苏丹饥荒事件的报道而获得全国新闻艾美奖。）

联想记忆

covering *n.* 遮盖物，覆盖物

单词	释义
accelerate	*v.* If the process or rate of something accelerates or if something accelerates, it gets faster and faster. 使加速；加速

双语例句

The airplane accelerates very quickly in the dive and when seen from the ground appears extremely fast.（飞机在俯冲时加速极快，从地面上看显得特别快。）

The excessive use of any electricity-powered machines like air conditioners will accelerate global warming.（过度使用空调等电器将会加速全球变暖进程。）

联想记忆

acceleration *n.* 加速；加速度
quicken *v.* 加快，加速
hasten *v.* 加快；急忙（进行）；赶往（某地）

145. Plans for the *statue* were *submitted* in June, attracting 177 letters in support and 100 letters of objection.

单词	释义
statue	*n.* A statue is a large sculpture of a person or an animal, made of stone or metal. 雕像

双语例句

New York's iconic Statue of Liberty is to close for a year for renovations.（纽约的标志性建筑自由女神像因要进行维修将关闭一年。）

One of the most stunning series of objects was a set of small bronze statues of horses.（这些物品中最令人惊叹的是一组小型的青铜马雕像。）

联想记忆

statute *n.* 法令，法规
stature *n.* 身高，身材

单词	释义
submit	*v.* If you submit a proposal, report, or request to someone, you formally send it to them so that they can consider it. 提交（建议、报告或请求）
	v. If you submit to something, you unwillingly allow something to be done to you, or you do what someone wants because you are not powerful enough to resist. 屈从

双语例句

The building could become a hotel, if plans submitted to the city council are approved.（如果提交给市议会的计划得到批准，这栋大楼将变成一家酒店。）

In desperation, Mrs. Jones submitted to an operation on her right knee to relieve the pain.（绝望中，琼斯夫人不得已接受了右膝手术以减轻疼痛。）

联想记忆

submission *n.* 投降；服从
submissive *adj.* 服从的；顺从的

146. The researchers hunted for quakes with nearly *identical* patterns of peaks and *troughs* on a seismograph reading.

单词	释义
identical	*adj.* Things that are identical are exactly the same. 完全相同的

双语例句

The newspaper found nearly identical rates of burglaries and stolen cars in these cities.（该报纸发现，这些城市的入室盗窃和汽车失窃率几乎相同。）

Each room is bright white and practically identical to the next, with only minor differences.（每个房间都是亮白色，和其他房间几乎相同，只有细微的差异。）

联想记忆

identically *adv.* 同一地；相等地

单词	释义
trough	*n.* A trough is a low point in a process that has regular high and low points. 低谷；波谷

双语例句

It's been 12 years since the economy hit its recession trough in June 2009.（自2009年6月经济触底以来，已经过去了12年。）

The demand has always been prone to peaks and troughs, but that inconsistency has worsened.（需求总是容易出现高峰和低谷，但这种不稳定的情况越来越糟了。）

联想记忆

trench *n.* 壕沟；沟槽
peak *n.* 顶点，巅峰；波峰

147. Fallen power lines were likely to have *sparked* the Tuesday *blaze*, since there were no other possible causes in the area.

单词	释义
spark	*v.* If a burning object or electricity sparks a fire, it causes a fire. 引起（一场火）；引发，触发
	n. A spark is a tiny bright piece of burning material that flies up from something that is burning. 火花；导火线；诱因

双语例句

The electricity sparked and sections of the subway began to catch fire.（电气引燃，地铁部分区域开始着火。）

This year has sparked fears of a second global food crisis after the devastating events of 2008.（继2008年灾难性事件之后，今年引发了人们对第二次全球粮食危机的担忧。）

Julian bought an electric heater, but under the fifteen-foot ceilings the device was like a spark at the North Pole.（朱利安买了一个电加热器，但天花板高达15英尺，这个装置就如同北极的一丝火花。）

联想记忆

sparkling *adj.* 闪闪发光的
glow *v.* 发光；容光焕发 *n.* 微弱稳定的光；红润光泽
catalyst *n.* 催化剂；诱因

单词	释义
blaze	*n.* A blaze is a large fire which is difficult to control. 大火
	v. When a fire blazes, it burns strongly and brightly. 熊熊燃烧

双语例句

In July and early August, firefighting crews have battled blazes in nearly every Western state.（七月和八月初，几乎在西部各州，消防队员都在为扑灭大火而奋战。）

Fire still blazed fiercely in front of the family, preventing any form of escape.（大火仍在他们一家人面前熊熊燃烧，阻断了屋里人任何逃生的途径。）

联想记忆

blazer *n.* 燃烧体；运动夹克，运动上衣
illumination *n.* 光亮，照明；启迪

148. There are dozens of versions of the new library scheme, and they range from *plausible* to *ridiculous*.

单词	释义
plausible	*adj.* An explanation or statement that is plausible seems likely to be true or valid.（解释或叙述）看似合理的

双语例句

Google says it was a mistake, and provided a completely plausible explanation for that mistake.（谷歌承认这是一个失误，并且为这次失误提供了完全合理的解释。）

Such asteroids could, in principle, be identified and, with plausible technology, nudged aside.（理论上，这样的小行星是可以识别出来的，并且可以通过合理的技术将其推开。）

联想记忆

plausibility *n.* 善变；似乎有理

单词	释义
ridiculous	*adj.* If you say that something or someone is ridiculous, you mean that they are very foolish. 荒谬的

双语例句

The majority of players do not live up to contracts that pay them a ridiculous amount of cash.（大多数球员都没有达到给他们支付巨额薪酬的合同所要求的条件。）

Luxury car makers typically build increasingly extreme and ridiculous versions of cars.（豪华汽车制造商通常会生产越来越极端和荒谬的车型。）

联想记忆

ridicule *v.* 嘲笑，奚落 *n.* 嘲笑
absurd *adj.* 荒谬的，可笑的

149. The presidency of the Council of Ministers ***rotates*** between the member governments at six-monthly ***intervals***.

单词	释义
rotate	*v.* If people or things rotate, or if someone rotates them, they take turns to do a particular job or serve a particular purpose. 轮流；使轮流
	v. When something rotates or when you rotate it, it turns with a circular movement. 旋转

双语例句

The meeting rotates between the G7 countries, and next year it will take place in France.（会议在七国集团之间轮流举办，明年将在法国举行。）

Venus rotates very slowly with the result that its cycle of rotation reaches as long as 243 days of the Earth.（金星自转极慢，其自转周期长达243个地球日。）

联想记忆

rotary *adj.* 旋转的；绕轴转动的 *n.* 环岛，环形交通枢纽
rotation *n.* 旋转；轮流

单词	释义
interval	*n.* An interval between two events or dates is the period of time between them.（时间上的）间隔
	n. An interval during a concert, show, film, or game is a short break between two of the parts. 幕间休息；中场休息

双语例句

The line has begun operating with just five Italian trains, running at 20-minute intervals.（这条线路已开始运营，只有5列意大利列车，每隔20分钟发一趟。）

Glen Johnson scored his first goal for the club with an excellent finish just before the interval.（格伦·约翰逊在中场休息前为俱乐部踢进了他的第一个球，为上半场画上了圆满的句号。）

联想记忆

intermittent *adj.* 断断续续的

intermission *n.* 间断；中场休息
interim *n.* 过渡期 *adj.* 临时的，过渡时期的

150. Nothing would be more ***detrimental*** to our ***prospects*** for success than cutting back on education.

单词	释义
detrimental	*adj.* Something that is detrimental to something else has a harmful or damaging effect on it. 有害的

双语例句

Human population growth on our planet is certainly detrimental to the environment.（地球上的人口增长必然对环境是有害的。）

The new policy would have a detrimental effect on the numbers of doctors entering the profession.（新政策将对进入该行业的医生人数产生不利影响。）

联想记忆

detriment *n.* 损害；危害
injurious *adj.* 有害的，致伤的

单词	释义
prospect	*n.* Someone's prospects are their chances of being successful, especially in their career. 成功的机会；前途
	n. If there is some prospect of something happening, there is a possibility that it will happen. 可能性；前景

双语例句

Students worry about their job prospects as technological advances transform professions in a way that cuts jobs.（学生担心他们的就业前景，因为技术进步使得各行各业发生转变，工作岗位减少了。）

Some welcome the prospect of economic development, and others fear the destruction of their rural lives.（有些人对经济发展的前景表示欢迎，另一些人则担心他们的乡村生活遭到破坏。）

联想记忆

prospective *adj.* 未来的，预期的
perspective *n.* 视角；观点；远景

单元练习 15

使用本单元核心词汇的适当形式填空,并将句子译为中文。

1. Officials point out that opponents of the dams have failed to propose a _____ alternative.
2. They _____ four manuscripts to American Geophysical Union journals for peer review.
3. The phone is _____ to the N8 in appearance, except for the missing camera pod in the back.
4. As mammals, they need to come to the surface to breathe at _____ of roughly 20 minutes.
5. For generations, salesmen have scratched their heads at the _____ of selling a Windows PC.
6. More attention must be paid to the plight of _____ African immigrants around the world.
7. When I interviewed the Secretary of State in Berlin, he was very _____ in rejecting that idea.
8. Hundreds of firefighters are tackling the fire, which was _____ during the Thursday morning rush hour.
9. Gino is a researcher at the Harvard Business School, who has conducted a _____ number of creative studies.
10. The city quickly regained its trade after the war and its growth _____ with the opening of the canal in 1825.

Unit 16

★ 本单元核心词汇 ★

sphere	boom	confess	implicate	obsession
drain	cherish	indispensable	utilize	minimize
prolong	revoke	scandal	affectionate	predator
duplicate	familiarize	withdraw	clamor	prevalent

★ 本单元拓展词汇 ★

uproar	pandemic	utility	priest	faculty
correspond	mania	retreat	buzz	prevail
xerox	relish	warrior	scope	crucial
vital	knit	relevancy	panel	filter
taskbar	upgrade	exposure	abolish	repeal
annul	deposit	humiliation	disgrace	gossip
tactic	predominant	cosmos	spin	

151. Not surprisingly, people in the developing world are *clamoring* for relatively cheap handsets, and their growth is ***booming***.

单词	释义
clamor	v. If people are clamoring for something, they are demanding it in a noisy or angry way. 强烈要求，大声呼吁
	n. Clamor is loud and confused noise, especially that of people shouting. 吵闹，喧嚣

双语例句

The minute that a new device is introduced the public is already clamoring for the next version.（一款新设备推出的那一刻起，公众就已经在吵着要下一代产品了。）

They came to Long Island for the season, or for a summer weekend away from the clamor and pandemic.（他们选择这个季节来长岛，或许想度过一个远离喧嚣和疫情的夏日周末。）

联想记忆

clamorous *adj.* 吵闹的
uproar *n.* 骚动，哗然

单词	释义
boom	v. If the economy or a business is booming, the number of things being bought or sold is increasing. 激增
	v. When something such as someone's voice, cannon, or a big drum booms, it makes a loud, deep sound. 发出低沉洪亮的声音
	n. Boom is also a NOUN. 激增；轰鸣

双语例句

Its digital book business is booming: Amazon has sold 105 e-books for every 100 printed books that left its warehouse.（数字图书业务正蓬勃发展：亚马逊每卖出100本纸质版图书，就会卖出105本电子书。）

The thunder and lightning boomed and crashed for a while and then it started to rain.（轰隆隆的雷声和闪电之后，不一会儿便开始下雨了。）

The city has experienced a recent boom of five-star restaurants, cafes, and hip nightclubs.（近年来，这座城市的五星级酒店、咖啡馆和时尚夜总会发展迅猛。）

联想记忆

boomer *n.* 生育高峰中出生的人
buzz *v.* 嗡嗡作响；匆忙走动 *n.* 蜂鸣声

152. According to police documents released in November, 19-year-old Nicholas *confessed* to the break-ins and *implicated* several others.

单词	释义
confess	*v.* If someone confesses to doing something wrong, they admit that they did it. 承认（做了某事）
	v. If someone confesses or confesses their sins, they tell God or a priest about their sins so that they can be forgiven. 忏悔

双语例句

Those who confess to cheating will also be required to complete a four-hour course in ethics.（承认作弊的人还必须完成一门四小时的道德教育课程。）

She believed that when she confessed her sins to the priest she was in fact confessing to God.（她认为，向牧师忏悔罪过实际上是在向上帝忏悔。）

联想记忆

confession *n.* 供认；忏悔；声明

单词	释义
implicate	*v.* To implicate someone means to show or claim that they were involved in something wrong or criminal. 与（罪行）有牵连

双语例句

Earlier this week, one of our faculty members at the main campus was implicated in an insider trading scandal.（本周早些时候，我们主校区的一名教职员工被卷入内幕交易丑闻。）

The Secret Service says 12 members of the agency have been implicated in the incident.（特勤局称，该机构有12名成员在此事件中受到牵连。）

联想记忆

implication *n.* 含义；暗示；牵连

153. Social media *obsession* can be a significant *drain* on creative productivity, which requires focused energy, attention and time.

单词	释义
obsession	*n.* If you say that someone has an obsession with a person or thing, you think they are spending too much time thinking about them. 迷恋

双语例句

Roth, a skilled storyteller, admits to an obsession with green grass around his corporate offices.（罗斯是一个擅长讲故事的人，他承认喜欢公司办公室周围的绿色草地。）

Most companies with such cultures were founded by people who had an obsession with data.（大多数拥有这种文化的公司都是由痴迷于数据的人创立的。）

联想记忆

obsess *v.* 使……着迷
mania *n.* 着迷，狂热

单词	释义
drain	*n.* Drain is a thing that uses up a particular resource. 消耗
	v. If something drains you, it deprived of strength or vitality; if something is drained, it means that it's used or spent completely. 耗尽；排干
	n. Drain is a channel or pipe carrying off surplus liquid, especially rainwater or liquid waste. 引流管；排水管；下水道

双语例句

The Christmas season means more than just crowds, traffic, and a massive drain on your wallet.（圣诞季不仅意味着人群拥挤，交通堵塞，还有疯狂购物。）

I've been totally drained of energy, and this morning I found it almost impossible to get myself out of bed.（我已经精疲力竭了，今天早上，我发现自己几乎无法下床。）

It's common that many surgeons take preventative measures by inserting a drain during surgery.（很多外科医生在手术中插入引流管来采取预防措施，这十分常见。）

联想记忆

drainage *n.* 排水；排水系统；污水

154. His stories of frontier lives are part of the ***cherished*** identity and the romantic history of the continent — an ***indispensable*** element of the American dream.

单词	释义
cherish	*v.* If you cherish something such as a hope or a pleasant memory, you keep it in your mind for a long period of time. 珍藏，珍视（希望、记忆等）
	v. If you cherish someone or something, you take good care of them because you love them. 珍爱

双语例句

The craft would realize a long-cherished dream: to fly non-stop from airport to cosmos.（这艘飞船将实现长久以来的一个梦想：从机场直飞宇宙。）

She deserves a reliable kind of guy, who will love her and cherish her.（她值得拥有一个可靠的男人，一个可以爱她并珍惜她的人。）

联想记忆

relish *v.* 享受；期盼 *n.* 乐趣；开胃小菜

单词	释义
indispensable	*adj.* If you say that someone or something is indispensable, you mean that they are absolutely essential. 必不可少的

双语例句

The horse is an indispensable character to most stories of Chinese warriors.（在大多数中国武士的故事中，马是一个不可或缺的元素。）

Microsoft, an iconic software company, now sees hardware as an indispensable part of its future.（微软是一家标志性的软件公司，现在它将硬件视为其未来发展的重要部分。）

联想记忆

crucial *adj.* 至关重要的
vital *adj.* 必不可少的；生命的

155. Cars will become more crash-worthy by design, and will ***utilize*** advanced technology to help drivers avoid getting into accidents or at least ***minimize*** their severity.

单词	释义
utilize	*v.* If you utilize something, you use it. 利用

双语例句

This knitting process utilizes individual color threads to create a multicolored pattern.（这种针织工艺采用单色线编织出彩色图案。）

Many young entrepreneurs are utilizing social media apps and websites to generate cash for their projects.（许多年轻企业家利用社交媒体应用程序和网站为他们的项目创收。）

联想记忆

utilization *n.* 利用,使用
utility *n.* 公用事业;实用,有用
exploit *v.* 利用,运用;剥削

单词	释义
minimize	*v.* If you minimize a risk, problem, or unpleasant situation, you reduce it to the lowest possible level. 减到最低数量;降到最低程度
	v. If you minimize a window on a computer screen, you make it very small, because you do not want to use it. 使最小化

双语例句

The patients spoke to relatives and friends from behind a glass panel to minimize the risk of infection.(病人从玻璃面板后面和亲友交谈,以最大限度减少感染的风险。)

Windows 95 featured the first appearance of the Start menu, taskbar, and minimize, maximize, and close buttons on each window.(Windows 95系统首次出现了开始菜单、任务栏以及每个窗口上的最小化、最大化和关闭按钮。)

联想记忆

minimal *adj.* 最低的;最小限度的
minimum *n.* 最小值;最小量 *adj.* 最小的;最低的

156. When later research showed Avastin didn't ***prolong*** life and brought more side effects, its approval for breast cancer was ***revoked***.

单词	释义
prolong	*v.* To prolong something means to make it last longer. 延长,拖延

双语例句

People at particular risk for the flu should avoid prolonged exposure to the sun.(特别易患流感的人应该避免长时间晒太阳。)

Mrs. Cadden joined the local Weight Watchers class, a move that she believes has prolonged her life.(卡登夫人参加了当地的减肥训练班,她认为这延长了她的寿命。)

联想记忆

lengthen *v.* 延长;加长
extend *v.* 延伸;扩展;扩大

单词	释义
revoke	*v.* When people in authority revoke something such as a licence, a law, or an agreement, they cancel it. 撤销，废除

双语例句

The fox hunting licence would be valid for a year but could be revoked at any time by the Scottish government.（猎狐许可证有效期为一年，但随时可能被苏格兰政府撤销。）

A letter was written to the university board to demand that her scholarship be revoked immediately.（有人给大学董事会写信，要求立即取消她的奖学金。）

联想记忆

abolish *v.* 废除，取消
repeal *v.* 废除，废止；撤销（法律、法案）
annul *v.* 废除；宣告无效

157. Sex *scandals* have been *prevalent* since the founding fathers established the United States Constitution.

单词	释义
scandal	*n.* A scandal is a situation or event that is thought to be shocking and immoral and that everyone knows about. 丑闻

双语例句

Barclays has come in for much criticism in recent years, following a series of scandals.（由于暴露出一系列丑闻，近年来巴克莱银行饱受非议。）

When a major newspaper asked him to write an op-ed about the Weiner scandal, he declined.（当一家主流报纸让他写一篇关于韦纳丑闻的特约稿时，他婉拒了。）

联想记忆

gossip *n.* 小道消息；流言蜚语 *v.* 闲聊
disgrace *n.* 耻辱；不光彩的事（或人）
humiliation *n.* 羞辱；耻辱

单词	释义
prevalent	*adj.* A condition, practice, or belief that is prevalent is common. 盛行的；普遍存在的

双语例句

Intelligent systems that will help control congestion will become more prevalent as time passes.（随着时间的推移，能控制交通拥堵的智能系统会变得越来越普遍。）

Imitation is more prevalent than innovation and, done well, can be a successful tactic.（模仿比创新更流行，如果做得好，也可以成为一种成功的策略。）

联想记忆

prevail *v.* 盛行，流行；获胜
prevalence *n.* 流行；普遍
predominant *adj.* 主要的，占主导地位的

158. Cats are warm and ***affectionate*** creatures to us, but viewed through the eyes of birds and mice they are vicious ***predators***.

单词	释义
affectionate	*adj.* If you are affectionate, you show your love or fondness for another person. 深情的，充满感情的

双语例句

My brother, though of few words, had been thoughtful and affectionate since his childhood.（我的兄弟虽然沉默寡言，但从小他就体贴人而且重情义。）

The church now has child-protection rules — so strict that they sometimes stifle healthy affectionate behavior.（现在教会有保护儿童的规定，有时候规则太严，会阻碍健康的亲情行为。）

联想记忆

affection *n.* 喜爱，感情
amiable *adj.* 亲切的，友善的

单词	释义
predator	*n.* A predator is an animal that kills and eats other animals. 捕食者
	n. People sometimes refer to predatory people or organizations as predators. 掠夺者

双语例句

Animals must be able to tell how quickly a potential predator is approaching.（动物必须能够判断潜在的捕食者正以多快的速度靠近。）

The frogs in the Caribbean are consumed by snakes and they in turn are major predators of mosquitoes.（在加勒比地区，蛇是青蛙的捕食者，而青蛙又是蚊子的主要捕食者。）

联想记忆

predatory *adj.* 捕食生物的；掠夺的
prey *n.* 猎物；受害者 *v.* 捕食

159. The ***duplicates*** were distributed to ***familiarize*** citizens with the new currency but police feel they might be used and have urged people to destroy them.

单词	释义
duplicate	*n.* Duplicate means one of two or more identical things. 复制；复制品
	v. If you duplicate something, you repeat or copy it. 复制；复印
	adj. Duplicate is used to describe things that have been made as an exact copy of other things. 复制的；完全一样的

双语例句

The results are displayed in order of relevancy, and duplicates are automatically filtered out.（结果按相关性顺序排列，重复项将被自动过滤掉。）

It is impossible to duplicate the Great Pyramid even if great resources and a trillion dollars were spent on the project.（即使投入大量资源和万亿美元，也不可能复制出大金字塔。）

The announcement was delayed after the FA received a number of what it described as "rogue" duplicate votes.（由于足协收到了一些其所称的"异常"重复选票，公告被推迟发布。）

联想记忆

duplication *n.* 复制；副本
xerox *n.* 复印机；复印件 *v.* 复印

单词	释义
familiarize	*v.* If you familiarize yourself with something, or if someone familiarizes you with it, you learn about it and start to understand it. 使熟悉

双语例句

Users are encouraged to change their passwords on a regular basis and to familiarize themselves with online safety tips.（我们鼓励用户定期更改密码，并了解网上安全提示。）

It has taken Mr. Clinton the better part of four years to familiarize himself with basic realities in Asia.（克林顿花了四年中的大部分时间来熟悉亚洲的基本情况。）

联想记忆

familiarity *n.* 熟悉；亲密

160. This development has major consequences, particularly for women who are often required to ***withdraw*** from the public ***spheres*** of society.

单词	释义
withdraw	*v.* If you withdraw from an activity or organization, you stop taking part in it. 退出
	v. When groups of people such as troops withdraw, they leave the place where they are fighting or where they are based. 撤退
	v. If you withdraw money from a bank account, you take it out of that account.（从银行）取钱

双语例句

Singapore withdrew from the Federation on August 9, 1965, and became an independent republic.（新加坡于1965年8月9日退出联邦，成为独立共和国。）

The US State Department has demanded that Hezbollah withdraw its fighters from Syria immediately.（美国国务院要求，真主党立即从叙利亚撤回战机。）

Thousands of customers were unable to withdraw cash or access their accounts after a software upgrade.（软件升级后，数千名客户无法取现或查询账户。）

联想记忆

retreat *v.*（军队）撤退；后退 *n.* 撤军；后退
deposit *v.* 储蓄；寄存；沉淀 *n.* 存款；押金；沉积物

单词	释义
sphere	*n.* A sphere of activity or interest is a particular area of activity or interest.（活动、兴趣的）领域
	n. A sphere is an object that is completely round in shape like a ball. 球体

双语例句

None of these technologies existed in 1997, when the Web in the public sphere was still in its infancy.（这些技术1997年都不存在，那时公共领域的网络还处于起步阶段。）

Because the earth spins, it is not a perfect sphere.（因为地球不断旋转，所以它不是一个完美的球体。）

联想记忆

scope *n.* 范围，领域
domain *n.* 领域；势力范围；（函数的）定义域

单元练习 16

使用本单元核心词汇的适当形式填空,并将句子译为中文。

1. The farms produce fruits, vegetables, dairy, and livestock _____ to our health.
2. Many users are unaware that their _____ handsets leave trails that can be followed by others.
3. They poured into the streets of New Delhi and _____ for stricter punishments for those criminals.
4. Two of the suspects have _____ to Saturday's attack, while the third denies any responsibility.
5. The operation was conducted in a way to _____ and avoid altogether, if possible, civilian casualties.
6. Most Japanese banks store _____ sets of data in computer centers 600 km apart in Osaka and Tokyo.
7. The pursuit of a youthful physical appearance is not the sole reason for their _____ with diet and exercise.
8. Video games can stimulate the mind in positive ways, but _____ exposure can lead to attention deficit problems.
9. The U.S. military announced it would _____ at least 2,500 troops from Southern Afghanistan.
10. Illegal logging has become _____, accounting for an estimated half of the annual production of timber.

Unit 17

★ 本单元核心词汇 ★

sensitive	moderate	intact	exterior	footage
ferocious	flare	refresh	advocate	devour
stumble	elude	conducive	temperate	hail
fascinate	heritage	prominent	compress	crave

★ 本单元拓展词汇 ★

reluctant	spire	external	mosque	slam
gulp	shuttle	status	humid	glitter
glint	energize	cabinet	blunder	dodge
cardiovascular	acclaim	stagger	delight	showcase
legacy	eminent	gobble	workaholic	opponent
applaud	commend	oppression	lag	

161. ***Moderate*** noise allows us to enter a state of mind ***conducive*** to creative breakthroughs, the study found.

单词	释义
moderate	*adj.* You use moderate to describe something that is neither large nor small in amount or degree. （数量或程度）适中的；温和的
	v. If you moderate something or if it moderates, it becomes less extreme or violent and easier to deal with or accept. 使缓和，变得缓和

双语例句

This moderate cardiovascular exercise will not only get the blood moving, but also help fight jet lag. （这种适度的心血管锻炼不仅让血液流动，而且有助于缓解时差反应。）

The Fed says it sees signs of slower growth that may moderate inflation pressures. （美国联邦储备委员会表示，经济增长有放缓的迹象，可能会缓解通胀压力。）

联想记忆

modest *adj.* 谦逊的；适度的

单词	释义
conducive	*adj.* If one thing is conducive to another thing, it makes the other thing likely to happen. 有益的，有助于……的

双语例句

It is generally believed that a relaxed classroom atmosphere is conducive to students' learning. （人们普遍认为，宽松的课堂环境有助于学生的学习。）

Many urban neighborhoods are not conducive to keeping a car, which some may be reluctant to give up. （许多城市社区都不适合买车，但一些人可能不愿放弃汽车。）

联想记忆

advantageous *adj.* 有利的，有益的
beneficial *adj.* 有益的

162. The home was extensively updated in 2006, though the original windows and ***exterior*** features were kept ***intact***.

单词	释义
exterior	*adj.* You use exterior to refer to the outside parts of something or things that are outside something. 外部的，外面的
	n. The exterior of something is its outside surface. 外部；外貌

双语例句

The new model of Mercedes-Benz performs well and delivers ample comfort, with an attractive exterior design.（这辆新款奔驰性能优异，舒适性好，外观设计也很吸引人。）

The buildings look distinctly Victorian from the exterior, with light-colored brick and red-roofed spires.（从外观上看，这些建筑具有鲜明的维多利亚风格，有着浅色的砖和红色的尖顶。）

联想记忆

external *adj.* 外部的；表面的；外国的

单词	释义
intact	*adj.* Something that is intact is complete and has not been damaged or changed. 完整无缺的

双语例句

The egg remained perfectly intact while it was in free fall under the action of gravity.（在重力作用下，鸡蛋在自由下落时依然完好无损。）

After the fire, hundreds of police surrounded the mosque, which was left largely intact.（火灾发生后，数百名警察包围了这座清真寺，所幸清真寺基本完好无损。）

联想记忆

undamaged *adj.* 完好的，未损坏的

163. Video ***footage***, which was available to the court, showed the moment when trouble ***flared*** in the early hours of the morning.

单词	释义
footage	*n.* Footage of a particular event is a film of it or the part of a film which shows this event. （描述某一事件的）片段镜头

双语例句

Local police were interviewing witnesses and watching video footage from security cameras.（当地警方正在问询目击者，并观看监控录像机拍摄的录像。）

Thirty years ago, footage of the Challenger space shuttle explosion streamed across television screens.（30年前，电视屏幕上播放了"挑战者"号航天飞机爆炸的画面。）

联想记忆

foot *n.* 脚；英尺 *v.* 步行；支付
footing *n.* 基础；立足处；社会关系

单词	释义
flare	*v.* If something such as trouble, violence, or conflict flares, it starts or becomes more violent. 爆发；激化
	v. If a fire flares, the flames suddenly become larger. （火）突然烧旺
	n. A flare is a sudden brief burst of bright flame or light. 闪光，闪耀

双语例句

In the years ahead tensions over water may flare in regions outside the Middle East as well.（在未来几年里，中东以外的地区也有可能爆发水资源紧张的局势。）

Some residents jumped from windows as the blaze flared through the building's entrance.（当大火蔓延至大楼的入口处时，一些居民从窗户里跳了出来。）

Witnesses said that a flare or firework lit by band members may have started the fire.（目击者称，火灾可能是由乐队成员点燃的火炬或烟花引起的。）

联想记忆

glitter *v.* 闪光，闪烁 *n.* 闪耀
glint *v.* 闪烁；发光 *n.* 微光；光亮

164. Not even the freezing mountain-water shower could *refresh* me and I crashed into my sleeping bag, desperately *craving* a full night's rest.

单词	释义
refresh	*v.* If something refreshes you when you are hot, tired, or thirsty, it makes you feel cooler or more energetic. 使清爽；使精神振作
	v. If you refresh something old or dull, you make it as good as it was when it was new. If you refresh a web page, you click a button in order to get the most recent version of the page. 更新；刷新

双语例句

Dancing not only energizes the body and refreshes the mind, but also brings about a lot of social interaction.（跳舞不仅可以健身和振奋精神，还能促进社交活动。）

Employers must make reasonable efforts to enable returning employees to refresh or upgrade their skills.（雇主必须努力使重返岗位的员工更新或提升他们的技能。）

Some refresh Facebook fifteen times an hour to track the likes on their status.（有些人每小时刷新"脸书"15次，查看他们朋友圈上的点赞。）

联想记忆

refreshing *adj.* 提神的；使人重新振作的
refreshment *n.* 点心；提神的东西

单词	释义
crave	*v.* If you crave something, you want to have it very much. 渴望得到

双语例句

Japan's population may be shrinking, but the Japanese crave bigger homes like everyone else.（日本的人口可能正在减少，但日本人和其他人一样渴望拥有大家庭。）

He craved the quiet security of academic life but abandoned it for the risks of public office.（他渴望安静又稳定的学术生活，但放弃了这种生活去冒险担任公职。）

联想记忆

craving *n.* 渴望

165. After the movie Jaws, sharks are considered as *ferocious* predators aggressively *devouring* innocent swimmers.

单词	释义
ferocious	*adj.* A ferocious animal, person, or action is very fierce and violent. 凶残的
	adj. A ferocious war, argument, or other form of conflict involves a great deal of anger, bitterness, and determination. 激烈的

双语例句

Far from being the ferocious beast of fishing tales, I have found sharks shy, and rarely aggressive.（我发现鲨鱼不是故事中描述的那样凶猛的野兽，而是很胆怯，很少有攻击性。）

Newspapers have become weapons in a ferocious battle for political power between Russia's tycoons.（报纸已成为俄罗斯大亨们争夺政治权力进行激烈斗争的武器。）

联想记忆

ferocity *n.* 凶猛；暴行

单词	释义
devour	v. If a person or animal devours something, they eat it quickly and eagerly. 狼吞虎咽地吃
	v. If you devour a book or magazine, for example, you read it quickly and with great enthusiasm. 急切地读

双语例句

As we settled down to supper, devouring the food hungrily, the front door slammed open.（当我们坐下，狼吞虎咽地吃晚餐时，前门"砰"地一声开了。）

Koretz started reading business books when he was 12 and devoured five a week until he was 16.（科瑞兹从12岁开始阅读商业书籍，直到16岁，他每周都要阅读5本。）

联想记忆

gulp v. 狼吞虎咽 n. 大口吞食
gobble v. 狼吞虎咽；大量消耗

166. In 2015, the group *stumbled* upon a solution that had been *eluding* medical professionals for years.

单词	释义
stumble	v. If you stumble upon something, you find or encounter it by chance. 偶然发现；偶然遇见
	v. If you stumble, you put your foot down awkwardly while you are walking or running and nearly fall over. Stumble is also a NOUN. 跟跄；绊脚

双语例句

As investigators were reviewing the crime-scene photographs, they stumbled upon a possible clue.（调查人员在查看犯罪现场的照片时，偶然发现了一条潜在的线索。）

I stumbled off a stair on the first day of vacation, breaking my foot and thus ending the trip before it really began.（假期的第一天，我从楼梯上摔下来导致腿脚骨折，旅行还没开始就这样结束了。）

联想记忆

stagger v. 蹒跚；大吃一惊 n. 跟跄，蹒跚
blunder v. 跌跌撞撞地走；犯错 n. 大错

单词	释义
elude	*v.* If a fact or idea eludes you, you do not succeed in understanding it, realizing it, or remembering it. 把……难住
	v. If you elude someone or something, you avoid them or escape from them. 躲避；不为……所获得

双语例句

Hampered by his impossible name and thick accent, success eluded him for many years.（拗口的名字和浓重的口音使他多年未能成功。）

The gang's leading members who have managed to elude arrest are either hiding in Nepal or have escaped to neighboring India.（该团伙尚未归案的主要成员要么躲在尼泊尔，要么已经逃往邻国印度。）

联想记忆

evade *v.* 回避，避开
dodge *v.* 躲开，巧妙躲避

167. They are a ***temperate***-climate crop, ***sensitive*** to temperature changes and requiring four distinct seasons.

单词	释义
temperate	*adj.* Temperate is used to describe a climate or a place which is never extremely hot or extremely cold.（气候或地区）温和的

双语例句

The temperate climate of the Austrian Alps attracts skiers in winter and walkers in summer.（奥地利阿尔卑斯山脉的温带气候吸引人们冬天来滑雪，夏天来爬山。）

Droughts and floods are likely to become a larger problem in many temperate and humid regions.（干旱和洪水很可能在许多温带和潮湿地区成为一个更严重的问题。）

联想记忆

tempered *adj.* 缓和的

单词	释义
sensitive	*adj.* Sensitive to something means it's quick to detect or respond to slight changes, signals, or influences. 敏感的
	adj. If you are sensitive to other people's needs, problems, or feelings, you show understanding and awareness of them. 有感知力的；能理解的
	adj. Sensitive documents or reports contain information that needs to be kept secret and dealt with carefully. 机密的

双语例句

Our brains behave like a highly sensitive radar constantly hunting a signal.（我们的大脑就像一台高度灵敏的雷达，不断地搜寻信号。）

An assessment of these may provide us with more accurate and more sensitive insights into the Indian past.（对这些进行评估可以使我们更准确、更好地了解印度的过去。）

Committee members were urged to keep all details of the meeting secret to prevent the sensitive information leaking into the public.（委员会成员要求对会议的所有细节保密，以防机密信息泄露出去。）

联想记忆

sensible *adj.* 理智的；合理的
sensitivity *n.* 敏感性；感知，察觉

168. For those *fascinated* by the great diversity of tropical rainforests, Queensland's World *Heritage* sites are well worth visiting.

单词	释义
fascinate	*v.* If something fascinates you, it interests and delights you so much that your thoughts tend to concentrate on it. 使着迷

双语例句

The scientists have long been fascinated with birth order and how it shapes our lives and careers.（长期以来，科学家们一直对出生顺序及其如何影响我们的人生和职业很感兴趣。）

Even as the future has aged, these concept cars continue to fascinate, as do the dream cars of Ford.（即使未来不断变化，这些概念车依然像福特梦幻汽车一样让人着迷。）

联想记忆

fascination *n.* 魅力，着迷
delight *v.* 使高兴 *n.* 令人高兴的人或事

单词	释义
heritage	*n.* Heritage is all the qualities, traditions, or features of life there that have continued over many years and have been passed on from one generation to another. 遗产；传统

双语例句

Many traditional dishes contain beans and corn, reflecting the Indian heritage of the country.（许多传统菜肴包含豆类和玉米，体现了美国印第安人的传统风俗。）

Kakadu National Park showcases the remarkable landscape, wildlife and cultural heritage of the Northern Territory.（卡卡杜国家公园展示了北部地区的秀丽风景、野生动物和文化遗产。）

联想记忆

inherit *v.* 继承；接手，承担
legacy *n.* 遗产；遗留问题

169. Western governments and ***prominent*** religious leaders have ***hailed*** him as the sort of man in whom to put their faith — and money.

单词	释义
prominent	*adj.* Someone who is prominent is important and well-known. 著名的
	adj. Something that is prominent is very noticeable or is an important part of something else. 突出的

双语例句

Men dominate business and politics, but many women have held cabinet posts or are prominent in arts and professions.（男性主导商界和政界，但许多女性也在内阁任职，或在艺术和专业领域成绩卓著。）

About two years ago I noticed a prominent bump on the inside of my right foot.（大约两年前，我注意到我的右脚内侧有一个突出的肿块。）

联想记忆

distinguished *adj.* 杰出的；著名的
eminent *adj.* 卓越的，杰出的

单词	释义
hail	*v.* If a person, event, or achievement is hailed as important or successful, they are praised publicly. 称赞
	v. If you hail a taxi, you wave at it in order to stop it because you want the driver to take you somewhere. 挥手呼叫
	n. Hail consists of small balls of ice that fall like rain from the sky. 冰雹

双语例句

Working too much damages people's health, yet most workaholics are hailed as heroes, or model employees.（过度工作会损害人们的健康，但多数工作狂被奉为英雄，或被评选为模范员工。）

We tried to hail a cab on 5th Avenue but hooked a silver Mercedes instead.（我们试图在第五大道上叫一辆出租车，却招来了一辆银色奔驰。）

Thunderstorms sometimes drop balls of ice known as hail in addition to rain.（除了下雨，雷暴有时会降下叫做冰雹的冰球。）

联想记忆

commend *v.* 赞扬，称赞
applaud *v.* 鼓掌；称赞
acclaim *v.* 赞扬，为……喝彩

170. ***Compressing*** the bachelor's degree into three years could be healthy for both colleges and students, ***advocates*** say.

单词	释义
compress	*v.* When you compress something or when it compresses, it is pressed or squeezed so that it takes up less space. 压缩；精简
	v. If an event is compressed into a short space of time, it is given less time to happen than normal or previously. 压缩（时间）

双语例句

The music is compressed by a factor of 12, without losing any noticeable sound quality.（这首歌被压缩至原来的1/12，而音质没有明显的损伤。）

The short life and lasting legend of the Irish freedom fighter was compressed into a 90-minute movie.（爱尔兰自由战士短暂而传奇的一生被拍摄成一部90分钟的电影。）

联想记忆

compression *n.* 压缩；浓缩
oppression *n.* 压迫；压抑

单词	释义
advocate	*v.* If you advocate a particular action or plan, you recommend it publicly. 提倡，主张
	n. An advocate of a particular action or plan is someone who recommends it publicly. 倡导者，支持者

双语例句

They advocate environmental education while on the job but are wasteful and polluting at home.（他们在工作中倡导环保教育，但在家里却浪费资源、污染环境。）

He was a strong advocate for human rights and for the fair treatment of African Americans.（他强力倡导人权，并提倡公平对待非洲裔美国人。）

联想记忆

opponent *n.* 对手；反对者

单元练习 17

使用本单元核心词汇的适当形式填空，并将句子译为中文。

1. Environments where employees are surrounded in blue are more _____ to creativity.
2. Movies and shows in digital form need to be _____ to be sent over broadband pipes.
3. The laser detectors on the machines aren't _____ enough to see a single DNA molecule.
4. Built in 1968, the 4-bedroom, 5-bath house is a European-style design with a stone _____.
5. As a teenager he _____ popular science fiction books and always had a wild imagination.
6. The church has been hit by two giant earthquakes but owing to its quake-resistant structure has remained _____.
7. Apple surprised observers by announcing its _____ Power Mac line of professional computers.
8. Talley _____ into chemistry at the University of Missouri after finding business classes unbearably dull.
9. The pace of life is slow and people socialize frequently with friends and family, drinking _____ amounts of wine.
10. The _____ Egyptian lawyer Nagla Al-Imam recently announced her conversion to Christianity in Cairo.

Unit 18

★ 本单元核心词汇 ★

commuter	exquisite	flash	appropriate	blur
scorching	vicinity	flock	dissipate	compliment
punctual	recruitment	notion	interact	abrupt
census	acknowledge	bizarre	implement	glorious

★ 本单元拓展词汇 ★

superb	censorship	hurricane	equator	gown
thunderclap	dental	squander	alumni	enlist
melody	rhythm	collaborate	weird	gadget
astronomical	gizmo	plantation	conception	peculiar
approximately	fuzzy	headquarter	reveal	sustain
situate	bureau			

Unit 18

171. The attraction isn't just the *exquisite* food, but the *glorious* vista of both the Mediterranean and the old town of Menton.

单词	释义
exquisite	*adj.* Something that is exquisite is extremely beautiful or pleasant, especially in a delicate way. 精美的

双语例句

These beautiful houses with exquisite carvings were built by eight brothers.（这些刻着精美壁画的漂亮房子是由兄弟八人共同建造的。）

He was working at Rochas in 2005, creating exquisite gown and dresses that were lavishly expensive.（2005年，他在罗莎时装工作，设计精美的礼服和裙子，其价格极其昂贵。）

联想记忆

exquisitely *adv.* 精致地；敏锐地

单词	释义
glorious	*adj.* Something that is glorious is very beautiful and impressive. 壮丽的
	adj. A glorious career, victory, or occasion involves great fame or success. 辉煌的；荣耀的；光荣的

双语例句

We bought a bright blue Chevrolet Impala which we drove thousands of glorious miles from Boston down to Key West in Florida.（我们买了一辆亮蓝色的雪佛兰黑斑羚，从波士顿开了几千英里，享受一路美景直到佛罗里达州基韦斯特。）

It was during his 104th Champions League match that the 34-year-old secured the defining image of his glorious career.（正是在他的第104场欧冠赛中，这位34岁的老将捍卫了他辉煌职业生涯中的完美形象。）

联想记忆

glory *n.* 光荣；壮丽
magnificent *adj.* 宏伟的，壮丽的
superb *adj.* 极好的，非同一般的

172. If the distinction between reality and fantasy is *blurred*, children may see violence on the screen as being *appropriate* in the real world.

单词	释义
blur	*v.* When a thing blurs or when something blurs it, you cannot see it clearly because its edges are no longer distinct. （使）变模糊
	n. A blur is a shape or area which you cannot see clearly because it has no distinct outline or because it is moving very fast. 模糊不清

双语例句

She looked at the letter but could not read it for the tears blurred her vision.（她盯着那封信，但无法看清，因为泪水模糊了她的视线。）

The lines between personal time and work time have become blurred at best, probably non-existent.（个人时间和工作时间的界限已经很模糊，甚至可能根本不存在。）

The first two and a half days of the Festival have been a blur of activity.（春节的前两天半是一片忙乱。）

联想记忆

blurry *adj.* 模糊的
fuzzy *adj.* 不清楚的，不明确的，含混的

单词	释义
appropriate	*adj.* Something that is appropriate is suitable or acceptable for a particular situation. 适当的
	v. Appropriate something is to take (something) for one's own use, typically without the owner's permission. 占用

双语例句

A spokesman for the railway said the company didn't feel it was appropriate to comment at this stage.（铁路部门的发言人表示，公司认为现阶段不宜作出评论。）

The governor thanked Congress for quickly appropriating billions of dollars in hurricane relief.（州长感谢国会迅速拨款数十亿美元用于飓风救援。）

联想记忆

appropriator *n.* 占用者；擅用者

173. The sun broke through the clouds and memories of summer's *scorching* hot days *flashed* through my mind.

单词	释义
scorching	*adj.* Scorching hot weather or temperatures are very hot indeed. 酷热的

双语例句

Situated almost directly on the equator, the mountain endures scorching days and freezing nights.（这座山几乎直接位于赤道上，白天炎热夜晚寒冷。）

The walk from the Colombian town to the beach took 15 minutes along a scorching hot dirt road.（从哥伦比亚的这个小镇到海滩，要冒着酷暑沿着土路步行15分钟。）

联想记忆

scorch *v.* 烧焦；枯萎 *n.* 焦痕
scorched *adj.* 烧焦的

单词	释义
flash	*v.* If something flashes through or into your mind, you suddenly think about it. 闪现；快速显示
	v. If a light flashes or if you flash a light, it shines with a sudden bright light, especially as quick, regular flashes of light. 闪光，闪亮
	n. A flash is a sudden burst of light or of something shiny or bright. 闪光

双语例句

As soon as Carley said those words, the image of her young son flashed through my head.（凯莉一说完这些话，她小儿子的模样就闪现在我脑海中。）

She only realized the man was not her husband when a ray of light flashed across his face.（当他的脸上闪过一道亮光时，她才意识到那人不是自己的丈夫。）

A flash of lightning lit her room followed by another thunderclap.（一道闪电照亮了她的房间，接着便是一阵雷鸣声。）

联想记忆

flashing *adj.* 闪烁的
flasher *n.* 发出闪光之物；闪光灯

174. These produce radiation at about the level of one dental X-ray in the immediate ***vicinity*** and quickly ***dissipate***.

单词	释义
vicinity	*n.* If something is in the vicinity of a particular place, it is near it. 附近

双语例句

Astronomical observations have revealed unexplained outflows of matter from the vicinity of black holes.（天文观测发现黑洞附近有物质向外涌出，这一点还无法解释。）

Violent and organized crime become involved in smuggling, especially in the vicinity of the Channel ports.（暴力和有组织的犯罪开始参与走私活动，特别是在海峡港口附近。）

联想记忆

locality *n.* 地方，地区

单词	释义
dissipate	*v.* When something dissipates or when you dissipate it, it becomes less until it disappears or goes away completely. 驱散；消散
	v. When someone dissipates money, time, or effort, they waste it in a foolish way. 浪费（金钱、时间、努力等）

双语例句

U.S. stocks have experienced sustained gains in January as uncertainty about taxes dissipated.（由于税收的不确定性消散，美国股市在1月份持续上涨。）

He wants to focus on the school rather than dissipating energy on risky foreign ventures.（他希望把精力集中在学校上，而不是浪费在高风险的海外投资上。）

联想记忆

dissipation *n.* 浪费；消散；损耗
squander *v.* 浪费；挥霍

175. Young Germans *flock* to Paris and love to watch French films, but the French seldom return the *compliment*.

单词	释义
flock	*v.* If people flock to a particular place or event, a very large number of them go there, usually because it is pleasant or interesting. 群集；蜂拥
	n. A group of people or things as a flock of them to emphasize that there are a lot of them. 一群，一批（人或物）

双语例句

Wealthy landowners flocked to the area, building plantations to grow Sea Island cotton, among other goods.（有钱的地主们蜂拥而至，建造庄园来种植海岛棉和其他商品。）

Flocks of tourists were collecting their baggage while a guide shouted to gather them for check-in.（游客们正在领取行李，一名导游大喊着让他们集合办理入住手续。）

联想记忆

cluster *v.* 群聚，聚集　*n.* 簇；一群人
bunch *v.* 捆，扎；使集中　*n.* 束，串；一群
herd *v.* 驱赶（兽群）；放牧　*n.* 兽群；民众

单词	释义
compliment	*n.* A compliment is a polite remark you make to someone to show that you like their appearance, appreciate their qualities, or approve of what they have done. 赞美，恭维，恭维话
	v. If you compliment someone, you give them a compliment. 赞美，恭维

双语例句

In her first weeks on the job, Ada frequently wandered around the newsroom floors giving compliments.（刚入职的前几周，艾达经常在新闻编辑室里走来走去，夸赞他人。）

Amateur beekeeper Ian Wallace of Newcastle said Prince Charles complimented him on his honey.（纽卡斯尔的业余养蜂人伊恩·华莱士说，查尔斯王子对他的蜂蜜大加赞扬。）

联想记忆

complimentary *adj.* 称赞的；免费赠送的
complement *v.* 补充

176. Replying to the debate on behalf of the government, the health minister *acknowledged* that one of the main challenges facing the NHS was *recruitment*.

单词	释义
acknowledge	*v.* If you acknowledge a fact or a situation, you accept or admit that it is true or that it exists. 承认（事实或情况）；认可
	v. If you acknowledge someone, for example, by moving your head or smiling, you show that you have seen and recognized them. 致意；致谢

双语例句

The health officer acknowledged that dozens of people had fallen sick due to lack of food and medicine.（卫生官员承认，数十人因缺乏食物和药品而患病。）

The Hunt Museum collection has been acknowledged as one of the most important private collections in the country.（亨特博物馆的藏品被公认为是该国最重要的私人收藏之一。）

The CEO finally acknowledged his female colleague who sat opposite him throughout the speech.（首席执行官最后感谢了在整个演讲过程中一直坐在他对面的女同事。）

联想记忆

acknowledgement *n.* 承认；感谢

单词	释义
recruitment	*n.* The recruitment of workers, soldiers, or members is the act or process of selecting them for an organization or army. 招聘

双语例句

Business schools can offer an expansive alumni network and recruitment opportunities across the world.（商学院可以提供世界各地广泛的校友网络和招聘机会。）

He moved the headquarters to Phoenix, figuring recruitment would be easier there than in remote New Mexico.（他把总部搬到了凤凰城，认为在那里招聘比在偏远的新墨西哥州容易一些。）

联想记忆

recruit *v.* 招聘；招募 *n.* 招聘；新兵
enlist *v.* 参军，入伍；招募

177. Schools with best practices have teachers who are *punctual* and *interact* with students in a friendly manner.

单词	释义
punctual	*adj.* If you are punctual, you do something or arrive somewhere at the right time and are not late. 准时的，守时的

双语例句

Our company remains committed to delivering punctual and reliable services.（我们公司始终致力于提供准时可靠的服务。）

Delhi Metro is clean and punctual, with 99% of all trains running on time since it began operating.（德里地铁干净准时，自运营以来，99%的列车都准点运行。）

联想记忆

punctuality *n.* 严守时间；准时性

单词	释义
interact	*v.* When people interact with each other or interact, they communicate as they work or spend time together. 相互交往；互动
	v. When one thing interacts with another or two things interact, the two things affect each other's behavior or condition. 相互作用，相互影响

双语例句

The teachers stay on after school hours to prepare for the next day's work and interact with students.（老师们在放学后留下来准备第二天的工作，并与学生们进行交流。）

What these songs have in common is the way that rhythm interacts with melody to produce a perfect effect.（这些歌曲的共同之处在于节奏与旋律融合，产生完美的效果。）

联想记忆

interactive *adj.* 交互式的；相互作用的
interaction *n.* 互动；相互作用
collaborate *v.* 合作，协作

178. The source of the current argument is the tax-cut plan itself, and the somewhat ***bizarre*** way in which it was ***implemented***.

单词	释义
bizarre	*adj.* Something that is bizarre is very odd and strange. 奇怪的，怪异的

双语例句

Though it sounds bizarre, mixing water into the fuel helps it burn better.（虽然听起来很奇怪，但是把水混合到这种燃料中可以使它燃烧更充分。）

The finding may help shed light on an even more bizarre aspect of the universe — dark energy.（这一发现可以帮助人们了解宇宙更奇异的一面——暗能量。）

联想记忆

bazaar *n.* 集市；义卖市场
weird *adj.* 奇怪的，古怪的
peculiar *adj.* 奇怪的；特别的，独特的
odd *adj.* 奇怪的；偶然出现的；奇数的

单词	释义
implement	*v.* If you implement something such as a plan, you ensure that what has been planned is done. 实施；执行
	n. An implement is a tool or other piece of equipment. 器具

双语例句

Wireless devices and networks must be properly planned and implemented to ensure the confidentiality of data.（无线设备和网络必须合理规划、妥善实施，以确保数据安全。）

The store sells clothing, household goods, small furniture and garden implements.（这家商店销售服装、家用物品、小型家具和园艺器具。）

联想记忆

gadget *n.* 小器具；小型装置
gizmo *n.* 小物件

179. The ***notion*** of retirement — an ***abrupt*** end to paid employment — is relatively recent but has been hugely popular.

单词	释义
notion	*n.* A notion is an idea or belief about something. 概念；想法

双语例句

There is a notion that the criminality is the product of poverty or government spending cuts.（有人认为，犯罪问题是贫困或政府削减开支导致的。）

Words like "family" are unclear, because people will have different notions of who makes up their family.（像"家庭"这样的词表意不清，因为人们对谁组成家庭持有不同观念。）

联想记忆

conception *n.* 概念，观念；构想

单词	释义
abrupt	*adj.* An abrupt change or action is very sudden, often in a way that is unpleasant. 骤然的，突然的
	adj. Someone who is abrupt speaks in a rude, unfriendly way. 唐突的

双语例句

After about four miles, the path comes to an abrupt end at the Museum of

Science.（经过大约四英里后，这条路突然在科学博物馆处到了尽头。）

Many of the e-mails that I receive are written in an extremely rude and abrupt tone.（我收到的许多电子邮件语气唐突，非常无礼。）

联想记忆

abruptly *adv.* 突然地；唐突地

180. The most recent *census* in 2016 showed that about four million are in *commuter* marriages, a 30% increase since 2010.

单词	释义
census	*n.* A census is an official survey of the population of a country that is carried out in order to find out how many people live there and to obtain details of such things as people's ages and jobs. 人口普查；（官方的）统计

双语例句

According to the U.S. Census Bureau, approximately 40 million people older than 65 live alone.（根据美国人口统计局的数据，大约有4 000万65岁以上的老人独居。）

The country's first national census of pollution sources is due to begin in February.（第一次全国污染源普查将于2月开始。）

联想记忆

censor *v.* 审查；检查 *n.* 检查员
censorship *n.* 审查制度

单词	释义
commuter	*n.* If you are a commuter, you travel a long distance every day between your home and your place of work. 通勤者

双语例句

Bus services will run every 30 minutes during peak commuter times and every hour at other times.（公共汽车在通勤高峰时段每30分钟一班，其余时段每小时一班。）

Traffic started to build up in the city at around 6 a.m., with thousands of commuters late for work.（每天早晨六点左右，城市交通就开始拥堵，成千上万的通勤者上班迟到。）

联想记忆

commute *v.* 通勤

单元练习 18

使用本单元核心词汇的适当形式填空,并将句子译为中文。

1. Friends said he was suffering from short-term memory loss and _____ vision.
2. Some companies such as General Assembly are reinventing the _____ of community college.
3. There are widespread complaints that drivers stopping _____ at lights are causing more accidents.
4. In South Dakota, a mobile home was destroyed when flames _____ 3,000 acres in the Black Hills.
5. In April Southwest departures were _____ only 76% of the time, worse than United and Delta.
6. Israel once had warm relations with some non-Arab countries in the _____, including Iran and Turkey.
7. The Kamppi Chapel of Silence is an example of _____ craftsmanship in the treatment of timber.
8. In the writing workshop she had signed up for, Maya received a lot of _____ from the instructor.
9. In healthy people, the discomfort lasts for about 30 seconds and then _____ after three minutes.
10. Corporations that _____ family-friendly practices were found to be more profitable than those without them.

Unit 19

★ 本单元核心词汇 ★

marvel	enchant	ultimately	swell	surpass
unfold	extinguish	plunge	activate	smash
evaporate	awkward	dilemma	succession	fabricate
transition	condense	squeeze	anonymous	riot

★ 本单元拓展词汇 ★

quench	stubborn	laud	prodigy	transaction
magnify	enlarge	overtake	skeptical	cognition
warfare	generator	revolt	earshot	sigh
momentum	vaporize	abridge	patriotism	punch
abbreviate	clumsy	cannon	uprising	stall
modify	predicament	plight	crush	

181. The torch itself was *extinguished* several times and *ultimately* loaded onto a bus where it was driven for much of the path.

单词	释义
extinguish	v. If you extinguish a fire or a light, you stop it from burning or shining. 使熄灭
	v. If something extinguishes a feeling or idea, it destroys it. 使破灭；消除

双语例句

More than 200 firefighters from Arlington, Va. extinguished a fire that burned for nearly three days.（来自弗吉尼亚州阿灵顿的200多名消防员扑灭了持续近三天的大火。）

Hopes that survivors might still be found have almost been extinguished.（发现生还者的希望几乎破灭了。）

联想记忆

extinguisher *n.* 灭火器
quench *v.* 扑灭；止渴；压制（感情）

单词	释义
ultimately	adv. Ultimately means finally, after a long and often complicated series of events. 最终
	adv. You use ultimately to indicate that what you are saying is the most important point in a discussion. 最重要地

双语例句

Google says the software platform ultimately may be used in devices beyond mobile phones.（谷歌表示，该软件平台最终可能会用于手机以外的设备。）

The energy will be transported to the most densely populated cities where it is ultimately required.（能源将被运送到人口最密集的城市，那里的需求最迫切。）

联想记忆

ultimate *adj.* 最终的；根本的
eventually *adv.* 最后，终于；终究

182. Visitors cannot help *marveling* at the super natural landscape, deeply *enchanted* by the leisurely life of the village.

单词	释义
marvel	*v.* If you marvel at something, you express your great surprise, wonder, or admiration. 大为赞叹
	n. You can describe something or someone as a marvel to indicate that they are wonderful. 奇迹

双语例句

I sat down once again, and stared out to the horizon, marveling at the wonders of the natural world.（我再次坐下来，凝视着地平线，惊叹于大自然的神奇。）

The railway was lauded as an engineering marvel when it opened in 1909.（这条铁路在1909年开通时被誉为一项工程奇迹。）

联想记忆

marvelous *adj.* 了不起的；非凡的
prodigy *n.* 奇迹；奇才，神童

单词	释义
enchant	*v.* If you are enchanted by someone or something, they cause you to have feelings of great delight or pleasure. 使陶醉；使入迷
	v. In fairy tales and legends, to enchant someone or something means to put a magic spell on them. 施魔法于

双语例句

David was enchanted with his beautiful young bride and she in turn appeared to be very happy.（戴维被他年轻漂亮的新娘迷住了，新娘看起来也非常幸福。）

They had to have enchanted glasses in there, because no matter how much champagne I drank, my glass never seemed to go down.（他们一定是给酒杯施了魔法，无论我喝多少，杯子里的香槟似乎都没有减少。）

联想记忆

enchanted *adj.* 着了魔的；有魔法的

183. The elderly population in the world is expected to *swell* by 200 million in the next decade to *surpass* one billion.

单词	释义
swell	*v.* If the amount or size of something swells or if something swells it, it becomes larger than it was before. 增加；使增大
	v. If something such as a part of your body swells, it becomes larger and rounder than normal. （身体部位等）肿胀

双语例句

Hundreds of thousands of refugees have swelled Monrovia's population to well over a million.（成百上千的难民涌入蒙罗维亚，使当地人口远超一百万。）

She was suffering from frequent headaches; her eye was watering and swelling up.（她经常头痛，眼睛流泪、肿胀。）

联想记忆

enlarge *v.* 扩大，扩展

magnify *v.* 放大；增大

单词	释义
surpass	*v.* If one person or thing surpasses another, the first is better than, or has more of a particular quality than, the second. 优于；超过

双语例句

Facebook has the lead in mobile advertising revenues, but Google will surpass it by 2025.（脸书在移动广告收入方面处于领先地位，但谷歌将在2025年超过它。）

Some are skeptical that AI will ever reach human levels of intelligence and cognition, let alone surpass it.（一些人认为人工智能无法达到人类的智力和认知水平，更不用说超越人类了。）

联想记忆

overtake *v.* 赶上；超越；超车

184. The European economic crisis has ***unfolded*** most dramatically in Greece, where the economy has ***plunged*** into a depression.

单词	释义
unfold	*v.* If a situation unfolds, it develops and becomes known or understood. 逐渐明朗
	v. If someone unfolds something which has been folded or if it unfolds, it is opened out and becomes flat. 展开；打开

双语例句

Many companies cling to the misguided idea that their plans will unfold exactly as written.（许多公司错误地认为，他们的规划将完全按照预期进行。）

She tore open the envelope and unfolded the paper inside, but sighed when she looked at it.（她撕开信封，把里面的纸展开，但是看到信时却叹了一口气。）

联想记忆

fold *v.* 折叠；倒闭 *n.* 折痕；褶皱
folder *n.* 文件夹

单词	释义
plunge	*v.* If a person or thing is plunged into a particular state or situation, or if they plunge into it, they are suddenly in that state or situation. 突然陷入
	v. If something or someone plunges in a particular direction, especially into water, they fall or throw themselves in that direction. 纵身跳向；猛冲向

双语例句

Millions of families across America were plunged into the deepest recession of their lifetimes.（美国数百万家庭陷入他们一生中最严重的经济衰退。）

She was running at full speed, glancing behind every few seconds, before plunging ahead with even greater speed.（她全速奔跑，每隔几秒钟向后看一眼，然后以更快的速度向前冲。）

联想记忆

plunger *n.* 活塞；潜水者；跳水者
leap *v.* 猛冲；跳起 *n.* 跳高，跳跃；激增

185. Four youths ***smashed*** windows at a supermarket and stole five televisions which were found abandoned in the car park after alarms were ***activated***.

单词	释义
smash	*v.* If you smash something or if it smashes, it breaks into many pieces, for example, when it is hit or dropped. 打碎；破碎
	v. If you smash through a wall, gate, or door, you get through it by hitting and breaking it. 撞破（墙或门）而入

双语例句

Firemen put ladders up to the bedroom window, smashed the glass and guided them to safety.（消防员将梯子搭在卧室的窗户上，砸碎玻璃，并引导他们到安全地带。）

More than 30 people were taken to hospital yesterday after a crowded underground train smashed into a tunnel wall.（昨天，一列拥挤的地铁撞上了隧道内墙，30多人被送往医院。）

联想记忆

punch *v.* 用拳猛击；打孔 *n.* 一拳；打孔器；果汁

单词	释义
activate	*v.* If a device or process is activated, something causes it to start working. 激活；启动

双语例句

The alarm signal activates the receiver, which then plays the warning to everyone in earshot.（报警信号激活接收器，然后接收器向附近的所有人发出警报。）

The 650-bed hospital experienced a power surge when emergency generators activated following the black-out.（这家拥有650个床位的医院在停电后启用紧急发电机，出现了电力过载。）

联想记忆

activator *n.* 催化剂；活化剂
activist *n.* 积极分子；活动家

186. Some of the ***evaporated*** seawater inside the greenhouse also ***condenses*** creating freshwater, which will be used to irrigate plants.

单词	释义
evaporate	*v.* When a liquid evaporates, or is evaporated, it changes from a liquid state to a gas, because its temperature has increased.（使）蒸发
	v. If a feeling, plan, or activity evaporates, it gradually becomes weaker and eventually disappears completely.（情绪、计划、活动）逐渐消逝

双语例句

While cooking the dish, check from time to time that the liquid has not completely evaporated.（烹饪这道菜时，需要时不时检查一下汤汁，确保没有完全蒸发。）

England's momentum quickly evaporated as South Africa took control of the first half of the game.（随着南非队控制了上半场比赛，英格兰队的势头很快就消失了。）

联想记忆

evaporation *n.* 蒸发；消失
vaporize *v.* 蒸发

单词	释义
condense	*v.* When a gas or vapor condenses, or is condensed, it changes into a liquid. （气体、蒸汽）冷凝
	v. If you condense something, especially a piece of writing or a speech, you make it shorter, usually by including only the most important parts. 压缩

双语例句

The air heats as it moves through the city to the center, then rises, cools and condenses into rain.（随着空气向城市中心流动，会逐渐变热，然后上升，冷却并凝结成雨。）

There are times when the movie has a rushed feel, as if a lot of action is being condensed into a short time.（电影有时会给人一种匆忙的感觉，好像大量的情节被压缩在很短的时间里。）

联想记忆

abridge *v.* 删节，简化
abbreviate *v.* 缩写；简化

187. That sometimes puts me in the *awkward* position of trying to figure out how to handle *anonymous* requests for medical advice.

单词	释义
awkward	*adj.* An awkward situation is embarrassing and difficult to deal with. 令人尴尬的
	adj. Something that is awkward is difficult to use or carry because of its design. A job that is awkward is difficult to do. （使用）不便的；棘手的
	adj. An awkward movement or position is uncomfortable or clumsy. 笨拙的

双语例句

It places South Koreans in the awkward position of weighing their patriotism against their vocation.（这让韩国人陷入尴尬的境地：在爱国主义和职业之间进行取舍。）

A more awkward question is whether the amount of dark energy in universe is changing.（一个更复杂的问题是，宇宙中的暗能量是否在变化。）

That gives the competitor a shot at grabbing a socially awkward but otherwise brilliant young engineer.（这让竞争对手有机会抓住一个不善交际，但才华横溢的年轻工程师。）

联想记忆

clumsy *adj.* 笨拙的，不灵活的

stubborn *adj.* 固执的；倔强的

单词	释义
anonymous	*adj.* If you remain anonymous when you do something, you do not let people know that you were the person who did it. 匿名的

双语例句

The museum bought the letters of Van Gogh from an anonymous private collector via Sotheby's in New York. （该博物馆通过纽约索斯比拍卖行从一位匿名私人收藏家手中购得梵高的信件。）

Threats of violence are more likely to be found on websites that allow posters to remain anonymous. （暴力威胁更容易出现在那些允许发帖者匿名的网站上。）

联想记忆

anonymity *n.* 匿名；匿名者

188. Employees trying to advance in their careers are finding it more challenging because the ***succession*** plans are unclear and, in many cases, ***fabricated***.

单词	释义
succession	*n.* A succession of things of the same kind is a number of them that exist or happen one after the other. 一连串
	n. Succession is the act or right of being the next person to have an important job or position. 继任；任权

双语例句

Several years ago, a succession of scandals rocked Jewish charities in New York and New Jersey. （几年前，纽约和新泽西的犹太慈善机构接连爆出丑闻。）

As second in the line of succession, Anna would only become queen if her sister died or became ineligible. （作为第二顺位继承人，安娜只有在她姐姐去世或失去王位继承权时，才能成为女王。）

联想记忆

succeed *v.* 成功；接替；继任

单词	释义
fabricate	*v.* If someone fabricates information, they invent or correct it in order to deceive people. 编造，捏造
	v. If something is fabricated from different materials or substances, it is made out of those materials or substances. 制造；装配；组装

双语例句

About 15% of researchers had seen their colleagues fabricate, falsify, alter or modify data.（约15%的研究人员曾看到同事伪造或篡改数据。）

It took this team almost two months to fabricate the weapon successfully.（这个团队花了近两个月的时间才成功研制出这种武器。）

联想记忆

fabrication *n.* 捏造，虚构的信息；装配
fake *v.* 伪造；伪装 *adj.* 伪造的 *n.* 假货；骗子

189. Traditional media companies were faced with the ***dilemma*** of ***transitioning*** to digital or holding forth.

单词	释义
dilemma	*n.* A dilemma is a difficult situation in which you have to choose between two or more alternatives. 困境；进退两难

双语例句

Brazil is caught up in its own dilemma between accelerated growth and environmental preservation.（巴西陷入经济加速增长和保护环境的两难境地。）

After he graduated from the University of Washington, Robert faced the dilemma of a career choice.（从华盛顿大学毕业后，罗伯特面临着职业选择的困境。）

联想记忆

predicament *n.* 困境
plight *n.* 处境，困境

单词	释义
transition	*v.* If someone transitions from one state or activity to another, they move gradually from one to the other. （逐渐地）转向
	n. Transition is the process in which something changes from one state to another. 转型

双语例句

The US Agency for International Development (USAID) will lead the way in transitioning from cash to electronic payments.（美国国际开发署将引领从现金支付转为电子支付。）

Marriage is a very important stage in a person's life, marking the official transition to adulthood.（婚姻是人一生中非常重要的阶段，标志着正式向成年过渡。）

联想记忆

transit *n.* 运送；交通运输系统　*v.* 经过，穿过
transitional *adj.* 转型的；过渡的
transaction *n.* 交易；业务

190. Since around 220,000 prisoners are *squeezed* into jails meant to hold 145,000, *riots*, gang warfare and mass escapes happen almost daily.

单词	释义
squeeze	*v.* If you squeeze a person or thing somewhere or if they squeeze there, they manage to get through or into a small space. 塞进；挤进
	v. If you squeeze something, you press it firmly, usually with your hands. （常指用手）挤压；紧捏
	n. Squeeze is also a NOUN. 紧捏；挤压

双语例句

The family of five squeezed into the bed of their tiny pick-up along with a giant refrigerator.（他们一家五口挤在小型皮卡的车厢里，旁边还有一个巨大的冰箱。）

At the beach there are stalls specializing in freshly squeezed fruit and vegetable juices.（海滩边有一些摊位专营鲜榨果蔬汁。）

A gentle squeeze will push the baby food in the bottle into the spoon attached in front.（轻轻一挤，就可以将瓶子里的婴儿食品挤到连接在前端的勺子里。）

联想记忆

squeezer *n.* 榨汁机
crush *v.* 挤压；捣碎；挤进（狭小空间）　*n.* 迷恋

单词	释义
riot	*n.* When there is a riot, people behave violently in a public place, for example, they throw stones, or damage buildings and vehicles. 暴乱
	v. If people riot, they behave violently in a public place. 闹事

双语例句

Economic inequality has remained a pressing problem and has led to riots and violent outbreaks.（经济发展不均衡仍然是一个紧迫的问题，已经导致多起暴乱和暴力事件发生。）

At several locations, riot police responded by firing rubber bullets and tear gas, and by using water cannon.（防暴警察在多处发射了橡胶弹和催泪瓦斯，并使用

了高压水枪。）

On March 18, prisoners rioted, breaking down a door and assaulting a police officer.（3月18日，囚犯发生暴动，他们砸倒房门并袭击了一名警官。）

联想记忆

rebellion *n.* 叛乱；反抗
uprising *n.* 起义；暴动
revolt *n.* 反抗，违抗 *v.* 反抗；拒不服从（权威、规定或法律）

单元练习 19

使用本单元核心词汇的适当形式填空，并将句子译为中文。

1. His mother opened a door in the master bedroom and _____ at the walk-in closet.
2. The earthquake crashed telephone networks and _____ parts of the city into darkness.
3. The building burned from the inside, and firefighters had _____ the flames before dawn.
4. The hope that California can recover its old luster in less than a generation may _____ as well.
5. Two pumps designed to start automatically during flooding failed to _____ in the early hours of November 25.
6. Windows have been _____ and cars damaged in more than a dozen separate incidents since March.
7. She received an _____ donation to attend college at UCLA, where she studied architecture.
8. The _____ arose when my sister announced a family reunion at her Lake Tahoe cabin in Nevada.
9. Haiti has experienced a _____ of aid programs with no coherency, co-ordination or long-term strategy.
10. He works with several employees who have _____ the retirement age for full Social Security benefits.

Unit 20

★ 本单元核心词汇 ★

outlaw	consent	embark	indigenous	alternate
merge	universality	eligible	obese	overlook
agony	naive	conspicuous	vow	ominous
hover	prosecution	offence	terminate	expire

★ 本单元拓展词汇 ★

dignity	outperform	dissent	gloomy	alien
disembark	aboriginal	seamless	unify	aisle
bonus	writhe	sedentary	adhere	plump
warranty	expectancy	facility	expiration	oath
pledge	aguish	linger	balcony	overhear
ward	radioactive			

191. The early songs are lyrically **naive** but that simplicity has given the Beatles a **universality** no other band has managed to achieve.

单词	释义
naive	*adj.* If you describe someone as naive, you think they lack experience and expect things to be easy or people to be honest. 幼稚的；天真的

双语例句

It would be dangerously naive to think that terrorism can effectively be fought in isolation.（孤立作战就可以有效地打击恐怖主义，这种想法不仅幼稚而且危险。）

She's had a rough childhood and still managed to stay sweet, innocent and a little naive.（她童年过得很苦，但仍然保持着善良、天真，甚至有些幼稚。）

联想记忆

naively *adv.* 天真地；无邪地

单词	释义
universality	*n.* Universality is the state or quality of being universal. 普遍性，广泛性

双语例句

The universality of its menu makes it easier to expand in different world markets.（其菜单具有普适性，这样更容易向全世界不同的市场进行扩张。）

Through their struggles and desire for dignity, slaves have contributed to the universality of human rights.（通过斗争和对尊严的渴望，奴隶为人权的普遍性作出了贡献。）

联想记忆

universal *adj.* 普遍的；宇宙的 *n.* 普遍特征；通用原理
universally *adv.* 普遍地，一般地

192. Physical punishment is **outlawed** already in UK schools, but not in the home — and not for childminders, with parental **consent**.

单词	释义
outlaw	*v.* When something is outlawed, it is made illegal. 宣布……为非法
	n. An outlaw is a criminal who is hiding from the authorities. 逃犯

双语例句

North Carolina, an important swing state, has just voted to outlaw gay marriage and partnerships.（北卡罗莱纳州是一个重要的摇摆州，刚刚投票禁止同性婚姻和同性关系。）

Bonnie and Clyde were notorious outlaws and criminals who traveled the central U.S. during the Great Depression.（邦尼和克莱德是臭名昭著的不法之徒，他们在大萧条时期穿越了美国中部地区。）

联想记忆

outlast *v.* 比……长久
outperform *v.* 胜过，比……更好

单词	释义
consent	*n.* If you give your consent to something, you give someone permission to do it. 同意，许可
	v. If you consent to something, you agree to do it or allow it to be done. 同意，准许

双语例句

The man's photograph had been obtained and published on the site without his consent.（这名男子的照片未经他本人同意就被发布在网站上。）

Most states, including Georgia, permit phone calls to be recorded as long as one party consents.（在包括佐治亚在内的大多数州，只要一方同意，就可以对电话进行录音。）

联想记忆

dissent *v.* 持异议 *n.* 不同意

193. To learn about the land and its people, walkers can *embark* on a journey guided by its *indigenous* inhabitants.

单词	释义
embark	*v.* If you embark on something new, difficult, or exciting, you start doing it. 开始从事
	v. When someone embarks on a ship, they go on board before the start of a journey. 登上（船）

双语例句

Carmike Cinemas has embarked on the most aggressive digital expansion of the theater chains.（卡麦克院线已经开始连锁影院模式中最激进的数字化扩张。）

Of the 1.7 million UK holidaymakers who went on cruises, nearly 700,000 embarked on a Mediterranean trip.（在170万英国游轮旅行者中，近70万人选择了地中海之旅。）

联想记忆

embarkment *n.* 装船；上船
disembark *v.* 登陆；上岸

单词	释义
indigenous	*adj.* Indigenous people or things belong to the country in which they are found, rather than being brought there from another country. 本土的

双语例句

Soybeans are indigenous to China and have long been a part of the country's diet.（大豆产于中国，长期以来一直是中国饮食原料的一部分。）

Those who speak indigenous languages or wear traditional dress are styled Indians.（那些讲土著语言或穿传统服饰的是地道的印第安人。）

联想记忆

aboriginal *adj.* 土著的 *n.* 土著居民；土生土长的生物
alien *adj.* 外来的；陌生的 *n.* 外星人；（植物或动物的）外国引进品种

194. Since then, his life *alternated* between music and spirituality to finally *merge* into a powerful combination.

单词	释义
alternate	*v.* When you alternate two things, you keep using one then the other. When one thing alternates with another, the first regularly occurs after the other. 交替
	adj. Alternate actions, events, or processes regularly occur after each other. 交替的；替换的
	n. An alternate is a person or thing that replaces another, and can act or be used instead of them. 替补

双语例句

The streets alternated between bombed-out buildings and stretches of fresh paint.（街道上随处都是被炸毁的建筑物，时而可以看到未干的交通标识线。）

Due to the heavy snow on Hwy. 36, all trucks and buses were advised to consider an alternate route.（由于36号公路上积雪严重，请所有卡车和公交车绕行其他路线。）

We'll select one of the alternates to take Ed's place in tomorrow's reenactment.（在明天的重演中，我们将从替补演员中选一个来代替艾德。）

联想记忆

alternative *adj.* 供选择的；交替的 *n.* 可供选择的事物
alternation *n.* 交替；轮流

单词	释义
merge	*v.* If one thing merges with another, or is merged with another, they combine to make one whole thing. You can also say that two things merge, or are merged. 合并，使合并

双语例句

Scotland's eight police forces are being merged into a single, national service next month.（苏格兰的八个警察部队将于下个月合并为一个全国性机构。）

Movies, TV programs, music, games and communications will merge seamlessly with each other.（电影、电视、音乐、游戏和通讯将实现无缝融合。）

联想记忆

unify *v.* 联合；统一

195. Only 25 percent of people, aged 17 to 24, are *eligible* to serve in the armed forces, partly because many are overweight or *obese*.

单词	释义
eligible	*adj.* Someone who is eligible to do something is qualified or able to do it. 有资格的；合格的

双语例句

In 1965, fewer than 7% of eligible blacks in Alabama were registered to vote.（1965年，阿拉巴马州有选举资格的黑人中只有不到7%登记投票。）

Teachers are eligible for annual salary increases and bonuses based on the classroom observations and student achievement.（根据听课情况和学生成绩，教师可以获得年度加薪和奖金。）

联想记忆

eligibility *n.* 适合；胜任

单词	释义
obese	*adj.* If someone is obese, they are extremely fat. 肥胖的

双语例句

Some experts have suggested smokers or obese women are dragging down life expectancy.（一些专家指出，吸烟者和肥胖女性的预期寿命正在降低。）

Moderate exercise, such as walking, can reduce the risk of diabetes in obese and sedentary people.（像散步这样的适度运动能够降低肥胖和久坐人群患糖尿病的风险。）

联想记忆

obesity *n.* 肥胖；肥胖症
plump *adj.* 胖乎乎的，丰满的

196. In spring and summer women whose ankles are too *conspicuous* are taken to police stations to sign statements *vowing* to dress more modestly.

单词	释义
conspicuous	*adj.* If someone or something is conspicuous, people can see or notice them very easily. 显著的，显而易见的

双语例句

He had exchanged words and a very conspicuous looking envelope with the head inspector.（他和探长说了几句话，然后将一个非常显眼的信封交给了探长。）

Mr. Vajpayee, conspicuous by his absence that day, describes the incident as "unfortunate".（瓦杰帕伊因那天的缺席而引人注目，他形容这一事件是"不幸的"。）

联想记忆

visible *adj.* 看得见的；明显的
evident *adj.* 清楚的，显然的

单词	释义
vow	*v.* If you vow to do something, you make a serious promise or decision that you will do it. 发誓
	n. A vow is a serious promise to do a particular thing. 誓言；誓约

双语例句

The president will vow to make facilities at the schools in the country fit for 21st century learning.（这位总统将发誓，使本国学校的设施能适应21世纪的学习。）

Her job is to help the couple choose every vow, blessing and prayer used in the wedding ceremony.（她的工作是帮助每对夫妇选择婚礼上使用的每一句誓言、祝福和祈祷。）

联想记忆

oath *n.* 誓言；誓约；咒骂
pledge *n.* 保证；承诺 *v.* 发誓

197. Patients showing up in the emergency room in ***agony*** were often ***overlooked*** or treated by unqualified clinicians.

单词	释义
agony	*n.* Agony is great physical or mental pain. 极大痛苦

双语例句

In a letter, she described the dreadful condition with soldiers writhing in agony in the wards.（在一封信中，她描述了可怕的情形，士兵们在病房里痛苦地挣扎。）

The crisis may well have lasting implications, even if the agonies of the Cyprus economy do not.（即使塞浦路斯的经济阵痛不会产生深远影响，这场危机也很可能会产生持久的影响。）

联想记忆

anguish *n.* 痛苦；剧痛

单词	释义
overlook	*v.* If you overlook a fact or problem, you don't notice it or realize how important it is. 忽视；忽略
	v. If a building or window overlooks a place, you can see the place clearly from the building or window. 俯瞰

双语例句

Despite a huge manhunt, police admit a key piece of information was initially overlooked.（尽管进行了大规模搜捕，但警方承认一开始就忽视了一个关键信息。）

Guests are served breakfast each morning on the balcony that overlooks the sea and village.（客人们每天早上在阳台上享用早餐，还可以俯瞰大海和村庄。）

联想记忆

oversee *v.* 监督，监管
overhear *v.* 偶然听到；偷听

overview *v.* 综述 *n.* 概览，概述

198. Behind us, the sun showed itself for the first time, but an ***ominous*** cloud still ***hovered*** above the island in the distance.

单词	释义
ominous	*adj.* If you describe something as ominous, you mean that it worries you because it makes you think that something bad is going to happen. 不祥的

双语例句

The news that radioactive elements are present in small amounts in some food seems ominous.（一些食物中含有少量放射性元素的消息似乎是不祥的预兆。）

The storm is just about to break; there's an ominous black cloud over Sheffield.（暴风雨即将来临，一片不祥的乌云飘在谢菲尔德上空。）

联想记忆

gloomy *adj.* 阴暗的；沮丧的；前景黯淡的

单词	释义
hover	*v.* To hover means to stay in the same position in the air without moving forward or backward. 盘旋
	v. If someone hovers, he stays in one place and move slightly in a nervous way; if something such as a price hovers around a particular level, it stays at more or less that level and does not change much. 徘徊；上下波动

双语例句

The roads were closed for security reasons and helicopters were hovering over head.（由于安全原因，道路被关闭，直升机在上空盘旋。）

My companion hovered over the fruit as if he'd never seen an orange before.（我的同伴在水果边上徘徊，好像从来没有见过橙子一样。）

The price of consumer goods is currently falling, and inflation overall is hovering around zero.（消费品价格目前正在下跌，通货膨胀率总体上在零附近徘徊。）

联想记忆

linger *v.* 继续存留；逗留；缓慢度过

199. Such attacks are not necessarily a criminal ***offence*** and it can be difficult to bring ***prosecutions***.

Unit 20

单词	释义
offence	*n.* An offence is a crime that breaks a particular law. 犯罪
	n. Offence is behavior that causes people to be upset or embarrassed. 冒犯

双语例句

Attacking a police officer is seen as an aggravated offence in the eyes of the Welsh law, and carries a prison sentence of up to six months.（根据威尔士法律，袭警被视为严重犯罪，最高可判6个月监禁。）

The comments would cause potential offence to those who adhere to Islam.（这些言论可能会对伊斯兰教信徒造成潜在的冒犯。）

联想记忆

offend *v.* 冒犯；违反；进攻
offensive *adj.* 攻击的；冒犯的 *n.*（军事）进攻；攻势

单词	释义
prosecution	*n.* Prosecution is the action of charging someone with a crime and putting them on trial. 起诉
	n. The party instituting or conducting legal proceedings against someone in a lawsuit are called the prosecution. 检方

双语例句

Individuals can bring private prosecutions in the criminal courts, but cases are rare.（个人可以在刑事法庭提起自诉，但这种情况很少。）

It's interesting that the prosecution haven't really referred to that video in court hearings.（有趣的是，公诉人并没有在法庭听证会上提及那段录像。）

联想记忆

prosecute *v.* 起诉；从事
prosecutor *n.* 检察官；公诉人

200. Midfielder Britton ***terminated*** his eight-year stay at Swansea in June 2010 to join the Blades after his contract ***expired***.

单词	释义
terminate	*v.* When you terminate something or when it terminates, it ends completely. 终止
	v. When a train or bus terminates somewhere, it ends its journey there.（火车或公共汽车）到达终点

双语例句

The Hero robot series was too difficult to produce and sell, and was soon terminated.（英雄机器人系列太难生产和销售，因此很快就被终止了。）

Trains are going to terminate at St Pancras, and the original station is being massively redeveloped.（列车将以圣潘克拉斯为终点站，原终点车站正在进行大规模重建。）

联想记忆

terminal *adj.* 末端的；晚期的 *n.* 终点；终端
termination *n.* 结束；终止

单词	释义
expire	*v.* When something such as a contract, deadline, or visa expires, it comes to an end or is no longer valid. 到期；失效

双语例句

The 62-year-old says he is planning a switch when his two-year Verizon contract expires.（这位62岁的老人说，他计划在两年的威瑞森公司合同到期后更换运营商。）

The one-year warranty has expired but they agree to carry out the repairs over the next three months.（一年的保修期已过，但他们同意在接下来的三个月内进行维修。）

联想记忆

expiry *n.* 逾期；终结
expiration *n.* 呼气；终结

单元练习 20

使用本单元核心词汇的适当形式填空,并将句子译为中文。

1. When he ended his career as an astronaut, he _____ on a successful political life.
2. Sadly, the political and business leaders are _____ among us only by their absence.
3. It is widely admitted that some of the _____ payment methods on the rise bring risks of their own.
4. Nearly 70% of the inhabitants are _____ to vote in Greenland, a Danish territory with partial autonomy.
5. Overnight lows _____ in the Northeast under 20 degrees and should not get above freezing Saturday.
6. Prior to the trip, parents were given full details and signed a _____ form before their child could take part.
7. San Francisco plans to set up free, _____ available wireless access to the Internet, otherwise known as Wi-Fi.
8. In 1939, Imperial Airways and British Airways _____ to form the British Overseas Airways Corporation.
9. School trips could broaden children's horizons but fear of _____ was often used as an excuse not to organize them.
10. The man would probably survive, but was destined to a life of physical _____ and psychological torment.

Unit 21

★ 本单元核心词汇 ★

overwhelm	dizzy	capsule	ingredient	resemble
spike	yearning	hoist	elliptical	dread
viable	withstand	saturate	derive	ample
slump	custody	auction	antique	detain

★ 本单元拓展词汇 ★

territory	prescribe	detach	shepherd	crane
skyline	constituent	dazzle	archeology	ellipsis
sanitation	crank	rage	miracle	surge
ceramic	arena	mute	viability	herb
derivational	sprout	property	plummet	cliff
inventory	fictional	consecutive	file	

201. Over the next 22 hours, one by one, the miners were *hoisted* to freedom in a red, white and blue metal *capsule*.

单词	释义
hoist	*v.* If you hoist something, you lift it or raise it by means of ropes and pulleys. 提起；吊起；升起（旗、帆等）
	n. Hoist is also a NOUN. 起重机；升起，吊起

双语例句

In New York City, cranes are prohibited from hoisting materials or equipment over city streets.（纽约市禁止使用起重机在城市街道上吊装材料或设备。）

The pool, equipped with hoists, will allow children to receive water therapy.（这个水池配有升降装置，孩子们可以享受水疗。）

联想记忆

hoister *n.* 提升机；起重机

单词	释义
capsule	*n.* A capsule is a small container with substances inside. 小容器
	n. A capsule is a very small tube containing powdered or liquid medicine, which you swallow. （装药的）胶囊
	n. A space capsule is the part of a spacecraft in which people travel, and which often separates from the main rocket. 太空舱

双语例句

The capsule contains the details of a safety deposit box in a Swiss bank.（这个容器里装有瑞士银行保险箱的详细资料。）

The herbs have long been used in traditional medicine, and are now sold in stores as capsules.（这些草药长期以来一直用作中药，现在以胶囊的形式在药店出售。）

About nine minutes out, the capsule detached from the spacecraft that had shepherded it from Earth.（大约9分钟后，太空舱与运载它离开地球的宇宙飞船分离。）

联想记忆

capsulate *adj.* 胶囊包裹的

202. It is normal for new mothers to feel *overwhelmed* with feeding schedules and *dizzy* from sleep deprivation.

单词	释义
overwhelm	*v.* If you are overwhelmed by a feeling or event, it affects you very strongly, and you do not know how to deal with it. （强烈地影响而）使不知所措
	v. If a group of people overwhelm a place or another group, they gain complete control or victory over them. 彻底制服；击败
	v. If you are overwhelmed by something, you are buried or drown beneath a huge mass of something, especially water. 淹没；覆盖

双语例句

The survivor may be overwhelmed by confusing emotions — fear, grief, guilt, rage.（恐惧、悲伤、内疚、愤怒，这些情绪交织在一起，让这位幸存者感到不知所措。）

Robertson overwhelmed his Indonesian opponent 15-6 at Birmingham's National Indoor Arena.（罗伯森在伯明翰国家室内体育馆以15比6击败了印度尼西亚选手。）

The restaurant reopened just five weeks after Hurricane Katrina hit and was immediately overwhelmed with customers.（这家餐厅在卡特里娜飓风袭击五周后就重新开张了，店里很快便食客如云。）

联想记忆

overwhelming *adj.* 压倒性的

单词	释义
dizzy	*adj.* If you feel dizzy, you feel that you are losing your balance and are about to fall. 眩晕的

双语例句

The physician twirled the patient around so fast, that the patient became dizzy and lost her balance.（医生迅速把病人转了个身，使得病人头晕目眩，失去了平衡。）

Despite the global recession, the skyline continues to sprout apartment towers of dizzy heights.（尽管全球经济衰退，高得令人眩晕的摩天大楼依然接连拔地而起。）

联想记忆

dazzle *v.* 使炫目，使眼花 *n.* 炫目，耀眼
drizzle *v.* 下毛毛雨 *n.* 蒙蒙细雨

203. As long ago as the 1950s, a perfumer noted that several ***ingredients*** of incense ***resembled*** scents of the human body.

单词	释义
ingredient	*n.* Ingredients are the things that are used when you are cooking a particular dish. （尤指烹调用的）原料；成分
	n. An ingredient of a situation is one of the essential parts of it. 要素

双语例句

Some Taco Bell franchisees were unwilling at first to pay more for the new ingredients.（一些塔可钟加盟商刚开始不愿意为新食材支付更多费用。）

Water and sanitation facilities are a key ingredient of social and economic progress.（水和卫生设施是社会和经济进步的一个关键因素。）

联想记忆

constituent *n.* 成分，构成要素；选民 *adj.* 组成的，构成的

单词	释义
resemble	*v.* If one thing or person resembles another, they are similar to each other. 像，与……相似

双语例句

The theory of dogs resembling their owners was put to the test at a fun dog show recently.（最近在一个有趣的狗展上，狗与主人长得相像这一理论得到了验证。）

What has been happening in Moscow over the past few days resembled a military operation, rather than national celebrations.（最近几天在莫斯科发生的事情更像是军事行动，而不是国庆庆典。）

联想记忆

resemblance *n.* 相似；相似之处

204. Fitness centers typically see a *spike* after the New Year, but treadmills and *elliptical* machines were alarmingly vacant this January.

单词	释义
spike	*n.* A spike is a sharp increase in the magnitude or concentration of something. 激增
	v. If something spikes, it rises quickly and reach a high value. 急剧增加
	v. When a person spikes a drink, he adds alcohol or poisonous substances to it. （向饮料中）掺入烈酒或毒药

双语例句

The recent spike in oil prices seems to have ended as increased production has boosted supplies.（近期油价大涨的局面似乎已经结束，因为产量增加推动了供应。）

As the chart shows, online interest in the currency has spiked in recent months.（如图所示，近几个月来，网民对这一货币的兴趣激增。）

Mr. Campbell claimed that while socializing with friends, including Harrison, his drink was spiked.（坎贝尔声称，在与包括哈里森在内的朋友们交谈时，他的饮料被下了毒。）

联想记忆

surge *n.* 激增；汹涌 *v.* 急剧上升；涌现

单词	释义
elliptical	*adj.* Something that is elliptical has the shape of an ellipse. 椭圆形的
	adj. Elliptical references to something are indirect rather than clear. 隐晦的

双语例句

He spent an hour on the elliptical machine in his home basement cranking through calories and some 50 emails.（他在地下室的椭圆仪上锻炼了一个小时来消耗热量，同时处理了约50封电子邮件。）

When the Prime Minister visited Africa this past March, he issued only an elliptical, half-baked apology.（今年3月，首相访问非洲时，他只是含糊其辞地进行了道歉。）

联想记忆

elliptic *adj.* 椭圆形的；省略的
ellipse *n.* 椭圆形；椭圆
ellipsis *n.* 省略；省略号

205. That *yearning*, coupled with a widespread *dread* of going to a nursing home, has led to more programs aimed at helping the elderly stay in their neighborhoods longer.

单词	释义
yearning	*n.* A yearning for something is a very strong desire for it. 渴望；向往

Unit 21

双语例句

Throughout the Middle East, there is a great yearning for the quiet miracle of a normal life.（在整个中东地区，人们向往出现奇迹，恢复平静的正常生活。）

He is a famous film actor who feeds a popular yearning for heroes, even fictional ones.（他是一位著名的电影演员，满足了大众对英雄的渴望，即便是虚构的英雄。）

联想记忆

yearn *v.* 渴望；思念

单词	释义
dread	*n.* Dread is a feeling of great anxiety and fear about something that may happen. 忧虑；恐惧
	v. If you dread something which may happen, you feel very anxious about it because you think it will be unpleasant or upsetting. 害怕；担忧

双语例句

It is the physician's dread of lawsuits that drives up the cost of health care.（正是医生对法律诉讼的恐惧才推高了医疗成本。）

Those are the phone calls both dreaded and hoped for among the families of Sept. 11 victims.（那些电话是911遇难者家属既害怕又期盼的。）

联想记忆

dreadful *adj.* 可怕的
fright *n.* 惊恐，惊吓

206. Building tsunami shelters along the coast is only a ***viable*** option if they can ***withstand*** the waves as well as shifting ground.

单词	释义
viable	*adj.* Something that is viable is capable of doing what it is intended to do. 可行的

双语例句

Skills education is crucial for domestic industry to remain viable into the 21st century.（技能教育对于国内产业在21世纪保持活力至关重要。）

When I lived in west-central Ohio, Verizon was the only viable option for most people.（当我住在俄亥俄州中西部时，威瑞森是大多数人唯一可选的运营商。）

联想记忆

viability *n.* 生存能力；可行性

单词	释义
withstand	*v.* If something or someone withstands a force or action, they survive it or do not give in to it. 抵御；经受住

双语例句

The country has not yet established an economic model that can withstand long-term tests.（该国尚未建立一个能经得起长期考验的经济模式。）

The police station at the scene withstood the explosion, with a single, bullet-proof window blown in.（位于现场的警察局在爆炸中未严重受损，只有一扇防弹窗户被炸开了。）

联想记忆

survive *v.* 幸免于；挺过来；设法应付

207. More than half of the firm's revenues are ***derived*** from selling in rural India, where demand for its products is growing five times faster than in ***saturated*** urban markets.

单词	释义
derive	*v.* If you derive something such as pleasure or benefit from a person or from something, you get it from them. 获得
	v. If you say that something such as a word or feeling derives or is derived from something else, you mean that it comes from that thing. 源于；衍生

双语例句

Thailand derives a large portion of its revenue from tourism, which has been diminished by the flooding.（泰国很大一部分收入来自旅游业，但洪灾使旅游收入减少了。）

Almost all Olympic uniforms we see today derive from religious or military forms of clothes.（我们今天看到的几乎所有奥运服都源于宗教服饰或军装。）

联想记忆

derivation *n.* 引出；来历
derivational *adj.* 得来的；派生的

单词	释义
saturate	*v.* If people or things saturate a place or object, they fill it completely so that no more can be added. 使饱和；使充满
	v. If someone or something is saturated, they become extremely wet. 湿透

双语例句

Facing a saturated car market at home, Chinese carmakers nearly doubled their exports last year.（面对国内饱和的汽车市场，中国汽车制造商去年的出口额几乎翻了一番。）

Murdock eats only fruits, vegetables and fish, exercises regularly and avoids saturated fats and sugar.（默多克只吃水果、蔬菜和鱼，他定期锻炼，不碰饱和脂肪酸和糖。）

After heavy rainfall the soil became saturated, leading to more of the cliff falling away.（大雨过后，土壤渗透着水，导致悬崖更多地方开始掉落。）

联想记忆

saturation　*n.* 饱和；渗透

208. The currency collapse that triggered the ***slump*** was ***ample*** proof of how helpless nations are before the tidal waves of global capital.

单词	释义
slump	*n.* If something such as the value of something experiences a slump, it falls suddenly and by a large amount. （价值等）暴跌
	n. A slump is a time when many people in a country are unemployed and poor. 经济萧条时期
	v. Slump is also a VERB. 暴跌，猛跌

双语例句

The land is now worth much less than originally hoped because of a slump in property prices.（由于地产价格暴跌，这块土地现在大不如原来期望的那么值钱了。）

During the economic slump, many retailers reduced prices in hopes of ridding themselves of excess inventory.（在经济萧条时期，许多零售商降低价格，希望消化过剩库存。）

Spain's economy shrank for a seventh consecutive quarter between January and March as domestic demand slumped.（由于国内需求大幅下滑，西班牙经济在1月至3月连续第七个季度萎缩。）

联想记忆

plummet *v.* 暴跌；坠落 *n.* 骤降

单词	释义
ample	*adj.* If there is an ample amount of something, there is enough of it and usually some extra. 充足的，充裕的

双语例句

Every visiting press member received a visitor's guide and ample opportunities to tour university facilities.（每位来访的新闻记者都收到了一份游客指南，有充分的机会参观大学设施。）

There is an ample supply of workers with a wide variety of education and job skills who can't get jobs.（有大量受过各种教育、拥有多种技能的工人找不到工作。）

联想记忆

plentiful *adj.* 丰富的；众多的

209. He had been ***detained*** in police ***custody*** but released Thursday after investigators said there was no evidence against him.

单词	释义
detain	*v.* When people such as the police detain someone, they keep them in a place under their control. 拘留
	v. To detain someone means to delay them, for example, by talking to them. 耽搁

双语例句

The security forces have detained a man on suspicion of anti-government actions.（安全部队拘留了一名涉嫌从事反政府活动的男子。）

The firemen were detained so long that by the time they reached the scene the building had burned to the ground.（消防员被耽搁太久，当他们到达现场时，房子已夷为平地。）

联想记忆

detainment *n.* 扣留；延误
detention *n.* 扣留；扣押；（放学后）留校

单词	释义
custody	*n.* If someone is being held in a particular type of custody, they are being kept in a place that is similar to a prison. 拘留
	n. Custody is the legal right to keep and take care of a child, especially the right given to a child's mother or father when they get divorced. 监护权

双语例句

The suspect can be held in police custody for 96 hours without charges being filed.（在没有提出指控的情况下，犯罪嫌疑人可以被关押96个小时。）

Both of the girls' natural parents, who live apart, are fighting for custody of the twins.（两个女孩的亲生父母处于分居状态，都在争取双胞胎姐妹的监护权。）

联想记忆

custodial *adj.* 保管的；保管人的
guardian *n.* 监护人；守护者

210. A slice of the 1871 wedding cake of her daughter, Princess Louise, was recently ***auctioned*** off at an ***antiques*** fair for $215.

单词	释义
auction	*v.* If something is auctioned, it is sold in an auction. 拍卖
	n. An auction is a public sale where items are sold to the person who offers the highest price. 拍卖

双语例句

Each year a fixed number of green cards or visas would be auctioned off to the highest bidder.（每年，固定数量的绿卡或签证将被拍卖给出价最高的人。）

The first book printed in the U.S. will tour various cities before the auction on Nov. 26.（在11月26日拍卖之前，美国印刷的第一本书将在多个城市巡回展出。）

联想记忆

auctioneer *n.* 拍卖商

单词	释义
antique	*n.* An antique is an old object such as a piece of china or furniture that is valuable because of its beauty or rarity. 古董

双语例句

Broomer, a native Londoner, opened her antique store in Manhattan in 1987, selling mainly ceramics.（布鲁默是土生土长的伦敦人，1987年她在曼哈顿开了一家古董店，主要销售陶瓷制品。）

The interior has a muted color palette with a mix of contemporary and antique furnishings.（室内色调柔和，装修风格是现代与古典的混搭。）

联想记忆

antiquity *n.* 文物，古物；古代
archeology *n.* 考古；考古学

单元练习 21

使用本单元核心词汇的适当形式填空，并将句子译为中文。

1. The strike has led to a _____ in crime, with more than 100 murders in Salvador.
2. A sense of purpose and basic life skills are the necessary _____ for a successful life.
3. Lit up at night, the couple's house _____ an art installation more than a suburban home.
4. Research suggests people _____ job satisfaction from being able to personalize their working environment.
5. The waiter was _____ for further questioning to make sure he was not in possession of stolen property.
6. Staffers dressed in everything from leather pants to business suits rush around looking _____ with work.
7. Rain returned to southwest England, bringing high river levels to areas already _____ by heavy downpours.
8. It's been tested in the University of Texas at Arlington's laboratory to _____ winds in excess of 250 mph.
9. Kaylor had always _____ going to physical education class, so she tried to offer fun options when she was in charge.
10. A college diploma has been the ticket to a good job, but the economic _____ has dampened the dreams of many U.S. college seniors.

Unit 22

★ 本单元核心词汇 ★

chronic	catastrophe	sprain	prone	reside
precede	dispense	anthem	dwell	void
giggle	fracture	stammer	curse	divert
rival	discriminatory	disruptive	constitution	stiff

★ 本单元拓展词汇 ★

collision	biography	calamity	interstate	liable
precedent	null	dweller	thigh	hymn
invalid	outage	constitute	toothpaste	stutter
subsequent	chuckle	switchboard	stiffen	twist
blessing	contend	distribute	sneer	acute
counterculture	rupture	wrench	rigid	

211. As individuals live longer, they are increasingly *prone* to such "old age" problems as diabetes and heart disease — *chronic* ailments that are usually expensive to treat.

单词	释义
prone	*adj.* To be prone to something, usually something bad, means to have a tendency to be affected by it or to do it. 易于（受某事影响或做某事）

双语例句

More than 68 million people now live in hurricane-prone coastal areas, up 31% since 1970.（现在有超过6 800万人生活在飓风多发的沿海地区，比1970年增加了31%。）

Backup generators are prone to performance problems, depending on the frequency of electric grid outages.（备用发电机容易出现性能问题，这取决于电网断电的频率。）

联想记忆

liable *adj.* 易于；有……倾向的；有责任的
apt *adj.* 易于；有……倾向的

单词	释义
chronic	*adj.* A chronic illness or disability lasts for a very long time. 慢性的；长期的

双语例句

Surprisingly, psychological therapy can also help treat various sorts of chronic pain.（令人惊讶的是，心理疗法也可以帮助治疗各种慢性疼痛。）

Iran has slashed local energy demand, reducing chronic pollution and leaving more oil for export.（伊朗大幅削减了国内能源需求，降低了长期以来的污染，留下更多石油用于出口。）

联想记忆

acute *adj.* 严重的；急性的；敏锐的

212. They are denied citizenship under *discriminatory* legislation from 1982, although many families have *resided* in Myanmar for generations.

单词	释义
discriminatory	*adj.* Discriminatory laws or practices are unfair because they treat one group of people worse than other groups. 歧视性的

双语例句

The act has long been a focus of criticism as the law is particularly discriminatory against immigrants.（该法案长期以来一直是人们批评的焦点，因为它特别歧视移民。）

The system assumes women are better parents than men, which is totally discriminatory.（这个体系认为女性比男性更适合当父母，这完全是歧视。）

联想记忆

discriminate *v.* 歧视；区别对待
discrimination *n.* 歧视；辨识力

单词	释义
reside	*v.* If someone resides somewhere, they live there or are staying there. 居住
	v. If a quality resides in something, the thing has that quality. 存在

双语例句

At that time, less than 10,000 non-Indians resided in what is today California.（当时，只有不到1万名非印第安人居住在今天的加利福尼亚州。）

Baseball's best team may reside in Washington, where the Nationals open Monday against the Miami Marlins.（最好的棒球队可能在华盛顿，国民队周一将在此迎战迈阿密马林鱼队。）

联想记忆

resident *adj.* 居住的；定居的 *n.* 居民
residential *adj.* 住宅的；与居住有关的
residence *n.* 住宅；住处；居住

213. It was the worst financial ***catastrophe*** the country has ever experienced and ***preceded*** the Great Depression.

单词	释义
catastrophe	*n.* A catastrophe is an unexpected event that causes great suffering or damage. 灾难

双语例句

The catastrophe may have encouraged a shift in policy at the top of government.（这场灾难可能促使政府高层的政策发生了转变。）

Unit 22

The Japanese face a huge bill for rebuilding after the earthquake, the most expensive natural catastrophe in history.（日本人面临着地震后重建的巨额费用，这是历史上付出代价最大的一次自然灾害。）

联想记忆

catastrophic *adj.* 灾难的；悲惨的
calamity *n.* 灾难，灾祸

单词	释义
precede	*v.* If one event or period of time precedes another, it happens before it. 先于（某事件）发生
	v. If a person precedes someone, or if a sentence, paragraph precedes another one, they just come before others. 走在前面；处于前面

双语例句

The accident was preceded by a minor collision, which had stopped traffic on Interstate 15 near Salt Lake City.（事故前发生了一起轻微碰撞，导致盐湖城附近的15号州际公路交通中断。）

There is a complete biography for virtually every artist, and each section is preceded by an introductory essay.（几乎每个艺术家都有一本完整的传记，传记中每部分之前都有一篇介绍性的文章。）

联想记忆

precedent *adj.* 在先的；前面的 *n.* 先例
preceding *adj.* 先前的；前述的
subsequent *adj.* 随后的，接着的

214. The crowd of thousands sang the national ***anthem***, which contains the prayer "may we ***dwell*** in unity, peace and liberty".

单词	释义
anthem	*n.* An anthem is a song that is used to represent a particular nation, society, or group and that is sung on special occasions. 国歌；赞歌；圣歌

双语例句

Lights are dimmed, and the audience rises as a recording of the national anthem comes over the speakers.（灯光暗了下来，观众起立，扬声器里传来国歌声。）

Released in May 1967, the song became a global hit and an anthem for the 1960s counterculture movement.（这首歌于1967年5月发行，当时风靡全球，并成为20

世纪60年代反文化运动的圣歌。）

联想记忆

hymn *n.* 圣歌；赞美诗

单词	释义
dwell	*v.* If one dwells in a particular place, he lives there. 居住
	v. If you dwell on something, especially something unpleasant, you think, speak, or write about it a lot or for quite a long time. 细想；详述

双语例句

Some squirrels, like the orange-colored species in the Grand Canyon, dwell in desert climates.（有些松鼠，比如大峡谷里的橙色松鼠，生活在沙漠气候中。）

Americans, perhaps even more than Europeans, like to dwell on their cultural links with Greece.（美国人可能比欧洲人更喜欢讲述他们与希腊的文化渊源。）

联想记忆

dweller *n.* 居民，居住者

215. The resultant April 2 general elections have already been declared ***void*** by the ***constitution*** court.

单词	释义
void	*adj.* Something that is void is officially considered to have no value or authority. 无效的
	adj. If you are void of something, you do not have any of it. 没有……的

双语例句

All regulations issued by the National Labor Relations Board over the past year are null and void.（全国劳资关系委员会在过去一年发布的所有规定都是无效的。）

He rose, his face void of emotion as he walked toward the door.（他站了起来，面无表情地朝门口走去。）

联想记忆

invalid *adj.* 无效的；（论据、理由等）站不住脚的

单词	释义
constitution	*n.* The constitution of a country or organization is the system of laws which formally states people's rights and duties. 宪法；章程

双语例句

Under the country's constitution, one or more of Iraq's 18 provinces may form federal regions.（根据国家宪法，伊拉克18个省中的一个或多个可以形成联邦区域。）

Under the NHS Constitution, patients have a right to be seen in 18 weeks.（根据英国国家医疗服务章程，在18周内得到治疗是病人的权益。）

联想记忆

constitute *v.* 组成，构成；建立
comprise *v.* 包含；由……组成

216. The girls at the back of the classroom couldn't help *giggling* when the inexperienced young teacher *stammered*.

单词	释义
giggle	*v.* If someone giggles, they laugh in a childlike way, because they are amused, nervous, or embarrassed. 咯咯地笑
	n. Giggle is also a NOUN. 咯咯的笑

双语例句

During our walk through the tiny village, the little girls kept running up behind us, touching our clothes and giggling.（穿过这个小村庄的时候，小女孩们不停地跟在我们后面跑，拽着我们的衣服，咯咯地笑。）

The giggles and laughs were silenced when another round of performance began.（当另一轮表演开始时，咯咯声和欢笑声都停了下来。）

联想记忆

grin *v.* 露齿而笑 *n.* 嬉笑
sneer *v.* 嘲笑，冷笑 *n.* 嘲笑
chuckle *v.* 轻声地笑 *n.* 轻笑，咯咯笑

单词	释义
stammer	*v.* If you stammer, you speak with difficulty, hesitating and repeating words or sounds. 结结巴巴地说
	n. Someone who has a stammer tends to stammer when they speak. 口吃

双语例句

But he still stammered in some situations, such as when he drank too much or was angry or tired.（但是，他在一些场合仍然会结巴，比如在醉酒、生气或疲惫的时候。）

Geddes is 63 and has been struggling with a stammer for most of his life.（戈德斯今年63岁，他一生中大部分时间都受口吃困扰。）

联想记忆

stutter *v.* 结结巴巴地说话 *n.* 口吃，结巴

217. The flight was *diverted* to Kansas City airport on Thursday after the woman became *disruptive*.

单词	释义
divert	*v.* To divert vehicles or travelers means to make them follow a different route or go to a different destination than they originally intended. 改道
	v. If someone diverts your attention from something important, they behave in a way that stops you thinking about it. 转移注意力
	v. To divert a phone call means to send it to a different number or place from the one that was dialed by the person making the call. 转接（电话）

双语例句

The accident forced the closure of the busy 22nd St., with traffic being diverted through South Riverside.（事故迫使繁忙的22街关闭，车辆改道滨河南路。）

By ordering an attack on Israel, Iran diverted their attention away from its nuclear program.（通过下令攻击以色列，伊朗转移了他们对其核试验的注意力。）

He instructed the switchboard staff to divert all Laura's calls to him.（他通知接线员把劳拉打来的所有电话都转给他。）

联想记忆

diversion *n.* 转移；消遣；分散注意力
distract *v.* 分心，转移注意力

单词	释义
disruptive	*adj.* To be disruptive means to prevent something from continuing or operating in a normal way. 妨碍的，扰乱的

双语例句

A whole generation of people moving abroad is disruptive to families, as well as the economy.（一整代人移居国外，无论是对家庭还是对国家经济都是巨大的打击。）

These and many other questions are confronting us as we adapt to truly disruptive technologies.（当我们适应真正的颠覆性技术时，便会面临这些以及其他许多问题。）

联想记忆

disrupt *v.* 破坏；使分裂；使中断 *adj.* 分裂的；中断的；分散的
disruption *n.* 破坏，毁坏；分裂，瓦解

218. The company faces ***stiff*** competition from ***rivals*** in Mexico and elsewhere in Central America.

单词	释义
stiff	*adj.* Stiff can be used to mean difficult or severe. 艰难的，激烈的
	adj. Something that is stiff is firm or does not bend easily. 硬的，不易弯曲的
	adj. Stiff behavior is rather formal and not very friendly or relaxed. 拘谨的

双语例句

They next face a stiff test against France away in Paris on Friday, 27 February.（接下来他们面临2月27日（周五）在巴黎对战法国队的严峻考验。）

His brother looked uncomfortable in his new clothes, pulling constantly at his stiff collar.（他哥哥穿着新衣服显得很不自在，不断拉扯硬硬的领子。）

Dancing with Angelina was difficult, as she refused to get close to him and was stiff and cold.（和安吉丽娜一起跳舞很难，因为她不愿意接近他，有些拘谨而冷漠。）

联想记忆

stiffen *v.* 变硬，使……变硬
stiffness *n.* 僵硬；坚硬；不自然
rigid *adj.* 严格死板的；不易弯曲的

单词	释义
rival	*n.* Your rival is a person, business, or organization who you are competing or fighting against in the same area or for the same things. 对手
	v. If you say that one thing rivals another, you mean that they are both of the same standard or quality. 与……相匹敌

双语例句

Efforts by foreign countries to persuade the rivals to return to peace talks have been fruitless.（外国敦促双方回归和平谈判，但最后无果而终。）

Few events in the technology world can rival the attention a new iPhone launch draws.（在科技界，几乎没有什么比苹果手机新品上市更吸引众人的目光。）

联想记忆

contend *v.* 声称，主张；竞争

219. Most villages have a witch who *dispenses* spells, removes *curses* and provides spiritual guidance.

单词	释义
dispense	*v.* If someone dispenses something that they own or control, they give or provide it to a number of people. 分发
	v. If you obtain a product by getting it out of a machine, you can say that the machine dispenses the product.（机器）售出（商品）

双语例句

The church runs monthly missions to the jails to dispense toothpaste, shampoo and basic food supplies.（该教堂每月都向监狱分发牙膏、洗发水和基本食品。）

The machine dispenses gold and silver bars, coins and a range of diamond with jewelry.（这台机器发售金条、银条、硬币以及一系列钻石和珠宝。）

联想记忆

dispenser *n.* 药剂师；分配者；自动售货机
distribute *v.* 分发；配送；分布

单词	释义
curse	*n.* Curse is rude or offensive language that some people use when they are very angry. Curse is also a VERB. 诅咒；咒骂
	n. You can refer to something that causes a great deal of trouble or harm as a curse. 祸根，祸因

双语例句

During his various periods in government in Poland, the name Balcerowicz was often a curse word.（他在波兰政府任职期间，巴尔切罗维茨这个名字经常是骂人的词。）

For agricultural companies and food producers, rising commodity prices can be a blessing or a curse.（对农业公司和食品生产商来说，商品价格上涨可能是福也可能是祸。）

联想记忆

cursed *adj.* 被诅咒的
blessing *n.* 祝福；祈祷；幸事

220. McGeechan was relieved that his teammate had *sprained* but not *fractured* his ankle during the second half of the game.

单词	释义
sprain	*v.* If you sprain a joint such as your ankle or wrist, you can accidentally damage it by twisting it or bending it violently. 扭伤
	n. A sprain is the injury caused by spraining a joint. 扭伤

双语例句

Antoine Mason, who had missed the last four games with a sprained ankle, returned for Niagara with 20 points.（安托万·梅森因脚踝扭伤错过了过去的四场比赛，这次他回归尼亚加拉队，得了20分。）

The player's injury problems were sparked by a sprain of his knee during the third round of game in April.（这位球员的伤病问题是由今年4月第三轮比赛中膝盖扭伤引发的。）

联想记忆

wrench *v.* 猛拉；扭伤 *n.* 扭伤；扳手
twist *v.* 弯曲；缠绕；扭伤 *n.* 扭动；拐弯处；波折

单词	释义
fracture	*v.* If something such as a bone is fractured or fractures, it gets a crack or break in it. 折断；破裂
	n. A fracture is a crack in something, especially a bone. 断裂；骨折

双语例句

About 40 gas engineers worked through the night to repair the fractured pipe, according to United Utilities.（据联合公用事业公司称，大约40名天然气工程师在连夜抢修破裂的管道。）

His 12-year-old daughter, from Glendale, suffered an open fracture to her thigh in the crash.（他12岁的女儿来自格伦代尔市，在车祸中大腿开放性骨折。）

联想记忆

rupture *v.* 破裂；断裂 *n.* 破裂

单元练习 22

使用本单元核心词汇的适当形式填空，并将句子译为中文。

1. In December alone three postal workers suffered _____ after falling in the snow.
2. Most of the casualties were due to the air strikes that _____ the ground incursion.
3. The new _____ requires parties to set at least 60 women (out of 395) in parliament.
4. The internal problems of the Congress have made it vulnerable to attacks from _____ parties.
5. He serves on a committee of local churches and nonprofits that _____ aid to those in need.
6. Diabetes is a _____, life-threatening illness that touches people of every age, ethnicity, and background.
7. Even today, _____ against gays and lesbians in Russia and Kazakhstan remains widespread.
8. Women are more _____ to interrupted jobs and careers since they are the primary caregivers for small children and the elderly.
9. The film, which tells the tale of how King George VI overcame his _____, was nominated for 12 Academy Awards.
10. Banner Health Center has been _____ trauma patients to other hospitals because it does not have enough surgeons.

Unit 23

★ 本单元核心词汇 ★

condemn	patriotic	veteran	rehearsal	scrawl
demonstrate	embryonic	strain	malnutrition	grid
equate	incentive	conservative	avenue	trek
eradicate	emancipation	shutter	monotonous	abide

★ 本单元拓展词汇 ★

embryo	conform	continent	proclamation	hum
capable	preliminary	draft	chauffeur	phase
boulevard	wearisome	crutch	motivation	scribble
graffiti	babble	approval	dedication	stem
tedious	maintenance	brook	trickle	outlet
vandal	pharmaceutical	lattice		

221. Tuesday's debate could be a dress ***rehearsal*** for the coming debate over ***embryonic*** stem cell research.

单词	释义
rehearsal	*n.* A rehearsal of a play, dance, or piece of music is a practice of it in preparation for a performance. 排练；预演

双语例句

The travelers were car-less so I volunteered to be chauffeur to rehearsal dinner and to the performance.（旅行者没有车，所以我自愿当司机送他们去彩排晚宴和表演现场。）

It takes hours of rehearsal to deliver a presentation without notes or the crutch of reading from slides.（如果没有笔记辅助，也不读幻灯片的话，做一场演讲需要几个小时的排练。）

联想记忆

rehearse *v.* 排练，预演

单词	释义
embryonic	*adj.* An embryonic process, idea, organization, or organism is one at a very early stage in its development. 萌芽阶段的，初期的

双语例句

Initially Grove was enthusiastic about the potential of embryonic stem cells as a treatment.（最初，格罗夫对胚胎干细胞作为治疗手段的潜力充满信心。）

Carroll focused on the organism in the embryonic stage as it was undergoing dramatic development.（卡罗尔关注的是处于最初阶段的生物体，因为该阶段发展很快。）

联想记忆

embryo *n.* 胚胎；胚芽；初期
embryology *n.* 胚胎学

222. Most importantly, the program is an ***avenue*** for the social ***emancipation*** of women, ethnic minorities and low class groups.

单词	释义
avenue	*n.* Avenue is a method or way of doing something. 途径，方法
	n. An avenue is a wide, straight road, especially one with trees on either side. 林荫大道；大街

双语例句

The mobile phone can serve as another avenue for the public to access important information.（手机可以作为公众获取重要信息的另一种途径。）

In the next phase, currently under planning, the path will extend a mile north to Mack Avenue.（下一阶段目前正在规划中，这条路将继续向北延伸一英里直至马克大街。）

联想记忆

boulevard *n.* 林荫大道；街道
venue *n.* （事件的发生）地点；（活动的）场所

单词	释义
emancipation	*n.* Emancipation is the process of giving people social or political freedom and rights. 解放

双语例句

The people of Africa are struggling to win the complete emancipation of the continent.（非洲人民正在为争取该地区的完全解放而斗争。）

On Sept. 17, he had finished the second draft of the preliminary *Emancipation Proclamation*.（9月17日，他已经完成了《解放宣言》初稿的第二稿。）

联想记忆

emancipate *v.* 解放；不受束缚
liberation *n.* 解放；自由

223. Several countries ***condemned*** the United States for failing to ***abide*** by the Geneva Conventions.

单词	释义
condemn	*v.* If you condemn something, you say that it is very bad and unacceptable. 谴责，责备
	v. If someone is condemned to a punishment, they are given this punishment. 宣判，判决

双语例句

Graham has the right to condemn his players for lack of ability, attitude and application.（格雷厄姆有权责备球员能力不足，态度不端正，不肯用功。）

In the second trial, after two court sessions, Helmut was again found guilty and condemned to death.（在复审中，经过两次开庭，赫尔穆特再次被认定有罪并判处死刑。）

联想记忆

denounce *v.* 谴责，严厉指责

单词	释义
abide	*v.* If you abide by a law, agreement, or decision, you do what it says you should do. 遵守

双语例句

The Supreme Court abided by the Constitution and ousted Zelaya because he had violated the law.（最高法院依据宪法驱逐了塞拉亚，因为他违反了宪法。）

Almost every movie theater abides by the 17 and over rule, which prevented me from seeing *Gladiator* as a thirteen-year-old.（几乎每家影院都遵守17岁及以上的观影规定，这让我无法在13岁时观看《角斗士》。）

联想记忆

conform *v.* 遵守；符合
comply *v.* 遵从；（商品）符合特定标准

224. Ever since then, politicians have *equated* homeownership with the American Dream and fallen all over themselves to *demonstrate* their fierce dedication to it.

单词	释义
equate	*v.* If you equate one thing with another, or if you say that one thing equates with another, you believe that they are strongly connected. 等同于

双语例句

The higher marks could possibly be equated to improvements in the quality of teaching.（分数高可能说明教学质量提高了。）

Ben Graham announced record production in their last quarter which equated to about 23% growth over the prior year.（本·格雷厄姆宣布上一季度的产量创下纪录，相比上一年增长了约23%。）

联想记忆

equation *n.* 方程式，等式；相等；化学反应式

单词	释义
demonstrate	*v.* If you demonstrate something, like a skill or quality, you show by your actions that you have it. 展现；证明；演示

双语例句

A selection of cosmetic companies will be there to demonstrate their new products.（一些化妆品公司会在那里展示他们的新产品。）

All candidates are anxious to demonstrate to the voters that they have practical policies.（所有候选人都急于向选民证明，他们有切实可行的政策。）

联想记忆

demonstration *n.* 示范；证明；示威游行

225. So far, many **patriotic** companies have answered the call, hiring more than 16,000 **veterans**.

单词	释义
patriotic	*adj.* Someone who is patriotic loves their country and feels very loyal towards it. 爱国的；有爱国精神的

双语例句

For two decades, Susan has proven to be an extraordinary, capable, patriotic, and passionate public servant.（二十年来，苏珊证明了自己是一名卓越能干、热爱祖国、热忱为民的公职人员。）

Very quickly what had begun as a business venture was transformed into a popular patriotic cause.（最初的商业冒险很快就变成了一项广受欢迎的爱国事业。）

联想记忆

patriot *n.* 爱国者
patriotism *n.* 爱国主义

单词	释义
veteran	*n.* A veteran is someone who has served in the armed forces of their country, especially during a war. 退伍军人
	n. You use veteran to refer to someone who has been involved in a particular activity for a long time. 经验丰富的人

双语例句

Sears is increasing the number of veterans and military spouses in their workforce by 10%.（西尔斯百货公司将把退伍军人和军属员工的数量增加10%。）

Dozens of high-ranking veteran eBay employees have left since Donahoe joined the company in 2005.（自从2005年多纳霍加入易趣网以来，数十名资深高级员工已经离职。）

联想记忆

novice *n.* 初学者，新手

226. The programs have strong support from *conservative* Republicans, who believe they give public schools greater *incentive* to improve.

单词	释义
conservative	*adj.* Someone who is conservative or has conservative ideas is unwilling to accept changes and new ideas.（观点）保守的
	n. Conservative is also a NOUN. 保守者；保守党

双语例句

People tend to be more liberal when they're young and more conservative as they get older.（人们在年轻时往往更开放，年纪越大越保守。）

Mr. Williams is a conservative who advocates fewer government controls on business.（威廉是一位保守人士，提倡减少政府对商业的控制。）

联想记忆

conservatism *n.* 保守主义；守旧性

单词	释义
incentive	*n.* If something is an incentive to do something, it encourages you to do it. 鼓励；刺激；激动

双语例句

Higher labor costs are the incentive for employers to find ways to use less labor.（越来越高昂的人工成本促使雇主们想方设法少用劳工。）

They moved quickly to create incentives for panel makers to open new factories in Florida.（他们迅速采取措施，鼓励面板制造商在佛罗里达州开设新工厂。）

联想记忆

motivation *n.* 动机；积极性；推动
stimulus *n.* 刺激；激励；刺激物

227. Some vandals at a state park ***scrawled*** "We broke in for free!" over a ***shuttered*** cabin, to the horror of local news outlets.

单词	释义
scrawl	*v.* If you scrawl something, you write it in a careless and messy way. 潦草地写
	n. You can refer to writing that looks careless and messy as a scrawl. 潦草的字迹

双语例句

The menu was scrawled across a whiteboard, and almost nothing cost more than five dollars.（白板上潦草地写着菜单，几乎没有什么东西超过五美元。）

In this note, her handwriting is almost a scrawl, and the blue ink looks pale against the page.（这张便条上，她的字迹潦草，蓝色笔墨在纸上显得苍白无力。）

联想记忆

scribble *v.* 潦草地写 *n.* 涂鸦
graffiti *n.* 涂鸦 *v.* 涂写，涂画

单词	释义
shutter	*v.* If someone shutters a place, they close the wooden or metal covers on the outside of the windows. 关闭
	n. Shutters are wooden or metal covers fitted on the outside of a window. They can be opened to let in the light, or closed to keep out the sun or the cold. 百叶窗

双语例句

The cost cutting involves those 8,000 job losses, two shuttered research sites and one manufacturing plant.（削减成本导致了8 000人失业，两处研究所和一家制造厂关停。）

The shops couldn't install security shutters without approval from local authorities.（未经当局批准，商店不得安装安全百叶窗。）

联想记忆

shuttle *n.* 穿梭（班机、班车、火车） *v.* 往返穿梭

Unit 23

228. When everyone turns on their air conditioners on a really hot summer afternoon, the *grid* is often placed under extraordinary *strain*.

单词	释义
grid	*n.* A grid is a network of wires and cables by which sources of power, such as electricity, are distributed throughout a country or area. 电网
	n. A grid is something which is in a pattern of straight lines that cross over each other, forming squares. On maps, the grid is used to help you find a particular thing or place. 网格；（地图上的）坐标方格

双语例句

Backup generators only run when the electric grid goes down or for scheduled maintenance.（备用发电机仅在电网故障或定期维护时启用。）

The city is broken into grids now, and contractors are being assigned blocks to clean.（现在，这座城市被划分成若干网格，承包商被分配到街区去打扫卫生。）

联想记忆

lattice *n.* 晶格；格子

mesh *n.* 网格；网状结构

单词	释义
strain	*n.* If strain is put on an organization or system, it has to do more than it is able to do. 压力
	n. Strain is an injury to a muscle in your body, caused by using the muscle too much or twisting it. Strain is also a VERB. 损伤；扭伤

双语例句

Unemployment for these people can be quite devastating, putting a great strain on their families.（失业对这些人来说是毁灭性的，给他们的家庭带来了巨大压力。）

The player revealed that the muscle strain in her legs was the most painful injury she had suffered.（这位选手透露，这次腿部肌肉拉伤是她所经受的最痛苦的伤痛。）

联想记忆

strained *adj.* 紧张的；勉强的；牵强附会的

229. The only sound to be heard was the *monotonous* hum of the engine as the car continued its *trek* down the long quiet street.

单词	释义
monotonous	*adj.* Something that is monotonous is very boring because it has a regular, repeated pattern which never changes. 单调的

双语例句

Her life felt like a monotonous journey, not the grand adventure she had imagined.（她的生活感觉像是一次单调的旅行，而不是想象中的那样充满冒险。）

The scenery can be monotonous, and there is a handful of worthy stops like the unreal Lake Baikal.（这里的景色很单调，但也有值得一去的地方，比如梦幻般的贝加尔湖。）

联想记忆

tedious *adj.* 单调乏味的；沉闷的
wearisome *adj.* 疲倦的；乏味的

单词	释义
trek	*n.* If you are on a trek, you go on a journey across difficult country, usually on foot. 徒步旅行
	v. Trek is also a VERB. 长途跋涉

双语例句

He made his name in 1982, with a global trek that covered 35,000 miles and extended to both poles.（他在全球范围内跋涉了3.5万英里，直至南北两极，于1982年一举成名。）

Visitors start their hike in grassy valleys, trekking past thick bamboo trunks and babbling brooks.（游客们在长满青草的山谷中徒步前行，穿过茂密的竹林和潺潺的小溪。）

联想记忆

trickle *v.* 滴，淌 *n.* 细流

230. ***Malnutrition*** and starvation have not been ***eradicated***, even in the developed world, and may only worsen as the population expands.

单词	释义
malnutrition	*n.* If someone is suffering from malnutrition, they are physically weak and extremely thin because they have not eaten enough food or the right type of food. 营养不良

双语例句

Egypt, Guatemala and India pushed up agricultural value-added yet their malnutrition rates rose. （尽管埃及、危地马拉和印度提高了农业附加值，但营养不良率仍在上升。）

An estimated 127,000 children under age 5 are already suffering from severe malnutrition, UNICEF says. （联合国儿童基金会称，估计有12.7万名5岁以下儿童遭受严重营养不良。）

联想记忆

nutrition *n.* 营养
nutrient *n.* 营养成分

单词	释义
eradicate	*v.* To eradicate something means to get rid of it completely. 根除

双语例句

Local authorities are working towards a commitment to eradicate homelessness by the end of this year. （当地政府正努力在今年底之前彻底解决无家可归这一问题。）

The pharmaceutical companies have been pursuing tracks to eradicate the disease altogether with vaccines. （制药公司一直在寻求用疫苗彻底根除这种疾病的途径。）

联想记忆

eradication *n.* 消灭，根除

单元练习 23

使用本单元核心词汇的适当形式填空，并将句子译为中文。

1. Ordinary Italians are being urged to do their _____ duty and to buy government bonds.
2. The Golden State Warriors have been known to _____ by a culture of winning at all costs.
3. Stretching prevents muscle _____, gets your blood pumping, and can help lower cholesterol.
4. Although _____ in many countries, cholera still infects 3 million people in Cuba each year.
5. Soon he got bored of the daily _____ task of sitting behind the computer and keying in data.
6. They approved a $1.5 billion package of pay increases for the _____ of the Persian Gulf War.
7. The Air Force scheduled a Tuesday evening _____ for a planned fly-over on Wednesday's ceremonies.
8. Sadly, medicare now creates _____ for doctors to select the most expensive drugs when treating patients.
9. The entrepreneurs are looking for people who _____ social consciousness through volunteer work.
10. Educators are putting more lights in classrooms and encouraging teachers to _____ more clearly on blackboards.

Unit 24

★ 本单元核心词汇 ★

preserve	regulate	eternal	metabolic	endow
tranquil	prosperity	endanger	fragrant	combat
smuggle	dramatically	scent	radically	disparity
fraud	primitive	proposition	manual	propel

★ 本单元拓展词汇 ★

enzyme	ozone	syrup	vanilla	abstain
administer	dispel	smuggler	violent	serene
depletion	marijuana	sneak	yogurt	scam
bestow	drastically	reservation	conservation	render
aroma	bankruptcy	category	jeopardize	blade
hearth	array	scooter	submarine	carp
exotic	wares	bison	wedge	

231. Studies of *primitive* societies show that humans are not inherently "good", but that goodness stems from *prosperity*.

单词	释义
primitive	*adj.* Primitive means belonging to a society in which people live in a very simple way, without industries or a writing system. 原始的，远古的
	adj. Primitive means belonging to a very early period in the development of an animal or plant. （动物、植物）早期的

双语例句

Children in the primitive society had to learn how to cope with their physical environment.（原始社会的孩子们不得不学习如何应对生存环境。）

Some of the lowest creatures in the plant and animal kingdoms may not be as primitive as once thought.（在动植物王国里，一些最低等的生物可能并不像曾经认为的那样原始。）

联想记忆

primitively *adv.* 最初地，原始地

单词	释义
prosperity	*n.* Prosperity is a condition in which a person or community is doing well financially. 繁荣；兴旺

双语例句

The prosperity created by Europe's economic freedoms has allowed its citizens to lead longer, healthier lives.（欧洲经济自由带来的繁荣使其公民更长寿、更健康。）

The great prosperity owes much to the increased participation of women in the work force.（经济的极大繁荣很大程度上是因为女性在劳动力中的比例提高了。）

联想记忆

prosper *v.* 繁荣，昌盛；成功
prosperous *adj.* 繁荣的；兴旺的

232. When I lived in California, land of *eternal* sunshine, *preserving* food by drying was almost effortless.

单词	释义
eternal	*adj.* Something that is eternal lasts forever. 永恒的

双语例句

The printed version has a six-month shelf life, yet eBooks are eternal and this makes them more environmentally friendly.（纸质书有六个月的上架期，而电子书是长期的，这也使电子书更加环保。）

The prime minister's chief problem, however, is the eternal chaos of Italian politics.（然而，总理面临的首要问题是意大利的政局一直很混乱。）

联想记忆

everlasting *adj.* 永恒的，永久的

单词	释义
preserve	*v.* If you preserve food, you treat it in order to prevent it from decaying so that you can store it for a long time. 保存，保藏
	v. If you preserve something, you take action to save it or protect it from damage or decay. 保护，维护
	n. Preserves are foods made by cooking fruit with a large amount of sugar so that they can be stored for a long time. 果酱

双语例句

While developing the yogurt, Danone discovered an enzyme that preserves fresh milk for up to four hours.（在制作酸奶的过程中，达能发现了一种酶可以使鲜奶保鲜长达四小时。）

Unlike global warming and ozone depletion, preserving bio-diversity remains a difficult problem.（保护生物多样性和全球变暖、臭氧损耗不同，仍然是一个难以解决的问题。）

The market offered a fabulous array of jams, preserves and syrups, along with smoked fish, and hearth breads.（市场上有各式各样的果酱、蜜饯和糖浆，还有熏鱼和炉烤面包。）

联想记忆

preservation *n.* 保存，保留
conservation *n.* 保存，保持；保护
reservation *n.* 保留；预定（房间、座位）

233. Water is necessary to transport nutrients around the body, remove wastes, and ***regulate metabolic*** processes in our bodies.

单词	释义
regulate	*v.* To regulate an activity or process means to control it, especially by means of rules. 控制；管理，监管

双语例句

It's true that the Board of Health regulates restaurants but it's the state that regulates grocery stores.（餐馆的确是由健康委员会监管，但杂货店是由州政府监管。）

The streets are wedged solid with the chaos of poorly regulated parking and near-constant traffic jam.（车辆随意停放和交通拥堵导致一片混乱，街道被堵得严严实实。）

联想记忆

regulation *n.* 管理；规章制度
administer *v.* 管理；执行

单词	释义
metabolic	*adj.* Metabolic means relating to a person's or animal's metabolism. 新陈代谢的

双语例句

Drinking ice-cold water may also help to boost your overall metabolic rate as well.（喝冰水也有助于提高你的整体代谢率。）

These chemicals are a by-product of the metabolic activity that powers the body.（这些化学物质是为身体提供能量的新陈代谢活动的副产品。）

联想记忆

metabolism *n.* 新陈代谢

234. We're dedicated to the ***proposition*** that all people are created equal and ***endowed*** with some inalienable rights.

单词	释义
proposition	*n.* A proposition is a statement or an idea that people can consider or discuss to decide whether it is true. 主张，观点
	n. A proposition is a suggestion usually concerning some work or business, or a question, statement about an issue of public policy. 建议；提案

双语例句

The consumer companies have begun to add health as a value proposition to their products.（消费品公司已经开始将健康作为一项价值主张添加到他们的产品中。）

The proposition was passed but very narrowly, with 23 in favour, 22 against and one abstaining.（这项提案以23票赞成、22票反对、1票弃权的微弱优势获得通过。）

联想记忆

propose *v.* 提出；提议；求婚
preposition *n.* 介词

单词	释义
endow	*v.* If a person or place is endowed with a particular desirable ability, characteristic, or possession, they have it by chance or by birth. 赋予
	v. If someone endows an institution or scholarship, they provide a large amount of money. 资助

双语例句

Geographically, this region is endowed with diversity of hills, valleys, forest, and streams.（从地理上看，这个地区具有丘陵、山谷、森林和溪流等各种地貌。）

Many universities are able to pay high salaries, largely because they are well-endowed private institutions.（许多大学能支付高额薪酬，主要是因为这些私立学校资金充足。）

联想记忆

endowment *n.* 捐赠；天资
bestow *v.* 赠予；授予

235. The animals are *endangered* in the wild and protected by international law, but are sometimes illegally *smuggled* as exotic pets.

单词	释义
endanger	*v.* To endanger something or someone means to put them in a situation where they might be harmed or destroyed completely. 危害

双语例句

The state wants to remove the carp to protect an endangered species native only to Utah Lake.（该州想要清除这些鲤鱼，以保护这种只存在于犹他湖的濒危物种。）

The gases, the agency says, contribute to air pollution and may endanger public health or welfare.（该机构称，这些气体会造成空气污染，可能会危害公众健康。）

联想记忆

endangered *adj.* 濒危的，濒临灭绝的
jeopardize *v.* 危及，危害

单词	释义
smuggle	*v.* If someone smuggles things or people into a place or out of it, they take them there illegally or secretly. 走私，偷运

双语例句

Authorities accuse her of trying to smuggle 12 pounds of marijuana under a bus seat.（当局指控她试图将12磅大麻藏在巴士座椅下进行走私。）

Iranian carpet exporters complain they face bankruptcy if they do not smuggle out their wares.（伊朗地毯出口商抱怨，如果他们不走私货物，就将面临破产。）

联想记忆

smuggler *n.* 走私犯
sneak *v.* 偷偷地走；私运

236. Statistics show the crime rate is rising more ***dramatically*** in those allegedly ***tranquil*** areas than in cities.

单词	释义
dramatically	*adv.* If something changes or improves dramatically, it happens by a strikingly large amount. 显著地；戏剧性地

双语例句

Manchester has changed dramatically in recent years and is growing as a tourist destination.（曼彻斯特最近几年发生了显著变化，它正发展成为旅游胜地。）

Elk and bison populations increased dramatically because there was no natural predator to keep their numbers in control.（麋鹿和野牛的数量急剧增加，因为它们没有天敌。）

联想记忆

dramatic *adj.* 戏剧的；引人注目的
substantially *adv.* 大量地；大幅

单词	释义
tranquil	*adj.* Something that is tranquil is calm and peaceful. 宁静的，安宁的

双语例句

Our lives are richer for having cycled through the tranquil villages of Laos.（因为有了骑单车穿越老挝宁静村庄的经历，我们的人生变得更加丰富。）

William set off to find another job and he ended up in Jamesport, a tranquil town that has "gone green".（威廉决定找另一份工作，最后来到了詹姆斯波特，那是一个"绿色的"宁静小镇。）

联想记忆

tranquility *n.* 宁静，安宁
serene *adj.* 平静的；安详的

237. Lauder invents new *scents* for the company, and she often replaces salt in her food with *fragrant* herbs and spices.

单词	释义
scent	*n.* Scent is a liquid which women use to make themselves smell nice; the scent of something is the pleasant smell. 香水；香味
	v. If something scents a place or thing, it makes it smell pleasant. 充满香味

双语例句

The soaps are available through Amazon.com and come in rose and vanilla scents. （这种香皂可以在亚马逊网站上买到，有玫瑰和香草两种香味。）

While scented baby products have sold well in Europe, the U.S. market tends to shy away from them. （虽然加香味的婴儿产品在欧洲卖得很好，但美国市场往往避而远之。）

联想记忆

aroma *n.* 芳香；氛围
odor *n.* 气味；臭味

单词	释义
fragrant	*adj.* Something that is fragrant has a pleasant, sweet smell. 芳香的

双语例句

The area is famous for its wonderfully fragrant wine which has no rivals in the Rhone. （该地区以其醇香浓厚的葡萄酒而闻名，在罗纳河地区首屈一指。）

With minimal noise pollution on the empty trails, it is easier to hear the birdcalls and smell the fragrant wildflowers. （空旷的小径上没有嘈杂声，更容易听到鸟鸣，闻到野花的芳香。）

联想记忆

fragrance *n.* 香味；芬芳

238. The changes in the vote registration system were introduced in an attempt to *combat* electoral *fraud*.

单词	释义
combat	*v.* If people in authority combat something, they try to stop it from happening. 打击，与……作斗争
	n. A combat is a battle, or a fight between two people. 战斗；搏斗

双语例句

The number of prisoners increased as a result of the government's determination to combat violent crime.（政府决心打击暴力犯罪，因此犯人数量增加了。）

Clashes between both sides have rendered the once-bustling shopping street into a combat wasteland.（双方的冲突使这条曾经熙熙攘攘的购物街变成了战斗的荒野。）

联想记忆

warfare *n.* 战争；斗争

单词	释义
fraud	*n.* Fraud is the crime of gaining money by a trick or by lying. 诈骗，欺诈

双语例句

In the city of Miami, Medicare fraud has now replaced drug trade as the number one criminal activity.（在迈阿密，医疗保险诈骗已经取代毒品交易，成为第一大犯罪活动。）

The most-reported category of fraud in January was connected to online shopping and auctions.（今年1月报道最多的欺诈类别包括网购和拍卖。）

联想记忆

scam *n.* 骗局 *v.* 欺诈

239. The economy is *radically* different than it was in the 1930s, when the majority of the work force did *manual* labor.

单词	释义
radically	*adv.* Radically means completely, thoroughly, or fundamentally. 彻底地

双语例句

The move could radically transform the way we exchange money with friends, family and even businesses.（这一举措将彻底改变我们与朋友、家人，甚至企业之间的交易方式。）

The landscape has been radically altered, severely damaging the wildlife.（地貌彻底改变了，严重危害到野生动植物的生存环境。）

联想记忆

radical *adj.* 根本的，彻底的；激进的 *n.* 激进分子
drastically *adv.* 彻底地；激烈地

单词	释义
manual	*adj.* Manual work is work in which you use your hands or your physical strength rather than your mind. 体力的；手工的
	n. A manual is a book which tells you how to do something or how a piece of machinery works. 使用手册

双语例句

Raised in poverty, Langan dropped out of college and has worked a series of manual labor jobs ever since.（兰根家境贫寒，大学辍学后曾经做过各种体力活。）

Even without reading the manual it was simple to transfer and manipulate video clips.（即使不阅读手册，传输和操作视频剪辑也很简单。）

联想记忆

manually *adv.* 手动地；用手

240. Addressing income ***disparity*** is more difficult than simply building the new roads, airports and other infrastructure projects that have helped ***propel*** the economy.

单词	释义
disparity	*n.* If there is a disparity between two or more things, there is a noticeable difference between them. 差异，不同

双语例句

The disparity in wealth, language, and culture across countries raises a number of hurdles.（各国之间的财富、语言和文化差异带来了许多障碍。）

We need to reduce the adult illiteracy rate, especially the disparity between male and female rates.（我们要降低成人文盲率，特别是男性和女性文盲率之间的差距。）

联想记忆

disparate *adj.* 不同的，不相干的 *n.* 无法相比的东西

单词	释义
propel	*v.* To propel something in a particular direction means to cause it to move in that direction. 推进；促进

双语例句

The success comes from strong sales of condensed soup, propelled by increased promotions from retailers.（在零售商大力促销的推动下，浓缩汤销售强劲，取得成功。）

The submarine was propelled by a motor scooter engine, connected to metal blades and two 12V batteries.（该潜艇由一台摩托车发动机推进，发动机连接着金属叶片和两组12伏电池。）

联想记忆

propeller *n.* 螺旋桨；推进器
impel *v.* 推动，驱使
repel *v.* 击退；排斥；抵制
dispel *v.* 驱散；消除

单元练习 24

使用本单元核心词汇的适当形式填空，并将句子译为中文。

1. While the mountain gorillas remains _____, their numbers have grown to nearly 800.
2. Lula has taken to daily walks and a diet to control his weight and _____ a sedentary lifestyle.
3. Skilled computing staff are in short supply, as are builders and even unskilled _____ workers.
4. Although they work small plots with _____ equipment, their handpicked cotton is better quality.
5. Numerous rivers, once the source of human _____ and rich wildlife, are now heavily polluted.
6. Wilkinson, an _____ optimist despite his injuries, hoped he might recover in time to join the game.
7. Vitamin D is well known for promoting bone health and _____ calcium levels — hence its addition to milk.
8. Argentina is one of the best _____ countries in the world, with vast energy reserves and an incredible geography for agricultural production.
9. Cycling through the _____ villages of southern Hungary, I had been met with a mixture of inquisitive stares and shy waves.
10. Retailers added the most jobs last month, _____ by higher auto sales as people replace aging cars.

Unit 25

★ 本单元核心词汇 ★

extract	proceed	endeavor	consensus	graze
toxic	expansive	immune	incredible	internal
retain	gracious	handicap	transplantation	alter
originate	hospitality	orphanage	prejudice	impair

★ 本单元拓展词汇 ★

transcript	excerpt	tissue	cognitive	caution
crumby	undermine	phenomenal	spotlight	noxious
humble	pasture	devastation	habitat	amend
altercation	asylum	stability	spacious	strive
graceful	unanimous	mastery	accord	medieval
pertain	spectrum	cripple	bias	

241. The *expansive* home has *incredible* views of the Golden Gate Bridge, San Francisco Bay and the Presidio from almost every room.

单词	释义
expansive	*adj.* If something is expansive, it covers or includes a large area or many things.（面积）广阔的，辽阔的
	adj. If you are expansive, you talk a lot, or are friendly, because you are feeling happy and relaxed. 健谈的；友好的

双语例句

We ended our tour walking through the Ciutadella, an expansive park in the middle of the city.（我们穿过丘塔德拉公园便结束了行程，这是一个位于城市中央的大公园。）

After drinking a cup of coffee, she was clearly relaxed and in an expansive mood.（喝了一杯咖啡后，她显得悠闲自在，心情豁然开朗。）

联想记忆

expand *v.* 扩大；详述；膨胀

spacious *adj.* 宽敞的；空旷的

单词	释义
incredible	*adj.* If you describe something or someone as incredible, you like them very much or are impressed by them, because they are extremely or unusually good. 极好的；难以置信的

双语例句

It's incredible that banks are working so shortly after the flood's devastation.（令人难以置信的是，银行在经历洪灾后很快就恢复营业了。）

Time and again we have seen that difficult times create incredible opportunities to innovate.（我们一次又一次看到，困难时期会出现令人难以置信的创新机会。）

联想记忆

exceptional *adj.* 极好的，杰出的；例外的

242. After the decision to *proceed* with *transplantation*, she began to experience feelings of anxiety and fear.

单词	释义
proceed	*v.* If you proceed with a course of action, you continue with it. 继续；开展

双语例句

After passing the first round, students from the University of Virginia proceeded to the final round.（来自弗吉尼亚大学的学生通过了第一轮比赛，进入到最后的决赛。）

Tanzania is proceeding with plans to build a road through its Serengeti National Park.（坦桑尼亚正在计划修建一条穿过塞伦盖蒂国家公园的公路。）

联想记忆

proceedings *n.* 诉讼；行动；会议记录

单词	释义
transplantation	*n.* An operation moving an organ from one organism (the donor) to another (the recipient). 器官移植

双语例句

Approximately 20% of these people develop chronic liver disease, and many require liver transplantation.（大约20%的人患有慢性肝病，其中许多人需要进行肝脏移植。）

Advances in medicine are being made every day, whether it's tissue transplantation or tissue regeneration.（医疗事业每天都在进步，无论是组织移植还是组织再生。）

联想记忆

transplant *n.* （器官）移植 *v.* 移植；迁移
transcript *n.* 抄本；听力文稿；成绩单

243. ***Extracting*** information about the large-scale composition of a planet from a sample weighing a millionth of a gram was a fascinating example of scientific ***endeavor***.

单词	释义
extract	*v.* If you extract a particular piece of information, you obtain it from a larger amount or source of information. 摘取（信息）
	v. To extract a substance means to obtain it from something else, for example, by using industrial or chemical processes. 提炼，提取
	n. An extract from a book or piece of writing is a small part of it that is printed or published separately. 摘录，选段

双语例句

NASA engineers and astronauts extracted a valuable lesson from this mission.（美国航空航天局的工程师和宇航员从此次任务中得到了一个有重要意义的教训。）

Despite her efforts to extract hope from tragedy, the war years continue to cast a long shadow over her life.（尽管她努力从这场悲剧中寻求希望，但战争年代还是给她的生活留下了很大阴影。）

A short extract from this film can be downloaded from the British Film Institute's Archive.（这部电影的选段可以从英国电影学院的档案中下载。）

联想记忆

excerpt *n.* 摘录，节选

单词	释义
endeavor	*n.* An endeavor is an attempt to do something, especially something new or difficult. 努力；尝试
	v. If you endeavor to do something, you try very hard to do it. 努力

双语例句

The active participation of individuals in environmental protection is a worthwhile endeavor.（人们积极参与环保是很有意义的举动。）

We endeavor to do that across a large spectrum of engagement with Asia, wherever and whenever we can.（无论何时何地，我们都会在与亚洲的广泛接触中努力做到这一点。）

联想记忆

strive *v.* 努力；力争
exertion *n.* 努力，尽力；运用

244. In Albania, *toxic* levels thousands of times higher than normal were found on land where children play, vegetables are grown and animals *graze*.

单词	释义
toxic	*adj.* A toxic substance is poisonous. 有毒的，引起中毒的
	adj. If a financial asset is described as toxic, it is likely to cause significant loss to the holder. 有风险的（资产）

双语例句

Formalin is a dangerous toxic chemical that should be handled with caution.（福

尔马林是一种危险的有毒化学品，使用时应小心谨慎。）

The Japanese never took those toxic assets off their banks and for that reason they experienced ten years crumby economy.（日本没有把那些不良资产从银行剥离出去，因此其经济衰退了十年。）

联想记忆

toxicant *adj.* 有毒的 *n.* 毒药；有毒物
noxious *adj.* 有毒的；有害的；令人讨厌的

单词	释义
graze	*v.* When animals graze or are grazed, they eat the grass or other plants that are growing in a particular place. 放牧；（牛、羊等）吃草
	v. If you graze a part of your body, you injure your skin by scraping against something. Graze is also a NOUN. 擦伤

双语例句

The sheep are allowed to graze on rangeland for a good part of the year and are very healthy.（每年大部分时间绵羊都可以在牧场吃草，它们都很健康。）

I grazed my skin on the rough pavement, and now had twin bleeding elbows.（我在粗糙的路面上擦破了皮，两个肘部都流血了。）

Damage to the skin is the most common source of infection, including infection in minor cuts and grazes.（皮外伤是最普遍的感染源，包括轻微的划伤和擦伤感染。）

联想记忆

pasture *n.* 牧场，牧草地 *v.* 放牧
abrasion *n.* 擦伤；擦伤处

245. The researchers found that the drug has the ability to *alter* humans' *internal* clocks (their "circadian rhythms").

单词	释义
alter	*v.* If something alters or if you alter it, it changes. 改变，更改

双语例句

The conflict in Syria will forever alter the lives of an entire generation of children.（叙利亚冲突将会永远改变整整一代孩子的命运。）

In many cases, human actions may merely alter the character of habitats rather than eliminate them.（在很多情况下，人类活动可能只是改变了栖息地的特征而不是让其消失。）

联想记忆

alteration *n.* 修改，更改
altercation *n.* 争论，争吵
modify *v.* 修改；修饰，限定
amend *v.* 修订；改善

单词	释义
internal	*adj.* Internal is used to describe things that exist or happen inside a particular person, object, or place. 体内的；内部的
	adj. Internal is used to describe things that exist or happen inside a country or organization. 国内的；组织内部的

双语例句

He published a book showing the exact position of the internal organs of the body and their relations.（他出版了一本书，书中展示了人体内部器官的确切位置以及它们之间的关系。）

Taxpayers can call the Internal Revenue Service for general guidance on tax return filing questions.（纳税人可以致电国税局，请他们对纳税申报表的申报问题进行指导。）

联想记忆

interior *adj.* 内部的；国内的 *n.* 内部；本质
intern *n.* 实习生

246. Since setting foot on this beautiful land, we have received the ***gracious hospitality*** of the government and its people.

单词	释义
gracious	*adj.* If you describe someone as gracious, you mean that they are very well-mannered and pleasant. 和蔼可亲的
	adj. If you describe the behavior of someone as gracious, you mean that they behave in a polite and considerate way. 有礼貌的

双语例句

I'd like to thank Fudan University's President Jin for his hospitality and his gracious welcome.（我要感谢复旦大学金校长的盛情款待和热情欢迎。）

Despite his phenomenal success over five decades, Cliburn remained humble and gracious.（尽管克莱本在过去50年里取得了非凡的成功，但他依然谦逊有礼。）

联想记忆

graceful *adj.* 优雅的；优美的

单词	释义
hospitality	*n.* Hospitality is friendly, welcoming behavior toward guests or people you have just met. 好客；殷勤
	n. Hospitality is the food, drink, and other privileges some companies provide for their visitors or clients at major sports events or other public events. （公司为客人提供的）食物、饮料和其他优待

双语例句

As you roll into small towns in the evening you will be greeted by larger-than-life hospitality.（当你晚上进入小镇时，便会感受到人们无比热情好客。）

The hospitality tents had equipment and supplies donated by people from all over the world.（接待帐篷里有来自世界各地人们捐赠的设备和用品。）

联想记忆

hospitable *adj.* 热情好客的

247. There has never been a settled ***consensus*** on how long British people should ***retain*** the vote after they give up their British residence.

单词	释义
consensus	*n.* A consensus is general agreement among a group of people. 一致；共识

双语例句

An effort has been made to reach a consensus on how to help Colombia reform its economy in the coming decade.（他们努力就如何帮助哥伦比亚在未来十年改革其经济达成了共识。）

There's been a general consensus on how to get ahead: Get a college education, and find a reliable job.（关于如何取得成功似乎有一个普遍的共识：接受大学教育，然后找一份稳定的工作。）

联想记忆

accord *n.* 协议；一致 *v.* 给予；一致，符合
echo *n.* 回音；共鸣 *v.* 发出回声；附和
unanimous *adj.* 一致同意的

Unit 25

单词	释义
retain	*v.* To retain something means to continue to have that thing. 保留；保存

双语例句

Well into the 20th century, the Channel Islands retained medieval structures of society and government.（直到20世纪，海峡群岛仍保留着中世纪的社会和政府结构。）

Head teachers had complained schools were struggling to retain staff under the new funding arrangements.（校长们抱怨说，学校在新的经费支持下很难留住教职工。）

联想记忆

pertain *v.* 与……相关；属于
sustain *v.* 维持，保持；遭受；支撑

248. They faced severe ***handicaps*** because of limited education and job skills, inadequate English, and racial ***prejudice***.

单词	释义
handicap	*n.* A handicap is a physical or mental disability. 残疾；不利条件
	v. If an event or a situation handicaps someone or something, it places them at a disadvantage. 将……置于不利地位；阻碍

双语例句

They donated funds to build handicap access structures in various locations throughout the community.（他们在整个社区的不同地方捐款修建了残疾人便利设施。）

Unlike its neighbors, Thailand is particularly handicapped by an almost complete absence of the mastery of foreign languages.（与邻国人不同的是，泰国人几乎完全没有掌握外语的能力，这非常不利于其发展。）

联想记忆

handicapped *adj.* 残疾的；有生理缺陷的

单词	释义
prejudice	*n.* Prejudice is an unreasonable dislike of a particular group of people or things, or a preference for one group of people or things over another. 偏见
	v. If you prejudice someone or something, you influence them so that they are unfair in some way. 使……有偏见

双语例句

People living with HIV and AIDS have to endure prejudice born out of ignorance and fear.（艾滋病毒携带者和艾滋病患者不得不忍受源于无知和恐惧带来的偏见。）

Many employers are prejudiced against older workers, as they are often less comfortable with new technology.（许多雇主对年长的员工持有偏见，因为他们往往不太适应新技术。）

联想记忆

prejudiced *adj.* 怀偏见的；偏颇的
bias *n.* 偏见；偏差 *v.* 有偏心

249. Their experiments on mice showed the virus ***impaired*** the ability of a specific part of the ***immune*** system.

单词	释义
impair	*v.* If something impairs an ability or the way something works, it damages it or makes it worse. 损害；削弱

双语例句

Alcohol can also impair judgment to the extent that you may not make the best decisions in an emergency.（酒精在一定程度上还会降低你的判断力，使你在紧急状况下无法做出最佳决定。）

Stress may lead to many changes within the body, including impaired cognitive function and energy drain.（压力会导致体内发生很多变化，包括认知功能受损以及体力不支。）

联想记忆

undermine *v.* 破坏；损害
cripple *v.* 严重损坏；致残 *n.* 残疾人

单词	释义
immune	*adj.* If you are immune to a particular disease or something that happens, you are not affected by it. 免疫的；不受影响的
	adj. Someone or something that is immune from a particular process or situation is able to escape it. 免除的

双语例句

This chemical in the body is a vital part of the immune system and helps to fight off infections.（人体内的这种化学物质是免疫系统的重要组成部分，有助于抵抗感染。）

Britain's booming cities are not immune to the social problems common to all western cities.（英国繁华的城市也不能免于西方城市常见的社会问题。）

联想记忆

immunity *n.* 免疫力；豁免权
immunization *n.* 免疫，免疫接种
resistant *adj.* 反抗的；有抵抗力的

250. The chimpanzees *originated* from all over Africa and groups were formed based on their date of arrival at the *orphanage*.

单词	释义
originate	*v.* When something originates or when someone originates it, it begins to happen or exist. 始创，起源

双语例句

Iceberg originated from ice sheets, which form on land from millions of years of snowfall.（冰山源于冰原，而冰原是陆地上数百万年以来的降雪形成的。）

The demand for water originates from four main sources, namely, agriculture, production of energy, industrial uses and human consumption.（对水的需求主要来自四个方面，即农业、能源生产、工业用途和居民生活用水。）

联想记忆

original *adj.* 最初的；独创的；新颖的 *n.* 原件；原作；原物
originality *n.* 创意；独创性；新奇

单词	释义
orphanage	*n.* An orphanage is a place where orphans live and are cared for. 孤儿院

双语例句

David had been living in this orphanage since he was two years old.（大卫从两周岁起就生活在这家孤儿院了。）

Laura and her co-founder have had a dream of opening an orphanage in the Dominican Republic.（劳拉和她的联合创始人一直梦想在多米尼加共和国开办一所孤儿院。）

联想记忆

orphan *n.* 孤儿 *v.* 使成孤儿
asylum *n.* 政治庇护；避难所；收容所

单元练习 25

使用本单元核心词汇的适当形式填空，并将句子译为中文。

1. On a hill we spotted a dominant male rhino _____ quietly in the tall grass.
2. The ultimate goal is to produce an efficient way of _____ hydrogen from water.
3. Babies of women exposed to the chemicals may suffer _____ memory and learning ability.
4. He had chronic back pain that _____ from a car accident on Hwy. 93 almost thirty years ago.
5. After consideration, the minister decided not to _____ with the introduction of this tax policy.
6. Located on the seventh floor, the eatery has floor-to-ceiling windows with _____ views of the San Francisco Bay.
7. Guests will meet Ken Burns, a _____, charming and brilliant personality, at the cocktail reception.
8. New York is one of the states to adopt new systems, though there is no _____ on how best to evaluate teachers.
9. When she speaks to the news media regarding her area of expertise, she _____ her communication style completely.
10. Companies are required to provide years of _____ data, which are carefully reviewed by various government agencies.

Unit 26

★ 本单元核心词汇 ★

assign	uniform	populate	appliance	volatile
sector	crack	domestic	evacuate	mentor
compel	revive	transmit	nuisance	stable
rational	gauge	legible	contaminate	phobia

★ 本单元拓展词汇 ★

vacuum	pronounce	apparatus	pillbox	tablet
cracker	sparsely	dormouse	recuperate	tame
panic	reservoir	contamination	futile	stabilize
counselor	polo	erratic	irrational	flaw
intensely	annoyance	illegible	signature	fungus
mosquito	specify	taint	peek	

251. Despite security and infrastructure challenges, Afghanistan's private *sector* is slowly *reviving* from the bottom up.

单词	释义
sector	*n.* A particular sector of a country's economy is the part connected with that specified type of industry.（经济的）部门
	n. A sector of a large group is a smaller group which is part of it. 部分

双语例句

Health care is the fastest-growing sector of the U.S. economy and is dominated by women.（医疗服务是美国经济增长最快的领域，而且是由女性主导的。）

Workers who went to the Gulf came from the poorest sectors of Pakistani society.（去海湾地区的工人来自巴基斯坦社会最贫困的阶层。）

联想记忆

section *n.* 部分；截面 *v.* 分成若干部分
segment *n.* 部分；片段 *v.* 分隔

单词	释义
revive	*v.* When something such as the economy, a business, or a trend is reviving, it becomes active, popular, or successful again. 复兴；恢复
	v. If you revive someone who has fainted or if they revive, they become conscious again. 使苏醒；苏醒

双语例句

The prime ministers exchanged ideas on how to revive negotiations between Syria and Israel.（两位首相就如何重启叙利亚和以色列之间的谈判交换了意见。）

Efforts to revive him were unsuccessful, and he was pronounced dead a short time later.（救护人员没能让他醒过来，不久之后他便被宣告死亡。）

联想记忆

revival *n.* 复兴；复活
recuperate *v.* 恢复，康复

252. The new tourism act will *compel* hotels, restaurants and resorts to charge Bulgarians and foreigners *uniform* prices.

单词	释义
compel	*v.* If a situation, a rule, or a person compels you to do something, they force you to do it. 迫使，促使

双语例句

The society recently called on the UN to compel the country to write a new constitution.（最近，全社会都呼吁联合国敦促这个国家制定新的宪法。）

With social media, companies are being compelled to pay attention to what consumers are saying.（随着社交媒体的发展，各家公司现在都感到必须密切关注消费者的意愿。）

联想记忆

compelling *adj.* 引人注目的；强制的；激发兴趣的

单词	释义
uniform	*adj.* If you describe a number of things as uniform, you mean that they are all the same. 同样的；一致的
	n. A uniform is a special set of clothes which some people wear at work and which some children wear in school. 制服，校服

双语例句

The measuring sticks are not uniform, and across Spain the vara therefore represented different lengths.（度量标准并不统一，在西班牙各地瓦拉的长度就不同。）

All Peninsula Hotels have pages who are dressed in all-white uniforms with pillbox hats.（所有半岛酒店的服务员都穿着白色制服，戴着圆顶礼帽。）

联想记忆

uniformity *n.* 均匀性；一致；同样

253. High-priced foreign cars are common in the country but the most popular household ***appliances*** are inexpensive ***domestic*** models.

单词	释义
appliance	*n.* An appliance is an electrical device or machine in your home that you use to do a job such as cleaning or cooking. 家用器械

双语例句

It was not difficult to learn to use the vacuum cleaner, the washing machine and other household appliances.（学习使用吸尘器、洗衣机和其他家用电器并不难。）

Domestic areas of comparable store sales growth included computers (including tablets), appliances and e-readers.（国内同类商店销售额增长的领域包括计算机（含平板电脑）、家电和电子阅读器。）

联想记忆

apparatus *n.* 设备；器具

单词	释义
domestic	*adj.* Domestic items and services are intended to be used in people's homes rather than in factories or offices. 家用的；家庭的
	adj. Domestic political activities, events, and situations happen or exist within one particular country. 国内的；本国的
	adj. A domestic animal is one that is not wild and is kept either on a farm to produce food or in someone's home as a pet. 家养的，驯养的

双语例句

Family doctors play an important role in helping resolve family problems, including domestic violence.（家庭医生在帮助解决家暴等各种家庭问题中起重要作用。）

The President is committed to continuing to expand domestic oil and gas production safely and responsibly.（总统承诺继续安全、负责地扩大国内油气生产。）

The species, which was about the size of a domestic cat, lived between 100 and 200 million years ago.（该物种大小和家养的猫差不多，生活在1亿到2亿年前。）

联想记忆

household *n.* 家庭；一家人 *adj.* 家用的；家喻户晓的
tame *adj.* 驯服的，温顺的 *v.* 驯化，驯服

254. Michelle Obama first met the young Barack when she was ***assigned*** to ***mentor*** him at their law firm.

单词	释义
assign	*v.* If someone is assigned to a particular place, group, or person, they are sent there, usually in order to work at that place or for that person. 分派，分配；布置

Unit 26

双语例句

There are four positions on a polo team, with players assigned numbers worn on their shirts. （马球队里有四个位置，队员的球衣上都有编号。）

Dory was assigned to work on a waste management project in a Dominican farm worker community. （多莉被分配到多米尼加农场工人社区的一个垃圾管理项目工作。）

联想记忆

assignment *n.* 分配；任务，作业

单词	释义
mentor	*v.* To mentor someone means to give them help and advice over a period of time, especially help and advice related to their job. 指导
	n. A person's mentor is someone who gives them help and advice over a period of time, especially help and advice related to their job. 导师

双语例句

He trained and mentored young photographers who captured many of the war's defining images. （他培养了一些年轻的摄影师，他们拍下了许多典型的战地照片。）

Lack of mentors and social networks were mentioned as major barriers to entry into the workforce. （缺乏指导和人脉关系被认为是进入职场的主要障碍。）

联想记忆

counselor *n.* 顾问；参事

255. I live in Beckenham in an area *populated* by many foxes, and they do sometimes make a *nuisance* of themselves.

单词	释义
populate	*v.* If an area is populated by certain people or animals, those people or animals live there, often in large numbers. 聚居；栖息

双语例句

The area is sparsely populated, leading to hopes that casualty figures may not climb much higher. （该地区人口稀少，因此估计伤亡数字可能不会上升太多。）

The dormice are known to populate nearby woodland and surveys at the reservoir had been futile. （众所周知，睡鼠生活在附近的林地中，人们在水库进行的调查徒劳无益。）

联想记忆

populous *adj.* 人口稠密的；人口多的

单词	释义
nuisance	*n.* If you say that someone or something is a nuisance, you mean that they annoy you or cause you a lot of problems. 讨厌的人（或事）

双语例句

Some Canadians consider the penny more of a nuisance than a useful coin.（一些加拿大人认为，与其说一便士的硬币有用，不如说其令人讨厌。）

Cars are great for getting people to buildings, but a nuisance once you arrive.（汽车很方便，可以将人们带到目的地，但一旦到了便是个麻烦。）

联想记忆

pest *n.* 害虫
annoyance *n.* 烦恼；令人讨厌的人或事

256. As I grew up and began to delve into myself a little more, I learnt the truth behind fears — from *phobias* to totally *rational* terrors.

单词	释义
phobia	*n.* A phobia is a very strong irrational fear or hatred of a particular object or situation. 恐惧症

双语例句

It has been approved for treating people who have phobias or suffer from panic attacks.（它已经获得批准，用于治疗患有恐惧症或恐慌症发作的人。）

Anxiety disorders include obsessive-compulsive disorder and social phobia, and are usually treated with prescription drugs, talk therapy, or both.（焦虑症包括强迫症和社交恐惧症，通常用处方药、谈话疗法或两者兼用的方法来治疗。）

联想记忆

panic *n.* 恐慌，惊慌 *v.* 惊慌失措

单词	释义
rational	*adj.* Rational decisions and thoughts are based on reason rather than on emotion. 理性的；理智的

Unit 26

双语例句

Rational fiscal policy would focus on reducing unemployment and getting the economy back on track.（合理的财政政策应着眼于减少失业率，使经济重回正轨。）

David was usually a rational person; always able to maintain a sense of control.（通常情况下，大卫是个理智的人，总能克制自己。）

联想记忆

ration *n.* 定量；口粮；配给量 *v.* 配给；定量供应
irrational *adj.* 不合理的

257. The deadly violence in Kenya, which had been a ***stable*** country in an otherwise ***volatile*** region, has sparked international outrage.

单词	释义
stable	*adj.* If something is stable, it is not likely to change or come to an end suddenly. 稳定的；稳固的
	n. A stable is a building in which horses are kept. 马厩

双语例句

The second patient, also male, was in stable but very serious condition, the hospital said.（医院方面称，第二名病人（也是男性）的病情目前比较稳定，但仍然很严重。）

She usually spent a few hours exercising the horse and cleaning out the stable.（通常，她遛马、清理马厩都会花上几个小时。）

联想记忆

stability *n.* 稳定，稳固；稳定性
stabilize *v.* （使）稳固；稳定

单词	释义
volatile	*adj.* A person or situation that is volatile is likely to change suddenly and unexpectedly. 变化无常的，情绪不稳定的
	adj. A volatile liquid or substance is one that will quickly changes into a gas. 易挥发的

双语例句

Renewable resources have helped reduce energy prices especially during those volatile periods.（可再生资源有助于降低能源价格，尤其是在动荡时期。）

Churchill was passionate, volatile and intensely emotional in much of his life.（丘吉尔一生中大部分时间都充满激情，但往往反复无常，是一个性情中人。）

It was not until 2007 that Strobel discovered the fungus emitted a remarkable mixture of volatile gases.（直到2007年，斯特罗贝尔才发现这种真菌释放出一种不同寻常的挥发性气体混合物。）

联想记忆

volatility *n.* 易变；挥发性
erratic *adj.* 不稳定的，难以预测的

258. The front seats are comfortable, and the speedometer and other *gauges* behind the steering wheel are stylish and clearly *legible*.

单词	释义
gauge	*n.* A gauge is a device that measures the amount or quantity of something and shows the amount measured. 测量仪器
	v. If you gauge people's actions, feelings, or intentions in a particular situation, you carefully consider and judge them. 判定

双语例句

Investigators determined the engine had run out of fuel, but that the fuel gauges were working properly.（调查人员发现燃油已经耗尽，但燃油表工作正常。）

In the experiment, participants easily gauged the difference between human and non-human images.（在实验中，参与者很容易就辨别出人像和非人像之间的区别。）

联想记忆

meter *n.* 表 *v.* 用表测量

单词	释义
legible	*adj.* Legible writing is clear enough to read. （字迹）清晰可辨的

双语例句

Documentation shall be legible and readily identifiable, maintained in an orderly manner and retained for a specified period.（所有文件均须书写规范、清晰可辨、妥善保管，并在规定时间内予以留存。）

This author left no writing in his own name, except for six crude signatures that are barely legible.（除了六个难以辨认的模糊签名，这位作者没有留下任何以自己名字写的文字。）

联想记忆

legibility *n.* 易读性；易辨认
illegible *adj.* 难以辨认的

259. The virus is ***transmitted*** to humans primarily through consumption of ***contaminated*** foods, such as undercooked meat products.

单词	释义
transmit	*v.* If one person or animal transmits a disease to another, they spread the disease to the other person or animal. 传播（疾病）
	v. When radio and television programs, computer data, or other electronic messages are transmitted, they are sent from one place to another, using wires, radio waves, or satellites. 传输；播送

双语例句

While mosquitoes transmit deadly diseases, they do not cause major harm in the UK.（虽然蚊子传播致命的疾病，但在英国没有造成重大伤害。）

The pictures were transmitted and published in every newspaper and news magazine around the world.（这些照片被传播开来，发表在世界各地的报纸和新闻杂志上。）

联想记忆

transmission *n.* 传播，播送
transmitter *n.* 发射机；发送器

单词	释义
contaminate	*v.* If something is contaminated by dirt, chemicals, or radiation, they make it dirty or harmful. 污染

双语例句

Industrial and biological pollution has contaminated almost 90 percent of the underground water in Bangladesh.（工业和生物废弃物已经污染了孟加拉国近90%的地下水。）

Crop production requires heavy use of agro-chemicals, which can contaminate the environment in health-harming ways.（农作物生产需要大量使用农药，这会污染环境并危害身体健康。）

联想记忆

contamination *n.* 污染

contaminant *n.* 污染物
taint *v.* 污染；玷污

260. Just a day before the collapse, the building was briefly *evacuated* when *cracks* appeared in the walls.

单词	释义
evacuate	*v.* To evacuate someone means to send them to a place of safety, away from a dangerous building, town, or area. 疏散；使……撤离

双语例句

The government has ordered citizens living within 20 kilometers of the nuclear plant to evacuate as soon as possible.（政府下令，核电站周围20公里内的居民须尽快撤离。）

The injured two soldiers were evacuated by helicopter to medical facility at Camp Bastion.（受伤的两名士兵由直升机运送撤离至巴斯顿军营的医疗中心。）

联想记忆

evacuation *n.* 疏散；撤离；排泄

单词	释义
crack	*n.* A crack is a line that appears on the surface of something when it is slightly damaged. 裂纹；缝隙
	v. If something hard cracks, or if you crack it, it becomes slightly damaged, with lines appearing on its surface. 破裂，裂开

双语例句

While I was checking that out, I noticed that there was a crack in the gas line, and it was leaking.（我在检查的时候，发现煤气管道有一条裂痕，而且正在漏气。）

The door to the room was cracked open just enough for John to peek through.（房间的门被推开一条缝，约翰刚好能看到里面。）

联想记忆

cracker *n.* 爆竹；饼干；胡桃钳
flaw *n.* 缺点，缺陷；裂痕

单元练习 26

使用本单元核心词汇的适当形式填空，并将句子译为中文。

1. Thanks to our brave men and women in _____, our nation has never been more secure.
2. Immigration seems to be a policy arena where _____ thought is in especially short supply.
3. The provision of this service could become a _____ revenue generator in the years to come.
4. Most tropical deforestation is driven by rocketing _____ and global demand for food and biofuel.
5. Energy Star offers a standard for energy efficiency for products such as computers and kitchen _____.
6. The new policy, in a way, _____ them to be not only police officers but social workers and counselors.
7. Wildlife was seen as a _____ and a danger, but over time people realize that they could attract tourists.
8. Parts of the document are difficult to read, and the signatures and notary stamp are barely _____.
9. Policemen arrived soon afterwards, surrounding the hospital complex and _____ nearby buildings.
10. The camera _____ the picture back to the central hub of the spacecraft, which then relayed the data to Earth.

Unit 27

★ 本单元核心词汇 ★

reinforce	casualty	particle	irritate	tease
swarm	orchestra	synthetic	compact	blast
substitute	internship	suspicion	accommodate	doom
acrobat	compromise	presume	sponsor	beam

★ 本单元拓展词汇 ★

affable	snug	detonation	bound	concede
concrete	concession	hormone	concerto	fortify
astound	flexibility	ambulance	undisguised	amber
substitution	reluctance	consolidate	symphony	stout
celebrity	agitated	coordination	impending	patron
glacial	philanthropic	gymnast	genetics	artificial
lengthy	protein	dome		

261. We drove into a hotel complex *swarming* with military men, many of whom eyed me with *suspicion* from under their peaked hats.

单词	释义
swarm	*v.* If a place is swarming with people, it is full of people moving about in a busy way. 挤满；（人群）涌往
	n. A swarm of bees or other insects is a large group of them flying together. 大群（蜜蜂等昆虫）

双语例句

Within minutes the area was swarming with police cars and dogs and helicopters.（几分钟内，这个区域到处都是警车、警犬和直升机。）

From schools of fish to a swarm of ants, animals exhibit extraordinary collective behavior.（从鱼群到蚁群，动物都表现出非凡的集群能力。）

联想记忆

cram *v.* 挤满，塞进；填鸭式学习 *n.* 拥挤；死记硬背

单词	释义
suspicion	*n.* Suspicion is a belief or feeling that someone has committed a crime or done something wrong. 怀疑
	n. If there is suspicion of someone or something, people do not trust them or consider them to be reliable. 猜疑

双语例句

The couple did not instantly recognize the man who came looking for a room, and their suspicions were aroused by his reluctance to leave.（这对夫妇并没有立刻辨认出看房的这个男人，但当他迟迟不愿离去的时候便起疑了。）

Those arrested are being questioned on suspicion of drug dealing, and possessing illegal weapons.（那些被捕的人因为涉嫌毒品交易和非法持有武器，正在接受审讯。）

联想记忆

suspicious *adj.* 可疑的；怀疑的
suspect *v.* 怀疑；猜想 *n.* 嫌疑犯

262. Two police officers who delivered first aid to injured *casualties* at the scene of a *blast* have been recognized for their bravery.

单词	释义
casualty	*n.* A casualty is a person who is injured or killed in a war or in an accident. 死伤者，伤亡人员
	n. Casualty is the part of a hospital where people who have severe injuries or sudden illnesses are taken for emergency treatment. 急救室

双语例句

Casualty figures are hard to verify as most foreign media are barred from Syria.（由于大多数外国媒体被禁止进入叙利亚，伤亡人数还难以确认。）

She was taken by ambulance to casualty at the hospital, after she lost consciousness at home.（她在家失去了意识，随后被救护车送到医院的急救室。）

联想记忆

casually *adv.* 随意地；漫不经心地

单词	释义
blast	*n.* A blast is a big explosion, especially one caused by a bomb.（尤指炸弹引起的）大爆炸
	v. If something is blasted into a particular place or state, an explosion causes it to be in that place or state. 爆炸；由爆炸生成
	v. If you blast something such as a car horn, or if it blasts, it makes a sudden, loud sound. If something blasts music, or music blasts, the music is very loud. 大声按响；发出巨响；大声放音乐

双语例句

Two bomb blasts and a bomb threat last week have caused tension and disturbance in the region.（上周的两起炸弹爆炸和一起炸弹威胁事件在这个地区引起了不安和骚乱。）

A disposal expert presses a button, triggering an explosion which blasts the mine to pieces.（一位爆破专家按下按钮引爆，将矿山炸裂开了。）

I almost fell asleep, only to be awoken by loud music blasting in my ears.（我快要睡着了，突然被传入耳朵里喧闹的音乐声吵醒了。）

联想记忆

detonation *n.* 爆炸；爆炸声

263. ***Compromising*** the education of girls and women will only ***reinforce*** the vicious cycle of poverty.

Unit 27

单词	释义
compromise	*v.* If you compromise with someone, you reach an agreement with them in which you both give up something that you originally wanted. 妥协，让步
	n. Compromise is also a NOUN. 妥协；折中

双语例句

The president urged the parties to compromise for the sake of stability.（总统敦促各党派为了国家稳定做出让步。）

Most countries thought Britain would eventually come round to accepting some version of that compromise.（大多数国家认为，英国最终将会接受某种程度的妥协。）

联想记忆

concession *n.* 让步，妥协
concede *v.* 承认；让步

单词	释义
reinforce	*v.* If something reinforces a feeling, situation, or process, it makes it stronger or more intense. 加强
	v. To reinforce an object means to make it stronger or harder. 加固

双语例句

The statement actually reinforced the idea that Rankin was well connected to the University.（声明实际上让人们更加相信，兰金与这所大学关系融洽。）

The concrete on the roof is 1.5 meters thick, reinforced with steel.（房顶上的混凝土有1.5米厚，而且用钢筋加固过。）

联想记忆

reinforcement *n.* 加固；增援；援军
consolidate *v.* 巩固；强化
fortify *v.* 加强；加固；筑防

264. In a crammed room, Evo Morales *beamed* for the cameras and *teased* the reporters about being paparazzi.

单词	释义
beam	*v.* When someone is beaming, they have a big smile on their face because they are happy, pleased, or proud about something. 绽开笑容
	v. If radio signals or television pictures are beamed somewhere, they are sent there by means of electronic equipment. 播送
	n. A beam of light is a line of light that shines from an object. （光）束

双语例句

Frances beamed at her friend with undisguised admiration.（弗朗西丝朝着她的朋友绽开了笑容，羡慕之情溢于言表。）

Digital cinema cuts distribution costs, as each movie can be beamed instantly via satellite around the world.（数字影院削减了发行成本，因为每部电影都可以通过卫星在全球各地播放。）

A burst of sunshine sent a beam of amber light through the window.（一道阳光透过窗户射进了一束琥珀色的光。）

联想记忆

ray *n*. 光线，光束；射线

单词	释义
tease	*v.* To tease someone means to laugh at them or make jokes about them in order to embarrass, annoy, or upset them. 嘲笑；取笑
	n. Tease is also a NOUN. 嘲笑；取笑

双语例句

Bodner's grandchildren tease him that he has become an Internet celebrity.（博德纳的孙子们取笑说，他已经成为一名网红。）

Forbes carried a lengthy tease for an interview in the second issue with John.（《福布斯》杂志在第二期对约翰进行的专访中，有大量调侃的内容。）

联想记忆

mock *v.* 嘲笑；模仿 *adj.* 假的；假装的

265. High levels of exposure to these ***particles*** can ***irritate*** the eyes and cause respiratory discomfort, according to government reports.

单词	释义
particle	*n.* A particle of something is a very small piece or amount of it. 微粒，颗粒
	n. In physics, a particle is a piece of matter smaller than an atom such as an electron or a proton. 粒子

双语例句

The association analyzed the data based on ozone pollution and year-round particle pollution.（该协会分析了基于臭氧污染和全年颗粒物污染的数据。）

Extensive work is under way to determine the source of radioactive particles at the beach.（目前正在开展大量工作，以确定海滩上放射性粒子的来源。）

联想记忆

particulate *adj.* 微粒的 *n.* 微粒状物质
grain *n.* 颗粒；细粒

单词	释义
irritate	*v.* If something irritates your skin or a part of your body, it causes it to itch or become sore. 刺激（皮肤或身体部位）
	v. If something irritates you, it keeps annoying you. 激怒

双语例句

These medicines may irritate your skin, especially in the first few weeks that you use them.（这些药物可能会刺激皮肤，尤其是在使用后的最初几周。）

When you're irritated by something, your stress hormones rise and your concentration levels decrease.（当你被某事激怒时，压力荷尔蒙会上升，注意力则会下降。）

联想记忆

irritation *n.* 恼怒；恼人的事；刺激
agitated *adj.* 激动的；焦虑不安的

266. The tiny theatre, equipped with an *orchestra* pit for a single musician, can *accommodate* an audience of just 17.

单词	释义
orchestra	*n.* An orchestra is a large group of musicians who play a variety of different instruments together. Orchestras usually play classical music. 管弦乐队

双语例句

The television drama told of an orchestra of prisoners at a Nazi camp during World War II.（这部电视剧讲述了二战期间纳粹集中营里一个囚犯管弦乐队的故事。）

Earlier this month, the pianist performed an original piano concerto with the Atlanta Symphony Orchestra.（本月早些时候，这位钢琴家与亚特兰大交响乐团合作了一首原创钢琴协奏曲。）

联想记忆

orchestrate *v.* 编管弦乐曲；精心安排

单词	释义
accommodate	*v.* If a building or space can accommodate someone or something, it has enough room for them. 容纳
	v. To accommodate someone means to provide them with a place to live or stay. 为……提供住宿
	v. If something is planned to accommodate a particular situation, it is planned so that this situation is taken into account. 使适应

双语例句

There are board rooms and theaters that can accommodate up to 200 guests, which overlook the glacial lake.（这里有能容纳200人的会议室和剧院，可以俯瞰冰川湖。）

Most houses here have multiple guest rooms to accommodate large groups and extended families.（这里的大多数房子都有多间客房，可以为大型团队和大家庭提供住宿。）

Sometimes to accommodate cultural and individual needs, the courses are arranged for evenings and weekends.（有时为了适应文化和个人的需要，课程安排在晚上和周末。）

联想记忆

accommodation *n.* 住宿，住处；调节

267. This *synthetic* chalk could *substitute* for some of the Portland cement now used in construction.

单词	释义
synthetic	*adj.* Synthetic products are made from chemicals or artificial substances rather than from natural ones. 合成的；人造的

双语例句

Genetics, nanotechnology, and synthetic biology are at least as important as information technologies.（遗传学、纳米技术和合成生物学至少和信息技术一样重要。）

Each year, over 1,000 new synthetic chemicals are introduced in the United States.（每年美国都会研发出上千种新的合成化学物质。）

联想记忆

synthesize *v.* 合成；综合
synthesis *n.* 综合，合成；综合体

artificial *adj.* 人造的，人工的

单词	释义
substitute	*v.* If you substitute one thing for another, or if one thing substitutes for another, it takes the place or performs the function of the other thing. 代替
	n. A substitute is something that you use instead of something else, or a player who is brought to a game to replace another player. 替代品；替补

双语例句

Natural gas has become so cheap that it can be substituted for coal as an electricity-generating fuel.（天然气已经变得非常廉价，以致可以代替煤作为发电燃料。）

Owen made an appearance as substitute midway through the second half, but he barely touched the ball.（欧文作为替补出现在下半场中间，但他几乎都没碰到球。）

联想记忆

substitution *n.* 代替；代替物

268. Earlier this year, *the New York Times* ***sponsored*** a debate about the morality and legality of unpaid ***internships***.

单词	释义
sponsor	*v.* If an organization or an individual sponsors something such as an event, they pay the expenses, often in order to get publicity for themselves. 赞助
	n. A sponsor is a person or organization that sponsors something or someone. 赞助人，赞助商

双语例句

Some of the best services for the seniors are sponsored by philanthropic organizations.（一些最好的老年人服务机构是由慈善组织资助的。）

Live streaming has opened up new opportunities for sponsors beyond the huge global events.（除全球大型赛事之外，直播为赞助商带来了新的机遇。）

联想记忆

sponsorship *n.* 赞助；发起
patron *n.* 赞助人；顾客
patronage *n.* 赞助；资助

单词	释义
internship	*n.* An internship is the position held by an intern, or the period of time when someone is an intern. 实习生的职位；实习期

双语例句

The application for the Summer 2022 White House Internship Program is now open.（2022年夏季白宫实习项目现在开始接受申请。）

The students will go through a three-month training program, ending in a nine-month paid internship.（学生们会进行为期3个月的培训，之后带薪实习9个月。）

联想记忆

intern *n.* 实习生 *v.* 做实习医师

269. Robbins is short and ***compact***, and he has the wiry physique of an ***acrobat*** beneath the softness of a few extra pounds.

单词	释义
compact	*adj.* A compact person is small but looks strong; a compact thing is small or takes up very little space. 矮小结实的；小巧的；简洁的
	n. A compact is an official contract or agreement. 合同，协议

双语例句

Martin Freeman, compact and affable, is a snug fit in the difficult role of Bilbo.（马丁·弗里曼身材矮小、和蔼可亲，很适合扮演比尔博这个难演的角色。）

Worldwide demand for compact cars began growing due to rising fuel costs and stricter controls on emissions.（由于燃油成本上升，排放控制趋严，全球对紧凑型汽车的需求开始增长。）

The compact is designed to ensure that governments do not build up excessive public deficits.（该协议旨在确保政府不会产生过多的公共赤字。）

联想记忆

pact *n.* 条约，协定

stout *adj.* 壮实的；矮胖的

单词	释义
acrobat	*n.* An acrobat is an entertainer who performs difficult physical acts such as jumping and balancing, especially in a circus. 杂技演员

双语例句

They realized that acrobats, gymnasts and stilt walkers needed a high protein diet. （他们意识到，杂技演员、体操运动员和高跷表演者都需要高蛋白饮食。）

The tourists were astounded by the talents of Chinese acrobats, performing feats of extreme flexibility and coordination. （游客们为中国杂技演员的才华而感到震惊，他们的表演集柔韧性和协调性于一体。）

联想记忆

acrobatics *n.* 杂技，杂技表演
gymnast *n.* 体操运动员

270. The declining share of the white male voter is ***presumed*** to ***doom*** the Republicans to its forty years in the wilderness.

单词	释义
presume	*v.* If you presume that something is the case, you think that it is the case, although you are not certain. 推测
	v. If you say that someone presumes to do something, you mean that they do it even though they have no right to do it. 擅自（做某事）

双语例句

It was presumed that the largest threat facing the country was the economic downturn. （据推测，该国面临的最大威胁是经济衰退。）

She would never presume to give anyone advice about how to run their lives. （她从不擅自给人提供有关如何经营人生的建议。）

联想记忆

presumably *adv.* 大概；推测起来
resume *v.* （中断后）重新开始，继续 *n.* 简历

单词	释义
doom	*v.* If a fact or event dooms someone or something to a particular fate, it makes certain that they are going to suffer in some way. 注定
	n. Doom is a terrible future state or event which you cannot prevent. 厄运

双语例句

That argument was the turning point for their marriage, and the one which doomed it to failure. （那次争吵是他们婚姻的一个转折点，注定了他们婚姻的失败。）

Despite the sense of impending doom, the government still thinks Germany is better off than other EU countries.（尽管有末日即将来临的感觉，政府仍然认为德国比其他欧盟国家更富裕。）

联想记忆

bound *adj.* 必然的；驶往……的；束缚的 *v.* 跳跃；反弹
dome *n.* 穹顶；圆顶状物

单元练习 27

使用本单元核心词汇的适当形式填空，并将句子译为中文。

1. Light, _____ and easy to use, the Acer LumiRead is the ultimate travel companion.
2. History shows that development strategies that overlook the cultural factor are _____ to fail.
3. The inevitable rush to complete construction has raised concerns that quality could be _____.
4. The ship can _____ 5,400 guests and has a park with live plants, a large auditorium and a carousel.
5. He recommends using meditation as a complimentary approach, rather than as a _____ for treatment.
6. The charity has launched a website, _____ by Halifax, offering advice on housing problems.
7. The entire Italy is _____ with museums and art, and the city of Florence too grounds a few wonderful ones.
8. The professor called _____ nitrogen fertilizer a "wonderful invention" because it increased food production.
9. Rich neighborhoods can afford better schools, which _____ the growing gap between different social groups.
10. His concert was scheduled to get under way at the Taj Mahal, from where it would be _____ by satellite around the world.

Unit 28

★ 本单元核心词汇 ★

poised	facilitate	delicate	appalling	brisk
barren	privilege	successor	navigate	blend
roam	versatile	filthy	conventional	evolve
polish	contemporary	gratitude	paralyze	fragile

★ 本单元拓展词汇 ★

amenity	revise	collagen	memento	desolate
ramble	huskiness	boutique	subtle	crispy
ruffle	predecessor	bittersweet	scribe	gratify
assortment	component	miscellaneous	grease	refine
nasty	plumage	specimen	brittle	stray
allege	fertile			

271. Although the prince was undoubtedly one of the most *privileged* students there, he *blended* in with the others.

单词	释义
privileged	*adj.* Someone who is privileged has an advantage that others don't have, often because of their wealth or connections with powerful people. 有特权的
	adj. If you feel privileged, you have an opportunity to do something that makes you feel proud. 荣幸的

双语例句

The medical advances, they agreed, must be used to benefit all people, not the privileged few.（他们一致认为，医学发展必须造福所有人，而不是少数享有特权的人。）

I was privileged to work on two concerts held for the queen in her garden at Buckingham Palace.（我有幸参与了在白金汉宫花园里为女王举办的两场音乐会。）

联想记忆

privilege *n.* 特权；荣幸 *v.* 给予特权

单词	释义
blend	*v.* If you blend substances together or if they blend, you mix them together so that they become one substance. 混合；融合
	n. A blend of things is a mixture or combination of them that is useful or pleasant. 调配；美妙的结合

双语例句

Built into a mountainside, the ultra-modern, Barcelona style is designed to blend into the landscape.（这座超现代的巴塞罗那风格建筑建在山腰上，与周围的风景融为一体。）

The public areas offer a subtle blend of traditional charm with modern amenities.（这些公共场所体现了传统魅力与现代设施的巧妙结合。）

联想记忆

blender *n.* 搅拌机；混合物
assortment *n.* 混合；各种各样

272. There is a growing trend of remote employment, *facilitated* online, that is *poised* to address the labor shortage problem.

单词	释义
facilitate	*v.* To facilitate an action or process, especially one that you would like to happen, means to make it easier or more likely to happen. 促进；使容易

双语例句

Vitamin C, found in citrus fruits, facilitates collagen production, a critical component for vibrant skin.（柑橘类水果富含维生素C，能促进胶原蛋白形成，而胶原蛋白是保持皮肤活力的关键成分。）

Each song comes with a link to Amazon Music Store to facilitate download sales.（每首歌都附有一条亚马逊音乐商城的链接，以增加下载销量。）

联想记忆

facility *n.* 设施；容易；灵巧

单词	释义
poised	*adj.* If someone is poised to do something, they are ready to take action at any moment. 准备行动的
	adj. If you are poised, you are calm, dignified, and self-controlled. 镇定的

双语例句

The Heat and Bulls may be poised to dominate the East for the next several years.（热火队和公牛队未来几年可能在东部地区占主导地位。）

Britain's first mainstream female football presenter is cool, poised and confident.（英国的首位主流足球女主持非常酷，镇定而自信。）

联想记忆

poise *n.* 姿势；镇定 *v.* 平衡；准备好；保持……姿势

273. His increasing interest in ***contemporary*** art was met with mixed emotions by his ***conventional*** Catholic family.

单词	释义
contemporary	*adj.* Contemporary things or people are related to the present time. 当代的；同时代的
	n. Contemporary is also a NOUN. 同时代的人

双语例句

Basquiat started out as a graffiti artist before finding fame as a contemporary artist.（巴斯奎特刚开始只是一名涂鸦艺术家，后来成为著名的当代艺术家。）

The living organisms defied contemporary scientific opinion that there was no life in deeper parts of the sea.（这些微生物推翻了当时科学界认为深海没有生命的观点。）

He spent nearly five years writing the biography of Isabella, who was a contemporary of William Wordsworth.（他花了近五年时间来写伊莎贝拉的传记，这是一位和威廉·华兹华斯同时代的人。）

联想记忆

contemporarily *adv.* 当今；时下

单词	释义
conventional	*adj.* Someone who is conventional has behavior or opinions that are ordinary and normal; a conventional method or product is one that has been in use for a long time. 传统的
	adj. Conventional weapons and wars do not involve nuclear explosives. 常规的（武器）；不用核武器的（战争）

双语例句

Scientists have known for some time that conventional explanations for how the brain works need to be revised.（科学家们早就知道，关于大脑如何工作的传统解释需要修正。）

Baghdad currently possesses only 20% of the conventional weapons it had during the Gulf War.（巴格达目前拥有的常规武器只有海湾战争时的20%。）

联想记忆

convention *n.* 惯例；习俗；大会
conventionalism *n.* 墨守成规；传统主义

274. The terrain was so ***barren*** that people could only survive there by ***roaming*** from place to place in search of water and grazing land.

单词	释义
barren	*adj.* A barren landscape has very few plants and no trees; barren land consists of soil that is so poor that plants cannot grow in it. 荒芜的；贫瘠的

双语例句

The results can be barren fields, destructive floods or sickened populations from exposure to contamination.（污染导致的后果是土地贫瘠、洪水和疾病肆虐。）

The landscape appeared almost lunar and barren, and it was impossible to imagine any kind of animals enduring here.（这里的景象几乎像月球一样荒凉，很难想象有什么动物能存活下来。）

联想记忆

desolate *adj.* 荒无人烟的；凄凉的
fertile *adj.* 富饶的；肥沃的

单词	释义
roam	*v.* If you roam an area or roam around it, you wander or travel around it without having a particular purpose. 闲逛；漫游

双语例句

Many young men reportedly roamed Tehran streets looking for a fight with the police.（据报道，许多年轻人在德黑兰街头游荡，伺机与警察打斗。）

In the more isolated corners, brown bears and packs of wolves still roam free.（在一些荒无人烟的地方，棕熊和成群的狼仍在野外游荡。）

联想记忆

ramble *v.* 闲逛；蔓生，蔓延 *n.*（乡间）漫游；闲逛
stray *v.* 迷路，走失；游荡 *adj.* 流浪的；走失的

275. A housekeeper was ***polishing*** a glass cabinet displaying ***delicate*** mementos from Norway and New Zealand.

单词	释义
polish	*v.* If you polish something, you put polish on it or rub it with a cloth to make it shine.（用抛光剂等）擦亮
	v. If you polish your technique, performance, or skill at doing something, you work on improving it. 使完美；改进

双语例句

In Botswana and Namibia there have been a few diamond-polishing factories backed by De Beers.（在博茨瓦纳和纳米比亚，有几家戴比尔斯投资的钻石抛光工厂。）

The statement was carefully polished and checked before release.（这项声明是经仔细检查润色后才发表的。）

联想记忆

refine *v.* 改进，改善；精炼

单词	释义
delicate	*adj.* Something that is delicate is small and beautifully shaped. 精美的
	adj. If something is delicate, it is easy to harm, damage, or break, and needs to be handled or treated carefully. 易碎的；脆弱的
	adj. You use delicate to describe a situation, problem, matter, or discussion that needs to be dealt with carefully and sensitively in order to avoid upsetting things or offending people. 微妙的

双语例句

The blend of delicate design and technology placed the emphasis on simplicity of the LG device.（精美的设计和技术完美结合，凸显了LG的这台设备简洁大方。）

They are keeping a close watch on threats to the delicate eco-system along the coastline.（他们正密切关注对海岸线脆弱生态系统的各种威胁。）

The lead singer sings with a delicate huskiness about bittersweet memories and missed romantic chances.（主唱用细腻沙哑的声音歌唱苦乐参半的回忆和错过的浪漫。）

联想记忆

delicacy *n.* 精美；微妙；佳肴
subtle *adj.* 微妙的；敏锐的；巧妙的

276. The ***versatile*** light truck was supposed to provide the latest ***successor*** to the ubiquitous jeep used by the U.S. troops.

单词	释义
versatile	*adj.* A tool, machine, or material that is versatile can be used for many different purposes. 用途广泛的
	adj. If you say that a person is versatile, you approve of them because they have many different skills. 多才多艺的

双语例句

Lemons are especially versatile — the juice helps remove kitchen grease, bleach our skin and repel mosquitoes.（柠檬用途特别广泛——柠檬汁可以清除油污，美白皮肤，驱走蚊虫。）

Professional armies were expected to be versatile enough to adapt as needed to the enemies they faced.（专业的军队应具备优良的综合素质，以便在不同作战环境下更好地应对敌人。）

联想记忆

miscellaneous *adj.* 混杂的，各式各样的；多才多艺的

单词	释义
successor	*n.* Someone's successor is the person who takes their job after they have left. It could also be a machine, system, etc. that exists after another one in a process of development. 继任者；接替物

双语例句

Years before Mr. Welch retired, GE began the process of lining up a successor.（在韦尔奇退休前几年，通用电气就开始考虑继任者。）

When people think of the iPhone and its inevitable successor, they will still think of Jobs.（当人们想到苹果手机和其换代产品时，他们仍然会想起乔布斯。）

联想记忆

successive *adj.* 连续的；继承的；接替的
predecessor *n.* 前任，前身

277. The mobile market continues to ***evolve*** rapidly with new smartphones and tablets being introduced at a ***brisk*** (almost monthly) pace.

单词	释义
evolve	*v.* When animals or plants evolve, they gradually change and develop into different forms. 进化
	v. If something evolves or you evolve it, it gradually develops over a period of time into something different and usually more advanced. 逐步发展

双语例句

The bright plumage of many male birds was thought to have evolved to attract females.（许多雄鸟的鲜艳羽毛被认为是为吸引雌鸟而进化来的。）

The purpose of the festival has evolved into raising scholarship money to help young musicians in the region.（该音乐节的目的已经演变为筹集奖学金，来帮助该地区的年轻音乐家。）

联想记忆

evolution *n.* 演变；进展
evolutionary *adj.* 进化的；发展的；渐进的

Unit 28

单词	释义
brisk	*adj.* A brisk action is done quickly and in an energetic way. 轻快的
	adj. If trade or business is brisk, things are being sold very quickly and a lot of money is being made. （买卖、生意）兴隆的
	adj. If the weather is brisk, it is cold and fresh. 寒冷而清新的

双语例句

Thirty minutes of brisk walking each day would bring substantial health benefits. （每天30分钟的快走对健康十分有益。）

Across Mumbai, Delhi and other Indian metropolitan cities, designer boutiques are running brisk business. （在孟买、德里和其他印度大城市，设计师精品店生意兴隆。）

There was no moon, and under the low cloud cover a brisk wind ruffled the old Norwegian maples. （天空没有月亮，低矮的云层下，古老的挪威枫树在寒风中摇曳。）

联想记忆

briskness *n.* 轻快；活泼
chill *adj.* 凉飕飕的 *n.* 寒冷，寒意 *v.* 惊吓，使恐惧

278. Conditions in the camps are often ***appalling*** — they are overcrowded, ***filthy*** and desperately short of food and drinking water.

单词	释义
appalling	*adj.* Something that is appalling is so bad or unpleasant that it shocks you. 骇人听闻的；糟透的

双语例句

The young men in the jail had to endure appalling living conditions. （监狱里的年轻人不得不忍受可怕的生活条件。）

The appalling tragedy aside, most disturbing are the conflict's implications for regional security. （除了这起骇人听闻的惨剧，最令人不安的是冲突对地区安全造成的影响。）

联想记忆

appall *v.* 使胆寒；使惊骇
scary *adj.* 可怕的，恐怖的

单词	释义
filthy	*adj.* Something that is filthy is very dirty. 肮脏的，污秽的

双语例句

The camps are overcrowded, filthy and desperately short of food and drinking water.（难民营人满为患，肮脏不堪，极度缺乏食物和饮用水。）

Masri described his prison as a filthy hole, with walls scribbled on in Arabic.（马斯里将他服刑的监狱形容为一个肮脏的洞穴，墙上涂满了阿拉伯文。）

联想记忆

nasty *adj.* 令人厌恶的；污秽的
foul *adj.* 难闻的，恶心的；下流的 *v.* 弄脏；犯规 *n.* 犯规

279. Kids with a sense of responsibility who know when to experience *gratitude* will be better at *navigating* the social life of college.

单词	释义
gratitude	*n.* Gratitude is the state of feeling grateful. 感激，感谢

双语例句

The soldiers often came home greeted not with gratitude or support, but with neglect.（士兵们回到家，迎接他们的不是感激和支持，而是冷落。）

The former coach left the region at the end of last term, having earned people's gratitude.（这位前教练在上个任期结束后离开了这里，赢得了人们的感谢。）

联想记忆

gratify *v.* 使高兴；使满意

单词	释义
navigate	*v.* When a person navigates, they find the right way to deal with a difficult situation. 找到方法
	v. When someone navigates a vehicle, ship or an aircraft somewhere, they decide which course to follow and steer it there. When an animal navigates somewhere, they find the right direction to go there. 导航，找到行进方向

双语例句

New ideas are needed now more than ever to navigate an increasingly varying landscape.（现在比以往任何时候都更需要新思想，来应对日益变化的形势。）

The car successfully navigated the 12.4 mile, 156-turn Pikes Peak International

Hill Climb, without a driver on board.（这辆车在没有司机的情况下，成功地完成了全长12.4英里、156个转弯的派克峰国际爬山赛。）

联想记忆

navigation *n*. 导航；航行；导引
steer *v*. 驾驶（交通工具），掌方向；行驶；引导

280. In its wake, the earthquake left behind destruction and death, and it *paralyzed* an already *fragile* government.

单词	释义
paralyze	*v.* If a person, place, or organization is paralyzed by something, they become unable to act or function properly. 使失去活动能力；使瘫痪

双语例句

The storm dumped at as much as 3 feet of snow on Connecticut, paralyzing much of the state.（这场暴风雪在康涅狄格州降雪达3英尺之厚，导致该州大部分地区陷入瘫痪。）

Ahmad had contracted polio, a disease that paralyzes — and sometimes kills — its victims.（艾哈迈德患有小儿麻痹症，这种疾病会导致瘫痪，甚至死亡。）

联想记忆

paralysis *n*. 瘫痪；瘫痪状态

单词	释义
fragile	*adj.* If you describe a situation as fragile, you mean that it is weak or uncertain, and unlikely to be able to resist strong pressure or attack. 脆弱的
	adj. Something that is fragile is easily broken or damaged. 易碎的

双语例句

The nation's fragile public health system is struggling to cope with a rising number of influenza cases.（该国不堪一击的公共卫生体系正在努力应对不断攀升的流感病例。）

Cleaning and restoration is thought to be too risky because the painting is fragile.（专家们认为清理和修复风险太大，因为这幅画非常易碎。）

联想记忆

brittle *adj*. 易碎的；不牢固的
crispy *adj*. （食物的外皮）酥脆的

单元练习 28

使用本单元核心词汇的适当形式填空，并将句子译为中文。

1. In order to _____ distribution and purchase we can look for more e-commerce solutions.
2. While Ramon has battled loneliness in America, Ana has had to _____ some cultural pitfalls.
3. Driving towards the peninsula's tip, we feel human settlement has hardly made a scratch on this _____ landscape.
4. Cell phones have come way down in price, and they will become much more _____, offering a host of digital services.
5. Mathematicians often present unfinished work at conferences and _____ it for publication afterwards.
6. The Louvre gets its particular character because it _____ into a museum rather than being designed as one.
7. Wolves _____ the mountains of Wyoming and Idaho until the 1930s, when they were hunted under a federal program.
8. Power outages threaten to _____ the country and leave many people at the mercy of a colder than usual winter.
9. McGrath said it was a _____ to be asked to lead the company and he looked forward to building on the predecessors.
10. Recently there has been an unprecedented explosion of international interest in traditional and _____ African art.

Unit 29

★ 本单元核心词汇 ★

engrave	cohesive	famine	wrinkle	elapse
twirl	exclaim	haze	obscure	peer
random	assault	profile	commence	vendor
nurture	alleviate	epidemic	rampant	stain

★ 本单元拓展词汇 ★

peerless	cosmic	galaxy	silhouette	veil
outrage	plague	poach	pedestrian	shroud
ambiguous	lapse	perish	ingenuity	revolve
warehouse	holocaust	ivory	contour	yell
tedium	arbitrary	stainless	microscope	gasp
commencement				

281. The thousands of stars once visible to the naked eye are *obscured* by the glare of industrial light and the *haze* of pollution.

单词	释义
obscure	*v.* If one thing obscures another, it prevents it from being seen or heard properly. 遮掩，遮蔽
	adj. If something or someone is obscure, they are unknown, or are known by only a few people. 鲜为人知的；费解的

双语例句

The oil and gas boom obscures the fact that Russia has little to sell apart from what it can dig out of the ground. （石油和天然气生产的繁荣掩盖了一个事实：俄罗斯除了能从地下挖出的东西外，几乎没有什么可出售的。）

Wireless phones that were once the obscure property of the super rich are now quite pedestrian. （无线电话以前是大富豪们把玩的稀罕物，如今却变得相当常见。）

联想记忆

veil *v.* 遮盖；掩饰 *n.* 面纱；遮盖物
ambiguous *adj.* 模糊的，有歧义的

单词	释义
haze	*n.* Haze is light mist, caused by particles of water or dust in the air, which prevents you from seeing distant objects clearly. 薄雾；霾

双语例句

On many summer days, haze shrouds the scenery in national parks from Yosemite to the Great Smoky Mountains. （夏日里，从优胜美地到大烟山等许多国家公园的美景都笼罩在一层薄雾中。）

All that pretty talk at presentations organized by underwriters disappeared in a haze of restructurings. （在承销商组织的展示会上，所有那些天花乱坠的言论都消失在重组的迷雾中。）

联想记忆

hazy *adj.* 雾蒙蒙的，模糊的
mist *n.* 薄雾，水汽；难以了解的事物

282. For all the challenges of isolation, drought, and *famine*, the country is peaceful and socially *cohesive*.

单词	释义
famine	*n.* Famine is a situation in which large numbers of people have little or no food, and many of them die. 饥荒

双语例句

Yesterday the UN issued a warning that the famine is spreading and the situation is getting worse.（昨日,联合国发出一则警告：饥荒正在蔓延,局势正在恶化。）

Military analysts know well that a sudden onset of famine is one of the surest triggers for civil unrest and all-out war.（军事分析人士十分清楚,一场突然爆发的饥荒无疑是引发内乱和全面战争的导火索之一。）

联想记忆

starvation *n.* 饥饿,挨饿

单词	释义
cohesive	*adj.* Something that is cohesive consists of parts that fit together well and form a united whole. 有聚合力的；使结合的

双语例句

Culture creates jobs, carries educational benefits and makes societies more cohesive, especially in urban areas.（尤其是在城市,文化创造就业,助益教育,团结社会。）

Conventional wisdom has it that a gaggle of regional parties will find it difficult to provide cohesive government.（传统观点认为,一众地区政党将很难建立一个团结的政府。）

联想记忆

cohesion *n.* 凝聚；结合；内聚力
cohere *v.* 凝聚；连贯

283. The tourists **peered** through the fog, trying to read what was **engraved** on the gravestone Shakespeare had chosen for himself.

单词	释义
peer	*v.* If you peer at something, you look at it very hard, usually because it is difficult to see clearly. 费力地看；盯着
	n. Your peers are the people who are the same age as you or who have the same status as you. 同龄人；同等地位的人

双语例句

Those infrared emissions will allow the telescope to peer through cosmic dust to see things like the evolution of early stars and galaxies.（那些红外辐射将使望远镜能够透过宇宙尘埃，观察到早期恒星和星系的演化过程。）

Statistics show that black children are more than twice as likely to drown as their white peers.（统计表明，黑人孩子溺亡的可能性是同龄白人孩子的两倍多。）

联想记忆

peerless *adj.* 无与伦比的；出类拔萃的
peep *v.* 瞥一眼；探出，露出 *n.* 偷看；一瞥

单词	释义
engrave	*v.* If you engrave something with a design or words, you cut the design or words into its surface. 雕刻，铭刻

双语例句

The design is first sketched on paper, and then engraved on stone, in reverse, with a knife.（先是将设计稿绘制在纸上，然后再用小刀将其反刻在石头上。）

The quotation is engraved on the northeast corner of the National Archives Building in Washington.（这句话被刻在位于华盛顿特区的国家档案馆大楼东北角上。）

联想记忆

carve *v.* 雕，刻

284. The girl tried on a minidress, ***twirled*** in front of the mirror and turned to her two friends to ***exclaim***, "Oh my God, I look so hot!"

单词	释义
twirl	*v.* If you twirl, you turn around and around quickly, for example, when you are dancing. If you twirl something or if it twirls, it turns around with a smooth, fast movement. 旋转，转动

双语例句

Then the music started and they would laugh and take each other's arms and twirl over the floor.（然后音乐声响起，他们一边欢笑着一边相互挽着胳膊在地板上绕圈圈。）

As expected, the temperature of the blades rose as they twirled faster and faster.（正如所料，随着叶片旋转得越来越快，其温度也随之上升。）

联想记忆

whirl *v.* 旋转；晕眩 *n.* 旋转；忙乱
revolve *v.* 旋转；以……为重要内容
spin *v.* 快速旋转；急转身；晕眩 *n.* 高速旋转；旋球

单词	释义
exclaim	*v.* Exclaim is used to show that someone is speaking suddenly, loudly, or emphatically, often because they are excited, shocked, or angry. 呼喊，惊叫

双语例句

The passengers gasped and exclaimed, because the trail was almost too small for the bus at times.（乘客们紧张地喘着气，并发出尖叫声，因为这条路有的地方对巴士来说太窄了。）

When I was giving up hope, one of the voices suddenly exclaimed, "I just read something that might help you!"（就在我快要放弃的时候，一个声音突然叫道："我刚刚看过的资料可能会帮到你！"）

联想记忆

scream *v.* 尖叫；大声喊 *n.* 尖叫声
yell *v.* 叫喊，大喊 *n.* 叫喊

285. Farmer also made product improvements — he started offering work wear with fabrics that resisted ***wrinkles*** and ***stains***.

单词	释义
wrinkle	*n.* A wrinkle is a raised fold in a piece of cloth or paper that spoils its appearance.（布或纸上的）皱褶
	n. Wrinkles are lines that form on someone's face as they grow old. 皱纹
	v. If cloth wrinkles, it gets folds or lines in it. 起皱褶

双语例句

Material treated with nanotechnology can be engineered to do almost anything — repel liquids, resist wrinkles, dry fast.（用纳米技术处理过的材料几乎无所不能：防水、抗皱、速干。）

The supermodel admitted using such injections to keep her skin firm and wrinkle-free.（这位超模承认，她曾使用这种注射剂来保持皮肤紧致无皱纹。）

The room was stuffy, but he never removed his long, wrinkled jacket.（房间里很闷，但他一直没有脱下那件皱巴巴的长夹克。）

联想记忆

wrinkled *adj.* 有皱纹的；皱巴巴的

单词	释义
stain	*n.* A stain is a mark on something that is difficult to remove. 污渍
	v. If a liquid stains something, the thing becomes colored or marked by the liquid. （在某物上）留下污渍

双语例句

The tiny stain was only uncovered after the jacket had been examined with a microscope.（这个微小的污渍是在用显微镜观察外套后才发现的。）

Many have teeth stained from cigarettes they smoke and tobacco they chew to relieve the tedium.（很多人为了解闷于是抽烟或者嚼烟叶，他们的牙齿也因此变得很脏。）

联想记忆

stainless *adj.* 不锈的；无污点的

286. They found that forty percent of the *profiles* chosen at *random* included information about alcohol or drug abuse.

单词	释义
profile	*n.* A profile of someone is a short article or program in which their life and character are described. 简介；描述
	n. Your profile is the outline of your face as it is seen when someone is looking at you from the side. （面部的）侧面轮廓

双语例句

These studies include detailed information on the personal behaviors as well as clinical profiles of participants.（这些研究包括参与者的个人行为和临床特征的详细信息。）

The new software recognizes faces even if they are in profile or tilted up at a 45-degree angle.（新软件可以识别人脸，即使是侧脸或以45度角向上倾斜的脸部。）

联想记忆

contour *n.* 轮廓；外形
silhouette *n.* 暗色轮廓；剪影

单词	释义
random	*adj.* A random sample or method is one in which all the people or things involved have an equal chance of being chosen and they do not seem to follow a definite plan or pattern. 随机的；随意的

双语例句

Ten winners were chosen at random from all of the entries using a random number generator.（十名获胜者是从所有的参赛选手中使用数字生成器随机选出的。）

Academics say that the stock market is random — there is no pattern to price movements.（学者们说股市随机性很大，价格走势并没有规律可循。）

联想记忆

arbitrary *adj.* 任意的，随心所欲的；专横的
discretionary *adj.* 酌情决定的；随意的

287. Three years have now *elapsed*, but no one was ever charged with a crime in connection with the *assault*.

单词	释义
elapse	*v.* When time elapses, it passes. （时间）流逝

双语例句

Twenty-five years have now elapsed since the country last conducted an underground nuclear test.（自从该国上一次进行地下核试验以来，已经过去了25年。）

The elapsed time from when a patient arrives at the ER to treatment is not more than 90 minutes.（从患者到达急诊室到接受治疗，所用的时间不超过90分钟。）

联想记忆

lapse *n.* 疏忽，过失；走神 *v.* （时间）流逝；陷入（某种状态）

单词	释义
assault	*n.* An assault on a person is a physical attack on them. An assault by an army is a strong attack made on an area held by the enemy. 袭击；攻击
	v. To assault someone means to physically attack them. 袭击

双语例句

The assault has led to outrage across India with demands for strict action against the policemen.（这起袭击事件在印度各地激起民愤，人们要求严惩涉案警察。）

The news agency's photographer was assaulted by protesters, who broke one of his cameras.（该通讯社的摄影师遭到抗议者袭击，他们摔坏了一台相机。）

联想记忆

raid *n.* 袭击，突袭；突击检查 *v.* 突袭；抢劫
stab *n.* 刺伤，戳 *v.* （用锐器或尖物）刺；（话语）刺痛

288. As the weekend ***commences***, the ***vendors*** emerge from street with tempting, colorful displays of local arts and crafts.

单词	释义
commence	*v.* When something commences or you commence it, it begins. （使）开始

双语例句

If planning permission is granted, the construction of this stadium is expected to commence late next year.（如果规划获批，这座体育场预计将于明年晚些时候动工。）

The president offered several reasons for why it is time to commence troop reductions.（总统提出了几个理由，说明为什么现在是开始裁军的时候了。）

联想记忆

commencement *n.* 开始；毕业典礼

单词	释义
vendor	*n.* A vendor is someone who sells things such as newspapers, cigarettes, or food from a small stall or cart. 小贩
	n. A vendor is a company or person that sells a product or service, especially one who sells to other companies that sell to the public. 供应商

双语例句

Many vendors spray warehouses regularly with pesticides as bugs are a nuisance to them.（许多小商贩定期向仓库里喷洒杀虫剂，因为虫子让人很讨厌。）

Hewlett-Packard remains the largest vendor, with 17.7% market share, up from 17.3% a year ago.（惠普仍然是最大的供应商，市场份额为17.7%，高于一年前的17.3%。）

联想记忆

vend *v.* 出售
hawk *v.* 叫卖，兜售 *n.* 鹰；鹰派人物

merchant *n.* 商人，批发商

289. ***Nurturing*** others — raising children, teaching, caring for animals — helps to ***alleviate*** loneliness.

单词	释义
nurture	*v.* If you nurture something such as a young child or a young plant, you care for it while it is growing and developing. 养育；培养
	n. Nurture is care and encouragement that is given to someone while they are growing and developing. 培育，养育

双语例句

Dumont is exceptional in terms of the number of children she has nurtured over six decades.（杜蒙在过去60年里养育了很多孩子，在这一点上她与众不同。）

He has promised to curb home prices, boost education, and nurture more high-tech industries.（他承诺抑制房价，促进教育，并培育更多的高科技产业。）

There is an element of both nature and nurture in explaining the evil actions of individuals.（在解释人们的恶行方面，既有先天也有后天的因素。）

联想记忆

foster *v.* 促进；培养
cultivate *v.* 培养；培育；耕作
rear *v.* 养育；饲养 *n.* 后部；后方 *adj.* 后面的

单词	释义
alleviate	*v.* If you alleviate pain, suffering, or an unpleasant condition, you make it less intense or severe. 减轻（不适），缓和

双语例句

Economic development that alleviates poverty is a vital step in boosting happiness.（经济发展应着眼于解决贫困问题，这是提升幸福感的关键一步。）

Prior to the procedure, Kelly had been in physical therapy for years, with no success of alleviating her misery.（在手术之前，凯莉已经进行了多年的物理治疗，但这并没有减轻她的痛苦。）

联想记忆

alleviation *n.* 缓和；镇痛物
lighten *v.* 减轻；照亮
relieve *v.* 减轻；缓解；救济

290. Their average life expectancy was only 30 years and *epidemic* diseases were *rampant*, with the result that the population decreased year after year.

单词	释义
epidemic	*n.* If there is an epidemic of a particular disease somewhere, it affects many people there and spreads quickly to other areas. （疾病）流行
	n. If an activity that you disapprove of is increasing or spreading rapidly, you can refer to this as an epidemic of that activity. （坏事）盛行

双语例句

With dedication, persistence, and ingenuity, we can put an end to the diabetes epidemic. （凭借专注、坚持和智慧，我们可以终结目前盛行的糖尿病。）

Not long ago, Michelle appeared on the show to talk about her effort to end the epidemic of childhood obesity. （不久前，米歇尔在节目中谈到她为结束儿童肥胖流行所做的努力。）

联想记忆

pandemic *n.* 流行病 *adj.* （疾病）大规模流行的

plague *n.* 瘟疫，传染病 *v.* 困扰，烦扰

单词	释义
rampant	*adj.* If something bad, such as a crime or disease, is rampant, it is very common and is increasing in an uncontrolled way. 猖獗的；泛滥的

双语例句

Fear of failure is rampant among students who have been drilled in standardized-test taking. （接受标准化考试训练的学生普遍对失败感到恐惧。）

Though selling African elephant ivory has generally been banned since 1989, poaching is once again rampant. （尽管1989年以来，出售非洲象牙已被普遍禁止，但偷猎行为又开始猖獗起来。）

联想记忆

rampage *v.* 狂暴；乱闹；发怒

单元练习 29

使用本单元核心词汇的适当形式填空，并将句子译为中文。

1. The medicine has found another, more popular application in reducing facial _____.
2. "It is worse than in-flight food, or at a cheap college cafeteria," _____ her boyfriend.
3. Effective warning systems had been put in place following the 1984 _____ in Ethiopia.
4. When I was in the grocery store, the woman in line behind me saw my foodstamps and _____ into my cart.
5. He was an _____ but efficient figure who handled the powerful National Intelligence Service since 1990.
6. Metro Police in London stopped _____ travelers by searching their bags before they boarded the subway.
7. Implementation of the project _____ in 2018 and was initially scheduled to be completed by 2025.
8. Education must provide the knowledge and _____ the creativity that will allow our nation to thrive in the new economy.
9. Plants release moisture into the air, _____ the dry atmosphere generated by air-conditioning and central heating units.
10. Only three minutes had _____ in the second half when the supporters of Lakers started their cries for the introduction of Kobe Bryant.

Unit 30

★ 本单元核心词汇 ★

reliant	integral	monopoly	sanction	trait
harsh	distort	allocate	fraction	verge
attic	maximum	manipulate	inhabit	fend
insert	commentary	glamour	spice	plot

★ 本单元拓展词汇 ★

regime	rigorous	enlighten	habitant	spur
shield	attribute	margin	conspiracy	scrap
ranch	mend	renaissance	cursor	pirate
telescopic	boundary	alphabetical	brink	ratify
robotic	seasoning	implant	faction	cruise
allure	commentator	ritual	soak	

Unit 30

291. Bike sharing is on the ***verge*** of becoming an ***integral*** part of public transportation in cities across the globe.

单词	释义
verge	*n.* The verge of something is the edge or rim of it. 边缘
	n. If you are on the verge of something, you are going to do it very soon or it is likely to happen or begin very soon. 即将

双语例句

The drum was spotted by a member of the public walking on the grass verge alongside a road.（一个市民在路边的草地上散步时发现了这个鼓。）

In a relatively short period of time, humans have driven most shark populations to the verge of extinction.（在相对较短的时间内，人类将多数鲨鱼种群逼到了濒临灭绝的地步。）

联想记忆

brink *n.* 边缘
margin *n.* 页边空白；边缘；利润
boundary *n.* 边界；界限

单词	释义
integral	*adj.* Something that is an integral part of something is an essential part of that thing. 构成整体所必需的；完整的

双语例句

Rituals, celebrations, and festivals form an integral part of every human society.（宗教仪式、庆典活动和节日传统是人类社会不可或缺的组成部分。）

Stan Lee remains an integral part of the annual San Diego Comic-Con since 1975.（自1975年以来，斯坦·李一直是一年一度的圣地亚哥国际动漫展上不可或缺的人物。）

联想记忆

integrate *v.* 使合并；加入；求积分
integrity *n.* 完整；正直，诚实
integer *n.* 整数

292. About 2,500 families, out of the 40,000 displaced people, have so far been ***allocated*** new ***plots*** to build homes and grow vegetables.

单词	释义
allocate	*v.* If one item is allocated to a particular person or for a particular purpose, it is given to that person or used for that purpose. 分配；划拨

双语例句

India remains energy starved despite 15% or more of federal funds being allocated to the power sector.（尽管15%或更多的联邦资金都被分配给了电力部门，但印度仍然能源短缺。）

These children and families must be the focus when health plans are developed and resources allocated.（在制定卫生计划和分配资源时，必须重点关注这些儿童和家庭。）

联想记忆

allocation *n.* 分配，配置；安置
allot *v.* 分配；分派

单词	释义
plot	*n.* A plot of land is a small piece of land, especially one that has been measured or marked out for a special purpose. 小块圈地
	n. A plot is a secret plan by a group of people to do something that is illegal or wrong, usually against a person or a government. 阴谋
	v. If people plot to do something or plot something that is illegal or wrong, they plan secretly to do it. 密谋

双语例句

The Greek government has put the full plot of land up for sale in an effort to raise revenues and spur growth.（希腊政府拟出售全部土地，以增加收入，刺激经济增长。）

Mr. Dissanayake openly accuses university lecturers of being part of a plot to bring about regime change.（迪萨纳亚克公开指责大学讲师参与了政权更迭的阴谋。）

It's unclear who plotted the attack against Twitter and what their motives may have been.（目前还不清楚是谁策划了针对推特的攻击，也不清楚他们的动机是什么。）

联想记忆

conspiracy *n.* 阴谋；谋反

293. Nancy was self-***reliant***, a ***trait*** that she possibly picked up while growing up on a farm in New Hampshire.

单词	释义
reliant	*adj.* A person or thing that is reliant on something needs it and often cannot live or work without it. 依赖的；依靠的

双语例句

America, as the country most reliant on computers, is probably most vulnerable to cyber-attack.（作为最依赖计算机的国家，美国可能最容易受到网络攻击。）

My grandma worked hard and had a decent income, but she was hugely reliant on Medicare at the end of her life.（我奶奶工作努力，收入可观，但她在生命的最后阶段还得完全依赖医疗保险。）

联想记忆

reliance *n.* 信赖；信心

单词	释义
trait	*n.* A trait is a particular characteristic someone or something has. 特征，特点

双语例句

Those traits helped him win the PFA young player of the year award last season.（这些特点使他赢得了上赛季职业球员联盟年度最佳年轻球员奖。）

This new business model will be the most important trait of Britain's manufacturing renaissance.（这种新的商业模式将是英国制造业复兴的最重要特征。）

联想记忆

attribute *n.* 属性；特质 *v.* 归因于

294. Like other utilities, American Water Works enjoys a government-*sanctioned monopoly* in most of its markets.

单词	释义
sanction	*v.* If someone in authority sanctions an action or practice, they officially approve of it and allow it to be done. Sanction is also a NOUN. 批准；认可
	n. Sanctions are measures taken by countries to restrict trade and official contact with a country that has broken international law. 制裁

双语例句

The Indian government has sanctioned a nationwide census of birds to establish how many remain.（印度政府批准了一项全国范围的鸟类普查，以确定鸟类数量。）

The Burmese President has urged Western countries to scrap all sanctions against his country.（缅甸总统敦促西方国家取消对缅甸的所有制裁。）

联想记忆

ratify *v.* 批准；正式签署

单词	释义
monopoly	*n.* If a company, person, or state has a monopoly on something such as an industry, they have complete control over it. 垄断
	n. A monopoly is a company which is the only one providing a particular product or service. 垄断企业

双语例句

American Indians have great economic and political influence thanks to their monopoly on gambling.（由于美国印第安人垄断博彩业，因此他们拥有巨大的经济和政治影响力。）

This company was born in 1922, and has all the features of a typical state-owned monopoly of the mid-20th century.（这家公司成立于1922年，具有20世纪中期典型国有垄断企业的所有特征。）

联想记忆

monopolize *v.* 垄断，独占
monopolism *n.* 垄断主义；垄断制度

295. Despite its reputation as a ***harsh*** environment, surveys have uncovered evidence that suggests St Kilda was ***inhabited*** as early as 3,000 BC.

单词	释义
harsh	*adj.* Harsh climates or conditions are very difficult for people, animals, and plants to live in. 严酷的；恶劣的
	adj. Harsh actions or speech are unkind and show no understanding or sympathy. 残酷的；严厉的

双语例句

Little is known about the creature because its harsh environment makes it difficult for scientists to conduct research.（人们对这种生物知之甚少，因为其恶劣的环境使科学家很难开展研究。）

Democrats and Republicans traded harsh words on the House floor Tuesday in the debate over the bill.（民主党和共和党周二在众议院就该法案进行辩论时唇枪舌剑。）

联想记忆

rigorous *adj.*（规则、制度等）严格的，苛刻的

单词	释义
inhabit	*v.* If a place or region is inhabited by a group of people or a species of animal, those people or animals live there. 居住于

双语例句

The enlightened world we inhabit is a result of 200-plus years of growth, starting with the Industrial Revolution.（我们现在生活的文明世界是自工业革命以来200多年发展的结果。）

Karrada is a mixed commercial and residential area inhabited mostly by Shiites and Christians.（卡拉达是一个商住混合区，主要居住着什叶派和基督徒。）

联想记忆

inhabitant *n.* 居民；居住者
habitat *n.* 栖息地

296. Access to health care was ***distorted***, with the best going to the wealthy and the poor left to ***fend*** for themselves.

单词	释义
distort	*v.* If you distort a statement, fact, or idea, you report or represent it in an untrue way. 歪曲；曲解
	v. If something you can see or hear is distorted or distorts, its appearance or sound is changed so that it seems unclear. 扭曲；失真

双语例句

The Fed's excess money creation is distorting economies and financial markets around the world.（美联储超额印币是在扰乱全球经济和金融市场。）

Traditional speakers can distort the way instruments sound, often making music seem flat and narrow.（传统扬声器会使乐器的声音失真，经常出现降半音，而且乐声变窄。）

联想记忆

distortion *n.* 变形；失真；扭曲
falsify *v.* 伪造，篡改；歪曲

单词	释义
fend	*v.* If you have to fend for yourself, you have to look after yourself without relying on help from anyone else. 照料（自己）
	v. To fend means to keep or ward off. 避开；挡开

双语例句

Abel's parents agreed to pay the rent for his apartment but otherwise left him to fend for himself.（亚伯的父母同意替他付房租，其他的则让他自己解决。）

A cruise ship with 1,500 people aboard fended off a pirate attack in the Indian Ocean.（一艘载有1 500人的游轮在印度洋上避开了海盗的袭击。）

联想记忆

shield *v.* 保护；遮挡 *n.* 盾，遮挡物
ward *v.* 保护 *n.* 病房

297. His self-published 2005 novel, an English-language romance *spiced* with *commentary* on Thailand, sold fewer than ten copies.

单词	释义
spice	*v.* If you spice something that you say or do, you add excitement or interest to it. 增加趣味；加香料
	n. A spice is a part of a plant, or a powder made from it, which you put in food to give it flavor. Cinnamon, ginger, and paprika are spices. 香料

双语例句

The cheeseheads can be found in plastic bags next to gas-station checkouts, usually spiced with garlic or ranch flavoring.（这种奶酪头放在加油站收银台旁的塑料袋里，通常会加大蒜或牧场风味的香料。）

The herbs and spices are arranged in alphabetical order on narrow open shelves.（草药和香料按字母顺序排列，放在狭窄的开放式货架上。）

联想记忆

spicy *adj.* 辛辣的；多香料的
seasoning *n.* 调味品；佐料

单词	释义
commentary	*n.* A commentary is an article or book which explains or discusses something. 评论；评论性文章（或书籍）
	n. A commentary is a description of an event that is broadcast on radio or television while the event is taking place. 实况报道

双语例句

Andy's commentary on national security, the law, and politics is featured regularly in the national media.（安迪关于国家安全、法律和政治的评论文章经常发表在全国性媒体上。）

Penn keeps up a running commentary to distract the audience while the magic tricks are being performed.（在魔术表演的时候，潘恩一直在解说，目的是分散观众的注意力。）

联想记忆

commentate *v.* 评论时事；实况报道
commentator *n.* 评论员，解说员；时事评论者

298. Carr worries that local school districts would ***manipulate*** texts of textbooks to ***insert*** political biases.

单词	释义
manipulate	*v.* If someone manipulates an event or situation, they use or control it for their own benefit, or cause it to develop in the way they want. 操纵；控制
	v. If you manipulate something that requires skill, such as a complicated piece of equipment or a difficult idea, you operate it or process it. 操作

双语例句

The military authorities have denied that they ever tried to influence or manipulate election results.（军方当局否认他们曾试图影响或操纵选举结果。）

Through this technology, patients can move a computer cursor by thinking and manipulate a robotic arm.（运用这项技术，患者可以通过意念来移动电脑光标，并操纵机械手臂。）

联想记忆

manipulation *n.* 操纵；控制
deploy *v.* 部署；调配

单词	释义
insert	*v.* If you insert something into another thing, you add it or put it inside the thing. 添加；插入；嵌入

双语例句

Mr. Kerr spent four days in hospital and had steel rods inserted to mend his leg.

读美句·学单词

（科尔在医院住了四天，并植入了钢条来修复他的腿。）

Users simply insert a SIM card with credit to begin making calls at local rates.（用户仅需插入一张有余额的电话卡，就可以按本地费率来拨打电话。）

联想记忆

implant *v.*（尤指医学）移植；灌输（观点或思想） *n.* 植入物

299. Mr. Hutomo was given 15 years, a *fraction* of the *maximum* possible life sentence, for paying two hitmen to gun down the judge.

单词	释义
fraction	*n.* A fraction of something is a tiny amount or proportion of it. 少量
	n. A fraction is a number that can be expressed as a proportion of two whole numbers. For example, 1/2 and 1/3 are both fractions. 分数

双语例句

Only a fraction of the hundreds of thousands of displaced Pakistanis are ending up in camps.（在成千上万流离失所的巴基斯坦人中，只有一小部分最终住进了难民营。）

Thirty years ago, pupils would sometimes convert decimals into fractions to solve a problem.（30年前，学生有时会把小数变成分数来解题。）

联想记忆

fractional *adj.* 部分的；分数的
faction *n.* 派系；小集团

单词	释义
maximum	*adj.* You use maximum to describe an amount which is the largest that is possible, allowed, or required. 最大的，最大限度的
	n. Maximum is also a NOUN. 最大值

双语例句

He faces a maximum sentence of 206 years in prison if convicted of all charges.（如果所有指控成立，他将面临最高206年的监禁。）

The amount of alcohol in his blood was triple the legal maximum.（他血液中的酒精含量是法定上限的三倍。）

联想记忆

maximize *v.* 取最大值；充分利用

Unit 30

300. Despite his outward ***glamour***, this famous young man was, at 25, living in the ***attic*** of his mother's London boarding house in Ebury Street and having his first nervous breakdown.

单词	释义
glamour	*n.* Glamour is the quality of being more attractive, exciting, or interesting than ordinary people or things. 魅力

双语例句

India has used Bollywood glamour to promote the Taj Mahal, one of the seven winners.（泰姬陵是七大奇迹之一，印度曾利用宝莱坞的魅力进行广泛宣传。）

Soaked in film history and glamour, Cannes makes a fortune every year by hosting entertainment-industry events.（戛纳有着悠久的电影史和独特魅力，每年通过举办电影节等活动大赚一笔。）

联想记忆

glamorous *adj.* 富有魅力的；迷人的
allure *n.* 吸引力；魅力 *v.* 吸引

单词	释义
attic	*n.* An attic is a room at the top of a house just below the roof. 阁楼；顶楼

双语例句

By converting the attic, they were able to have two extra bedrooms.（通过改建阁楼，他们又多出了两间卧室。）

They brought in sniffer dogs and telescopic cameras over a number of days, even searching the attic.（他们带着警犬和可伸缩摄像机搜查了几天，甚至还搜查了阁楼。）

联想记忆

loft *n.* 阁楼；顶楼寓所
antic *adj.* 古怪的；滑稽可笑的 *n.* 滑稽动作；小丑

单元练习 30

使用本单元核心词汇的适当形式填空，并将句子译为中文。

1. The stock price is easy for executives to _____, sometimes over long periods of time.
2. These six personal _____ can help you survive divorce both emotionally and financially.
3. The species was hunted to the _____ of extinction before a ban was introduced in the 1960s.
4. The exhibition documents how images of Asians were _____ by American pop culture over the years.
5. Armstrong remained modest and never allowed himself to be caught up in the _____ of space exploration.
6. Those over 65 currently receive generous health insurance for which they pay only a small _____ of the cost.
7. A private chef dinner in Buenos Aires serves a _____ of 15 people and guests eat together around one large table.
8. The UN Security Council voted overwhelmingly to _____ Iran for its continued failure to live up to its obligations.
9. Almost two-thirds of the investment will be _____ to increase production facilities at the group's electronics businesses.
10. This old-fashioned neighborhood, footsteps away from the bustling market, was originally _____ by immigrants from Yemen.

参考文献

[1] 曹明伦. 英汉翻译二十讲[M]. 增订版. 北京: 商务印书馆, 2019.

[2] 何刚强. 笔译理论与技巧[M]. 北京: 外语教学与研究出版社, 2009.

[3] 教育部高等学校大学外语教学指导委员会. 大学英语教学指南: 2020版[M]. 北京: 高等教育出版社, 2020.

[4] 林六辰, 陈星伊, 周正履. 英语阅读训练200篇[M]. 西安: 西北工业大学出版社, 2022.

[5] 刘季春. 实用翻译教程[M]. 3版. 广州: 中山大学出版社, 2016.

[6] 刘毅. 突破英文词汇10 000[M]. 北京: 外语教学与研究出版社, 2004.

[7] 梅德明. 新编英语教程: 1[M]. 3版. 上海: 上海外语教育出版社, 2012.

[8] 梅德明. 新编英语教程: 2[M]. 3版. 上海: 上海外语教育出版社, 2012.

[9] 柯林斯出版公司. 柯林斯高阶英汉双解学习词典[M]. 北京: 外语教学与研究出版社, 2017.

[10] 谭卫国. 综合教程: 1[M]. 3版. 上海: 上海外语教育出版社, 2019.

[11] 张春柏. 综合教程: 2[M]. 3版. 上海: 上海外语教育出版社, 2020.

附录 I　参考答案

单元练习 1

1. ［答案］optimistic
   ［译文］赛后亨曼表达了他的失望，但对未来充满信心。
2. ［答案］potential
   ［译文］该团队专注于纳米技术的研究及其商业应用潜力。
3. ［答案］associate
   ［译文］她目前是该杂志的副主编，负责摄影方面的报道。
4. ［答案］enrollment
   ［译文］另一方面，商科、工程和计算机科学的入学人数却大幅上升。
5. ［答案］pursuit
   ［译文］为了实现公司扩张的目标，这些高管一直在加班加点工作。
6. ［答案］exhausted
   ［译文］繁忙的工作和复杂的人际交往环境往往让人身心俱疲。
7. ［答案］option
   ［译文］一些非常优秀的女性放弃了选择教育作为自己的职业，导致学校教育质量逐渐下降。
8. ［答案］departures
   ［译文］迈阿密国际机场在上午8点到10点之间只有15个航班离港，3个航班抵达。
9. ［答案］furious
   ［译文］许多商店和餐馆正处于最繁忙的时期，他们对于这些软件问题非常恼火。
10. ［答案］intimate
    ［译文］脸书（Facebook）具有独特的优势，可以为品牌方提供他们的所需：与目标客户保持亲密的关系。

单元练习 2

1. ［答案］renovate
   ［译文］政府计划对通往刚果和赞比亚的庞大铁路网进行改造。
2. ［答案］spectators

［译文］在城市，足球比赛现在可以吸引超过7万名观众，而棒球比赛只能吸引2万名观众。
3. ［答案］underlined
  ［译文］在一个快速变化的世界里，跨文化能力的重要性再怎么强调也不为过。
4. ［答案］adversity
  ［译文］虽然有些人能在逆境中破浪前行，但很多人一看到失败的迹象就会放弃。
5. ［答案］occupational
  ［译文］我们熟悉的职业姓氏有数百个，比如阿彻、卡特、费希尔、泰勒等。
6. ［答案］cautious
  ［译文］摩根大通被誉为全球大型银行中管理更好、更谨慎的银行之一。
7. ［答案］disposal
  ［译文］马萨诸塞州的一项法律禁止将尖锐的医疗物品（针头、柳叶刀等）扔到家庭垃圾中。
8. ［答案］ushered
  ［译文］将军被领到国王所坐的宝座前，便单膝跪地以示敬意。
9. ［答案］longevity
  ［译文］她位于地中海岛上的家乡以居民长寿而闻名，据说有370位百岁老人。
10. ［答案］encountered
  ［译文］社会学教授爱德华·谢尔斯回忆起他年轻时在宾夕法尼亚大学遇到的一位老师。

单元练习 3

1. ［答案］uncover
  ［译文］这些仪器或许能揭示那些矿物质形成时火星是什么样子。
2. ［答案］innocent
  ［译文］周一，波士顿马拉松赛发生恐怖袭击，造成数十人受伤，3名无辜者死亡。
3. ［答案］diverse
  ［译文］博尔特表示，他很期待见到肯尼亚各种各样的野生动物，但害怕遇到狮子。
4. ［答案］controversial
  ［译文］堕胎在任何地方都是一个敏感问题，在北爱尔兰争议更大。
5. ［答案］ensure
  ［译文］在英国国家医疗服务体系（NHS）工作的每个人都有责任确保个人信息受到保护。
6. ［答案］inverse
  ［译文］你说话的多少和在销售或说服他人方面的成功率呈负相关。
7. ［答案］identifying

[译文] 随着电子仪器的使用，识别和跟踪风暴方面取得了巨大进展。
8. [答案] accessible
[译文] 乘坐地铁很方便就可以到这个有7 500个座位的公园，那里可以俯瞰大西洋和康尼岛游乐园。
9. [答案] symptoms
[译文] 大约43%的志愿者有感染和感冒症状，如鼻塞、咳嗽和喉咙疼痛。
10. [答案] launched
[译文] 当时人们争先恐后要加入扎克伯格的社交网络，该网络最初只面向哈佛大学的学生。

单元练习 4

1. [答案] adjacent
[译文] 许多小径连接着卡梅隆自然保护区和邻近的马里布溪州立公园。
2. [答案] nourished
[译文] 一些病人出院时比他们入院的时候身体还差。
3. [答案] entitled
[译文] 虽然他在丹麦出生，但他从未申请过可以获得的丹麦国籍。
4. [答案] abundant
[译文] 该国丰富的自然资源使其成为投资兴业的好地方。
5. [答案] recessions
[译文] 严重的经济衰退通常会导致失业和经济活动减弱两者形成恶性循环。
6. [答案] resort
[译文] 这个海滨度假胜地也成为美国南部富有的庄园主们避暑的好去处。
7. [答案] scarcity
[译文] 一船一船绝望的索马里人不断地非法抵达欧洲，这表明索马里当地缺乏体面的工作。
8. [答案] competent
[译文] 通用汽车公司的管理层非常能干，受到董事会的密切监督。
9. [答案] devastated
[译文] 飓风桑迪10月袭击了美国，风暴造成的洪水摧毁了新泽西州数以千计的房屋。
10. [答案] contracted
[译文] 据估计，美国有2 200万人感染了这种病毒，截至9月15日，约有9万人住院治疗。

单元练习 5

1. [答案] intrusion
[译文] 詹姆斯被突如其来的巨响惊呆了，迅速站了起来。

2. ［答案］indifferent
   ［译文］当布莱克夫人把我介绍给她丈夫时，他不冷不热同我握了握手。
3. ［答案］relocate
   ［译文］当地部落不必搬迁，不过一旦水位下降，他们可能会面临生活方式的改变。
4. ［答案］isolation
   ［译文］越来越多的证据表明，社会孤立与疾病风险增加有关。
5. ［答案］decline
   ［译文］教师的薪水增加了，因此做家教的人变少了。
6. ［答案］confronted
   ［译文］就像美国各行各业一样，保险公司正面临着越来越多的诉讼。
7. ［答案］reminder
   ［译文］这座博物馆体现了该岛悠久的航海史，这里收藏着多艘20世纪的救生艇。
8. ［答案］violates
   ［译文］政府未能向公立学校学生提供教科书，这侵犯了宪法赋予他们受教育的权利。
9. ［答案］aggravated
   ［译文］报告称，太平洋西北地区的极端干旱状况将使加州的问题加剧。
10. ［答案］captured
    ［译文］新西兰各地的人们提交了350张照片，这些照片捕捉了该国生物多样性的不同元素。

单元练习 6

1. ［答案］elaborate
   ［译文］他们的厨房里根本没有地方来放这么精致的烘焙食品。
2. ［答案］diagnosis
   ［译文］如今，计算机已进入从医疗诊断到自动驾驶等各个领域。
3. ［答案］deteriorated
   ［译文］他被关押在莫斯科的一所监狱里，条件非常恶劣，导致他的健康状况迅速恶化。
4. ［答案］stuffy
   ［译文］在一个低矮的闷热房间里，美国职业橄榄球联盟和通用电气宣布启动一个新项目。
5. ［答案］compulsory
   ［译文］超过200名议员签署了一项动议，呼吁将金融教育纳入学校的必修课。
6. ［答案］dispute
   ［译文］很少有人会质疑，女性受教育具有巨大的社会效益和经济效益。

7. ［答案］permanent
   ［译文］在1977年以前，移民制度一般许可外国出生的内科医生永久居留。
8. ［答案］transferred
   ［译文］在沃顿商学院学习两年后，巴菲特转学到了内布拉斯加大学林肯分校，在那儿修完了大学最后一年的课程。
9. ［答案］maiden
   ［译文］作者回忆起1936年5月27日的情景，当时游轮从南安普敦出发，首次航行前往纽约。
10. ［答案］autonomous
    ［译文］内华达州已经通过了一项法律，允许自动驾驶汽车在道路上行驶，俄勒冈州也在考虑类似的立法。

单元练习 7

1. ［答案］distinct
   ［译文］在当前的经济环境下，Nexus 7相比任何一款iPad都有明显的优势。
2. ［答案］exceed
   ［译文］我们正面临着一场全球危机，这将超过历史上所经历的一切。
3. ［答案］quoted
   ［译文］新闻媒体援引匿名消息人士称，"莫斯科"可能会终止与这个岛国的外交关系。
4. ［答案］undergo
   ［译文］在过去的几年里，我目睹了许多人的职业发生转变。
5. ［答案］equivalent
   ［译文］每天有200人搬到拉斯维加斯，每年新增人口相当于一个密苏里州圣约瑟夫市。
6. ［答案］boosts
   ［译文］迈阿密大学的一项研究发现，工作时短暂的自我按摩可以减轻压力，提高工作效率。
7. ［答案］notorious
   ［译文］近年来，这所学校因一些教员与恐怖主义有关联而臭名昭著。
8. ［答案］pension
   ［译文］超过70%的受访公司表示，他们允许高管在60岁退休时领取全额养老金。
9. ［答案］circulation
   ［译文］《华尔街日报》的发行量很小，因为它是专门面向对商业新闻感兴趣的读者出版的。
10. ［答案］reassure
    ［译文］里根总统发表讲话，他向全国人民承诺，这场悲剧不会阻止美国探索太空的脚步。

单元练习 8

1. ［答案］priorities
   ［译文］健康和教育是雅各布·祖马总统政府的首要任务。
2. ［答案］luxurious
   ［译文］挪威邮轮公司决定将它们打造成水上最豪华的游轮。
3. ［答案］deserves
   ［译文］足球现在比以往任何时候都更是一项全球性的运动，值得在世界各地分享。
4. ［答案］shattered
   ［译文］爆炸发生在马拉松比赛终点线附近，窗户被震碎，浓烟腾空而起。
5. ［答案］transformed
   ［译文］经过几个世纪的扩建，故宫最终变成了一座皇家博物院。
6. ［答案］advent
   ［译文］随着数码摄影技术的出现，白银的工业需求量急剧下降。
7. ［答案］elevated
   ［译文］随着时间的推移，这些新奇的事物变得流行起来，其中一些最终上升为艺术形式。
8. ［答案］ground
   ［译文］美国农业部对伊利诺伊州一家公司生产的碎牛肉已经发布了高危预警。
9. ［答案］myth
   ［译文］有一个有趣的说法是，你必须去纽约或加州这样的大地方才能功成名就。
10. ［答案］approved
    ［译文］药品研发是一个耗费时间的过程，需要食品药品管理局多轮审验，最终才能获批。

单元练习 9

1. ［答案］contagious
   ［译文］一项新的研究发现，肥胖可能在家人和朋友之间具有社会传染性。
2. ［答案］commemorate
   ［译文］邮局发行了三枚邮票，以纪念2014年在巴西举行的世界杯。
3. ［答案］abandoned
   ［译文］许多欧洲政府已经放弃了过去鼓励人们提前退休的政策。
4. ［答案］withered
   ［译文］虽然很多地方戏已经凋零甚至消亡，但是万邦戏却出奇地受欢迎。
5. ［答案］soared
   ［译文］自桑迪胡克小学枪击案造成20名儿童死亡以来，全国范围内的枪支

销量飙升。
6. [答案] deprived
   [译文] 2009年的政变使马达加斯加被国际社会孤立,并失去了外国援助。
7. [答案] destined
   [译文] 它由66个巨型射电望远镜组成,旨在以毫米和亚毫米波长观测深空。
8. [答案] shrinking
   [译文] 芯片制造商可以通过缩小半导体尺寸和在单一硅片上集成更多芯片来降低成本。
9. [答案] embrace
   [译文] 许多教师希望在教学上有更多自由,愿意改变讲授这一教学模式。
10. [答案] capacity
    [译文] 该发电厂从12月到来年5月通常满负荷运行,然后进行两周的维护。

单元练习 10

1. [答案] eliminated
   [译文] 自2009年以来,加拿大的汽车行业已经减少了约1.5万个就业岗位。
2. [答案] profound
   [译文] 早期的生活经历可能对儿童时期及之后的身心健康产生深远影响。
3. [答案] commensurate
   [译文] 他们热心奉献,但得到的回报与付出的时间和精力并不匹配。
4. [答案] exclusively
   [译文] 这是目前世界上唯一专门为"左撇子"提供服务的在线吉他店。
5. [答案] initiated
   [译文] 劳动节是为了纪念工人阶级、于1882年在美国开始设立的。
6. [答案] triggering
   [译文] 不良的饮食习惯和不规律的作息可能会引发一些心理问题。
7. [答案] virtually
   [译文] 虽然大学入学人数创历史新高,但毕业率在过去30年里几乎没有变化。
8. [答案] victims
   [译文] 总统希望这场悲剧的受害者能够得到他们所需的医疗救助和心理疏导。
9. [答案] aggressive
   [译文] 大量研究表明,暴力游戏即使没有直接导致暴力行为,也会使人产生暴力的想法。
10. [答案] courteous
    [译文] 波特兰人是全美最不会路怒的,其次是礼貌的克利夫兰人和巴尔的摩人。

单元练习11

1. ［答案］supervised
   ［译文］政府对上周举行的大选准备工作进行了监督。
2. ［答案］imminent
   ［译文］他频繁受伤,人们传言他即将退役。
3. ［答案］vanished
   ［译文］布伦达于2012年2月失踪,她最后一次被人看到是送孩子去上学。
4. ［答案］authentic
   ［译文］这个宁静的社区有很多上等餐厅,供应正宗的当地美食。
5. ［答案］disclosed
   ［译文］该学区本周披露,已于2021年11月展开内部调查。
6. ［答案］occurrence
   ［译文］那里很少发生盗窃案,因为惩罚力度极大。
7. ［答案］temporary
   ［译文］周五即将生效的车辆禁令适用于挂黑色临时牌照的汽车。
8. ［答案］diminish
   ［译文］随着12月25日临近,所有商店的库存量将不断下降。
9. ［答案］flourished
   ［译文］在这个耳机制造商衰落的年代,有的公司挺过来了,甚至发展得很好。
10. ［答案］confidential
    ［译文］根据所谓的红旗规则,汽车经销商将以最严格的安全措施保护您的个人信息。

单元练习12

1. ［答案］triumph
   ［译文］人们用鞭炮和彩灯来庆祝这一胜利,以示正义战胜邪恶。
2. ［答案］enforced
   ［译文］迪亚斯声称,教会的政策并没有对男性和女性一视同仁。
3. ［答案］erupted
   ［译文］该国与种族主义的长期斗争终于爆发了,成千上万的人们走上街头。
4. ［答案］addicted
   ［译文］人们可能会对不同的东西上瘾——酒精、毒品、某些食物,甚至是电视。
5. ［答案］promptly
   ［译文］2016年,弗雷德来到怀俄明州拉勒米市,很快便在那里购买了新的住所。

6. ［答案］mission
   ［译文］20多年来，坚宝果汁公司一直致力于简化和改善健康生活。
7. ［答案］enhance
   ［译文］尽管人们为维护阿富汗女性的权益做出了很多努力，但虐待事件仍不断发生。
8. ［答案］flexible
   ［译文］我们希望建立一个灵活的教育体系，让孩子们练习应对社会问题。
9. ［答案］was delivered
   ［译文］他以书面声明的形式对周日的突发事件做出了初步回应。
10. ［答案］considerably
    ［译文］布朗小姐十分愤怒地从桌前站起来，流着眼泪乘坐轿车径直回家了。

单元练习13

1. ［答案］amateur
   ［译文］他曾是一名业余养蜂人，但现在他养蜂更加商业化。
2. ［答案］acquaintance
   ［译文］排队结账时，他被一个在旧金山时认识的老熟人认出来了。
3. ［答案］inadequate
   ［译文］据估计，全世界有8.8亿人无法获得安全的饮用水。
4. ［答案］mutual
   ［译文］这两家公司还将探索包括网络共享在内的其他合作领域。
5. ［答案］partial
   ［译文］虽然手有残疾，但他写出了两本著作和十多篇科技文章。
6. ［答案］highlights
   ［译文］布兰多里尼没有经过正规训练便取得成功，这一点更凸显了她的天赋。
7. ［答案］emissions
   ［译文］这个亚洲国家在减少温室气体排放和促进可持续发展方面行动迅速。
8. ［答案］skepticism
   ［译文］他的战略一直受到广泛质疑，但在去年最后两个月取得了成效。
9. ［答案］lessen
   ［译文］在未来某个时候，全新的能源技术和节能技术将减少我们对石油的依赖性。
10. ［答案］perceived
    ［译文］在STEM（科学、技术、工程和数学）领域，人们认为男性比女性更擅长。

单元练习14

1. ［答案］pervasive

[译文] 汽车尾气对健康的不良影响无处不在，且难以衡量。
2. [答案] prohibit
   [译文] 政府应该禁止人们重建被暴风雨损毁的建筑物。
3. [答案] dominates
   [译文] 在非洲销售的手机中，约90%都是功能机，诺基亚仍然占据主导地位。
4. [答案] coincided
   [译文] 他作为制作人的职业生涯恰逢流行音乐史上蓬勃发展的一段时期。
5. [答案] proportion
   [译文] 这些商品一旦售出，就会失去很大一部分价值。
6. [答案] prestigious
   [译文] 在某些学科上，英国大学是世界一流的，甚至领先于最负盛名的美国大学。
7. [答案] stationary
   [译文] 我们的客户，尤其是那些乘坐国际航班的客户，经常会几小时都不动。
8. [答案] chaotic
   [译文] 他于上周抵达爱丁堡，由于数十名记者参加其新闻发布会，现场一片混乱。
9. [答案] inferior
   [译文] 美国人购买的医疗服务质量往往不如其他国家的医疗服务。
10. [答案] vacant
    [译文] 这条街上到处都是折扣店和纪念品店，也不乏一些空置多年的商铺。

单元练习15

1. [答案] feasible
   [译文] 政府官员指出，反对修建大坝的人并没有提出可行的替代方案。
2. [答案] submitted
   [译文] 他们向美国地球物理联盟期刊提交了四份手稿，供同行评议。
3. [答案] identical
   [译文] 这款手机在外观上与N8完全相同，只是没有后置摄像头。
4. [答案] intervals
   [译文] 作为哺乳动物，它们大约每隔20分钟就需要到水面呼吸一次。
5. [答案] prospect
   [译文] 几代人以来，销售人员一直对销售Windows个人电脑的前景感到头疼。
6. [答案] vulnerable
   [译文] 全世界弱势非洲移民的艰难处境必须得到更多关注。
7. [答案] explicit
   [译文] 当我在柏林采访美国国务卿时，他非常明确地拒绝了这个想法。

8. ［答案］sparked
   ［译文］这场火灾是在周四早高峰时段引发的，数百名消防员正在灭火。
9. ［答案］ridiculous
   ［译文］吉诺是哈佛大学商学院的一名研究员，他开展了大量原创性研究。
10. ［答案］accelerated
    ［译文］这座城市在战后迅速恢复了贸易，其发展随着1825年运河的开通进一步加速。

单元练习 16

1. ［答案］indispensable
   ［译文］农场生产水果、蔬菜和奶制品，并饲养牲畜，这些对我们的健康都不可或缺。
2. ［答案］cherished
   ［译文］许多用户并没有意识到，他们珍爱的手机留下了他人可以追踪的痕迹。
3. ［答案］clamored
   ［译文］他们涌上新德里的街头，要求对这些罪犯实施更严厉的惩罚。
4. ［答案］confessed
   ［译文］两名嫌疑人对周六的袭击事件供认不讳，而第三名嫌疑人否认对此事负责。
5. ［答案］minimize
   ［译文］这次行动的目的是尽量减少平民伤亡，如可能的话则完全避免。
6. ［答案］duplicate
   ［译文］日本大部分银行都将数据备份在相距600公里的大阪和东京两市的计算中心。
7. ［答案］obsession
   ［译文］对年轻外表的追求并不是他们痴迷于节食和锻炼的唯一原因。
8. ［答案］prolonged
   ［译文］电子游戏能有效地刺激大脑，但长时间接触会导致注意力下降。
9. ［答案］withdraw
   ［译文］美国军方宣布，将从阿富汗南部撤出至少2500名士兵。
10. ［答案］prevalent
    ［译文］非法采伐已经很普遍，估计占木材年产量的一半左右。

单元练习 17

1. ［答案］conducive
   ［译文］员工周围的环境都是蓝色的话，则更有利于激发创造力。
2. ［答案］compressed

[译文] 数字形式的电影和节目需要压缩才能通过宽带进行传送。
3. [答案] sensitive
   [译文] 机器上的激光探测器不够灵敏，无法探测到单个DNA分子。
4. [答案] exterior
   [译文] 这座四室五卫的房子建于1968年，其设计为欧式风格，外墙由石头砌成。
5. [答案] devoured
   [译文] 在青少年时，他如痴如醉地阅读流行科幻小说，总是有着天马行空的想象力。
6. [答案] intact
   [译文] 这个教堂经历了两次大地震，但由于其抗震结构好，因此仍然完好无损。
7. [答案] refreshed
   [译文] 苹果公司发布了全新的Power Mac专业电脑系列，令观察人士感到意外。
8. [答案] stumbled
   [译文] 塔利发现商科课程乏味透顶，于是选择了密苏里大学化学专业。
9. [答案] moderate
   [译文] 生活节奏缓慢，人们经常与朋友和家人交流，并且会适量饮酒。
10. [答案] prominent
    [译文] 埃及著名律师纳格拉·阿尔伊玛目最近在开罗宣布皈依基督教。

单元练习 18

1. [答案] blurred
   [译文] 朋友们说，他的短时记忆丧失，视力模糊。
2. [答案] notion
   [译文] 通用会议（General Assembly）等公司正在重塑社区大学的概念。
3. [答案] abruptly
   [译文] 人们普遍抱怨，司机在红绿灯前突然停车导致交通事故增多。
4. [答案] scorched
   [译文] 在南达科他州，大火吞噬了布莱克山脉3000英亩的区域，一座移动房屋被烧毁。
5. [答案] punctual
   [译文] 今年4月，美国西南航空的航班准点率仅为76%，比美联航和达美航空还低。
6. [答案] vicinity
   [译文] 以色列曾经与一些邻近的非阿拉伯国家关系友好，包括伊朗和土耳其。
7. [答案] exquisite

[译文] 康比静思教堂是精湛木工工艺的一个典范。
8. [答案] compliments
[译文] 在玛雅报名参加的写作工作坊中，老师对她大加赞扬。
9. [答案] dissipates
[译文] 对于身体健康的人，这种不适感持续约30秒，三分钟后完全消失。
10. [答案] implemented
[译文] 人们发现，家庭友好型公司相比其他公司效益更好。

单元练习 19

1. [答案] marveled
[译文] 他母亲打开主卧的一扇门，对步入式衣橱感到非常惊异。
2. [答案] plunged
[译文] 地震导致电话网络崩溃，该城市的部分地区陷入一片黑暗。
3. [答案] extinguished
[译文] 大楼从内部开始着火，消防队员在黎明前扑灭了明火。
4. [答案] evaporate
[译文] 在不到一代人的时间里要恢复往日辉煌，加利福尼亚州的这一梦想也可能破灭。
5. [答案] activate
[译文] 11月25日凌晨，设计在洪水期间自启动的两台水泵未能启动。
6. [答案] smashed
[译文] 3月以来发生了十多起案件，车窗被砸，车辆受损。
7. [答案] anonymous
[译文] 她收到了一笔匿名捐赠，得以去加州大学洛杉矶分校上学，主修建筑学。
8. [答案] dilemma
[译文] 姐姐说将在她位于内华达州太浩湖的湖滨小屋举行家庭聚会时，我感到左右为难。
9. [答案] succession
[译文] 海地得到了一系列援助项目，但缺乏连贯性、协调性和长期战略性。
10. [答案] surpassed
[译文] 与他共事的几名员工已经过了领取全额社会保障福利的退休年龄。

单元练习 20

1. [答案] embarked
[译文] 他结束了作为宇航员的职业生涯，开启了一段成功的政治生涯。
2. [答案] conspicuous

[译文] 遗憾的是，政界和商界领袖只有在他们缺席的时候才格外显眼。
3. [答案] alternate
　　　[译文] 人们普遍认为，一些正在兴起的替代支付方式本身也会带来风险。
4. [答案] eligible
　　　[译文] 在拥有部分自治权的丹麦领地格陵兰岛，近70%的居民有投票资格。
5. [答案] hovered
　　　[译文] 东北部夜间最低气温在20华氏度以下，周六应该不会超过冰点。
6. [答案] consent
　　　[译文] 在孩子参加出游前，家长们会获得完整的详细信息，并签署一份同意书。
7. [答案] universally
　　　[译文] 旧金山计划搭建随处可用的免费无线互联网接入，也就是人们所说的Wi-Fi。
8. [答案] merged
　　　[译文] 1939年，帝国航空公司和英国航空公司合并，成立英国海外航空公司。
9. [答案] prosecution
　　　[译文] 郊游可以开阔孩子们的视野，但是担心被起诉往往是学校不组织该类活动的原因。
10. [答案] agony
　　　[译文] 该男子可能会幸存下来，但他注定要终生承受身体上的痛苦和心理上的折磨。

单元练习 21

1. [答案] spike
　　　[译文] 这次罢工导致犯罪率飙升，在萨尔瓦多发生了100多起谋杀案。
2. [答案] ingredients
　　　[译文] 设定人生目标并掌握基本生活技能，这些是成功生活的必备要素。
3. [答案] resembles
　　　[译文] 晚上亮起灯来，这对夫妇的房子更像是一件艺术品，而不是郊区的一所住宅。
4. [答案] derive
　　　[译文] 研究表明，人们可以通过个性化其工作环境来获得职业满足感。
5. [答案] detained
　　　[译文] 这名服务员被拘留接受进一步讯问，以确保他没有侵占被盗财物。
6. [答案] overwhelmed
　　　[译文] 从皮裤到西装，员工们穿什么的都有，他们四处奔走，看起来忙得不可开交。

7. ［答案］saturated
   ［译文］英格兰西南部再次降雨，已经被暴雨淹没的地区水位变得更高了。
8. ［答案］withstand
   ［译文］德克萨斯大学阿灵顿分校的实验室对其进行了测试，可以承受超过每小时250英里的风速。
9. ［答案］dreaded
   ［译文］凯勒过去一直害怕上体育课，所以她在负责此项工作时，尽量安排有趣的活动供学生选择。
10. ［答案］slump
    ［译文］大学文凭一直是找到一份好工作的敲门砖，但经济衰退击碎了众多美国高校应届毕业生的梦想。

单元练习 22

1. ［答案］fractures
   ［译文］仅在12月，就有三名邮政工人在雪地摔倒而骨折。
2. ［答案］preceded
   ［译文］大部分伤亡是由于地面入侵之前的空袭造成的。
3. ［答案］constitution
   ［译文］新宪法要求各政党在议会中至少有60名女性（共395个席位）。
4. ［答案］rival
   ［译文］国会内部的问题使其很容易受到对手的攻击。
5. ［答案］dispenses
   ［译文］他在一个由当地教会和非营利组织组成的委员会任职，该委员会向有需要的人提供援助。
6. ［答案］chronic
   ［译文］糖尿病是一种危及生命的慢性病，任何年龄、种族和背景的人都有可能患上。
7. ［答案］discrimination
   ［译文］即使在今天，在俄罗斯和哈萨克斯坦，人们对同性恋的歧视仍然很普遍。
8. ［答案］prone
   ［译文］女性的工作和事业更容易中断，因为她们主要照顾小孩和老人。
9. ［答案］stammer
   ［译文］这部电影讲述了乔治六世如何克服口吃的故事，它获得了12项奥斯卡提名。
10. ［答案］diverting
    ［译文］由于没有足够的外科医生，班纳健康中心一直将创伤患者转至其他医院。

单元练习 23

1. ［答案］patriotic
   ［译文］意大利普通民众被敦促发扬其爱国主义精神，购买政府债券。
2. ［答案］abide
   ［译文］金州勇士队一直奉行不惜一切代价取胜的团队精神。
3. ［答案］strain
   ［译文］拉伸可以防止肌肉扭伤，促进血液流动，还有助于降低胆固醇。
4. ［答案］eradicated
   ［译文］尽管霍乱在许多国家已被根除，但古巴每年仍有300万人感染。
5. ［答案］monotonous
   ［译文］没过多久，他就厌倦了每天坐在电脑前输入数据的单调工作。
6. ［答案］veterans
   ［译文］他们批准了为参加海湾战争的退伍军人增付15亿美元薪资的一揽子计划。
7. ［答案］rehearsal
   ［译文］美国空军定于在周二晚上为周三的飞行仪式进行彩排。
8. ［答案］incentives
   ［译文］可悲的是，医疗保险现在让医生在治疗病人时选择最昂贵的药物。
9. ［答案］demonstrate
   ［译文］企业家们正在寻觅那些通过志愿者工作表现出强烈社会责任感的人。
10. ［答案］scrawl
    ［译文］教育工作者在教室里安装了更多的灯具，并鼓励老师们在黑板上书写清楚。

单元练习 24

1. ［答案］endangered
   ［译文］尽管山地大猩猩仍处于濒危状态，但其数量已增长到近800只。
2. ［答案］combat
   ［译文］卢拉开始每天散步和节食来控制体重，并以此来改变久坐不动的生活方式。
3. ［答案］manual
   ［译文］熟练的计算机人员需求量很大，建筑工人甚至不熟练的体力劳动者也同样短缺。
4. ［答案］primitive
   ［译文］虽然他们用原始的设备耕种小块土地，但他们亲手采摘的棉花质量更好。

5. ［答案］prosperity
   ［译文］许多河流曾经是人类繁荣和生物繁衍的发祥地，如今却受到了严重污染。
6. ［答案］eternal
   ［译文］威尔金森尽管受伤了但一直很乐观，他希望自己及时康复，以便参加比赛。
7. ［答案］regulating
   ［译文］众所周知，维生素D能促进骨骼健康并调节钙质水平，因此经常添加到牛奶中。
8. ［答案］endowed
   ［译文］阿根廷是世界上资源最丰富的国家之一，拥有巨大的能源储备和极好的农业生产地理条件。
9. ［答案］tranquil
   ［译文］骑车穿过匈牙利南部宁静的村庄时，我发现人们的目光里带着好奇，挥手致意时略显羞涩。
10. ［答案］propelled
    ［译文］由于人们更换老旧汽车导致销量攀升，汽车零售商上个月增加的就业岗位最多。

单元练习 25

1. ［答案］grazing
   ［译文］在一座小山上，我们发现一头雄性犀牛在高高的草丛中默默吃草。
2. ［答案］extracting
   ［译文］最终目的是找到一种从水中提取氢的有效方法。
3. ［答案］impaired
   ［译文］接触过这些化学物质的妇女所生的孩子，其记忆力和学习能力可能会受损。
4. ［答案］originated
   ［译文］他长期背疼，起因是大约三十年前在93号高速公路上发生的一起车祸。
5. ［答案］proceed
   ［译文］经过考虑，部长决定暂停推行这项税收政策。
6. ［答案］incredible
   ［译文］餐厅位于七楼，设有落地窗，可以俯瞰旧金山湾的壮丽景色。
7. ［答案］gracious
   ［译文］客人们在鸡尾酒会上会见到和蔼可亲、极具魅力、才华横溢的肯·伯恩斯。
8. ［答案］consensus
   ［译文］纽约是采用新评价体系的州之一，尽管对于如何最有效地评估教师尚未达成共识。

9. ［答案］alters
   ［译文］当她向新闻媒体谈及自己的专业领域时，则完全改变了交流风格。
10. ［答案］internal
    ［译文］企业需要提供多年的内部数据，交由政府各机构仔细审查。

单元练习 26

1. ［答案］uniform
   ［译文］我们要感谢英勇的军人们，正是因为有了他们，我们的国家才如此安全。
2. ［答案］rational
   ［译文］移民似乎是一个特别缺乏理性思考的政策领域。
3. ［答案］stable
   ［译文］提供这项服务可能会成为未来几年稳定的收入来源。
4. ［答案］domestic
   ［译文］热带森林砍伐主要是由于国内外对粮食和生物燃料的需求激增造成的。
5. ［答案］appliances
   ［译文］能源之星为电脑和厨房电器等产品提供了能源效率标准。
6. ［答案］compels
   ［译文］在某种程度上，这一新政使他们不仅要当警察，还要充当社会工作者和咨询人员。
7. ［答案］nuisance
   ［译文］野生生物曾经令人讨厌，也很危险，但随着时间的推移，人们意识到它们可以吸引游客。
8. ［答案］legible
   ［译文］该文件的部分内容难以阅读，签名和公章也很难辨认。
9. ［答案］evacuating
   ［译文］警察很快便到达现场，他们包围了医院，并疏散附近建筑物里的居民。
10. ［答案］transmitted
    ［译文］摄像机将照片传回航天器的中心枢纽，然后再传回地球。

单元练习 27

1. ［答案］compact
   ［译文］宏碁 LumiRead 阅读器轻便小巧、易于使用，是终极旅行伴侣。
2. ［答案］doomed
   ［译文］历史表明，忽视文化因素的发展战略注定会失败。
3. ［答案］compromised
   ［译文］工人们不得不抓紧完成施工，这引发了人们对质量可能打折扣的担忧。

4. ［答案］accommodate
   ［译文］这艘船可以容纳5 400名客人，船上有公园、大礼堂和旋转木马。
5. ［答案］substitute
   ［译文］他建议将冥想作为治疗的一种辅助手段，而不是替代手段。
6. ［答案］sponsored
   ［译文］该慈善机构在哈利法克斯公司的赞助下推出了一个网站，就住房问题提供咨询。
7. ［答案］swarming
   ［译文］整个意大利博物馆林立，到处都是艺术品，佛罗伦萨市自然也有几座不错的博物馆。
8. ［答案］synthetic
   ［译文］这位教授称合成氮肥是一项"奇妙的发明"，因为它提高了粮食产量。
9. ［答案］reinforces
   ［译文］富裕社区的孩子能上更好的学校，这使得不同社会群体之间的差距越来越大。
10. ［答案］beamed
    ［译文］他的演唱会将在泰姬陵举行，届时将通过卫星向全世界转播。

单元练习28

1. ［答案］facilitate
   ［译文］为了便于分销和购买，我们可以寻求更多的电子商务解决方案。
2. ［答案］navigate
   ［译文］拉蒙在美国感到异常孤独，而安娜则面临着诸多文化陷阱。
3. ［答案］barren
   ［译文］驱车前往半岛的最前端时，我们感到人类几乎没有在这片贫瘠的土地上留下任何痕迹。
4. ［答案］versatile
   ［译文］手机价格已经大幅下降，其功能也会更加丰富，提供各种各样的数字化服务。
5. ［答案］polish
   ［译文］数学家们经常在学术会议上分享尚未完成的研究论文，之后对其进行润色以便发表。
6. ［答案］evolved
   ［译文］卢浮宫的独特之处在于它是逐渐演变成了一座博物馆，而不是被设计成博物馆。
7. ［答案］roamed
   ［译文］许多狼在怀俄明州和爱达荷州的山区游荡，直到20世纪30年代，人们才根据一项联邦计划对其进行猎杀。

8. ［答案］paralyze
　　［译文］断电可能使这个国家陷入瘫痪，许多人在比以往更寒冷的冬季里束手无策。
9. ［答案］privilege
　　［译文］麦格拉斯表示，他很荣幸将带领公司发展，并期待在前几任领导的基础上再接再厉。
10. ［答案］contemporary
　　［译文］最近，国际社会对传统的非洲当代艺术的兴趣空前高涨。

单元练习 29

1. ［答案］wrinkles
　　［译文］该药物还有一种更受欢迎的用途，可以减少面部皱纹。
2. ［答案］exclaimed
　　［译文］"这比飞机上的餐食和便宜的大学食堂饭菜还糟糕，"她男朋友叫道。
3. ［答案］famine
　　［译文］埃塞俄比亚在1984年发生饥荒事件后，便建立了有效的预警系统。
4. ［答案］peered
　　［译文］我在杂货店结账时，排在我后面的女人看到了我的食品券，并窥探购物车里的东西。
5. ［答案］obscure
　　［译文］他是一个低调但高效的人，自1990年以来一直掌管着强大的国家情报机构。
6. ［答案］random
　　［译文］伦敦地铁警察随机拦住乘客，检查行李后才让上车。
7. ［答案］commenced
　　［译文］该项目于2018年开始实施，初步计划于2025年完工。
8. ［答案］nurture
　　［译文］教育应传授知识，培养创造力，使我们国家能在新经济形势下蓬勃发展。
9. ［答案］alleviating
　　［译文］植物向大气中释放水分，缓解空调和中央供暖设备造成的干燥环境。
10. ［答案］elapsed
　　［译文］下半场才过了三分钟，湖人队的支持者就开始呼喊让科比·布莱恩特上场。

单元练习 30

1. ［答案］manipulate
　　［译文］高管们很容易操纵股价，有时这种情况会持续很长一段时间。

2. ［答案］traits
   ［译文］这六种个人特质可以帮助你在情感上和经济上挺过离婚阶段。
3. ［答案］verge
   ［译文］在20世纪60年代颁布禁令之前，该物种遭到猎杀，濒临灭绝。
4. ［答案］distorted
   ［译文］该展览展示了多年来美国流行文化是如何扭曲亚洲人形象的。
5. ［答案］glamour
   ［译文］阿姆斯特朗一直谦逊低调，从不允许自己戴着曾探索太空的光环。
6. ［答案］fraction
   ［译文］65岁以上的老人目前享受高额医疗保险，他们只需支付一小部分费用。
7. ［答案］maximum
   ［译文］布宜诺斯艾利斯的私人厨师晚宴最多接待15人，客人们围坐在一张大桌子旁用餐。
8. ［答案］sanction
   ［译文］联合国安理会以压倒性票数通过了对伊朗的制裁，因为伊朗一直未履行其义务。
9. ［答案］allocated
   ［译文］近三分之二的投资将用于扩充集团电子业务的生产设备。
10. ［答案］inhabited
    ［译文］这个老式社区距离繁华的市场仅几步之遥，这里最初居住的是来自也门的移民。

附录 II 词汇索引

A

abandon
abbreviate
abide
abolish
aboriginal
abortion
abrasion
abridge
abrupt
absolutely
abstain
abstract
absurd
abundant
abuse
accelerate
accent
accessible
accidental
acclaim
accommodate
account
accumulate
accuse
acknowledge
acquaint
acre
acrobat
activate
acute
addict
adhere
adjacent
administration
adolescent
advent
adventure
adversity
advocate
affable
affirm
afflict
afloat
aftermath
aggravate
aggression
agitate
agony
ailment
aisle
alarming
album
alien
allegedly
alleviate
allocate
allot
allowance
allure
almond
alter
alteration
altercation
alternate
altitude
alumni
amateur
ambassador
amber
ambiguous
ambition
ambulance
amend
amenity
amiable
ample
amplify
anguish
animation
ankle
anniversary
annoyance
annual
annul
anonymous

anthem	asylum	beam
anticipate	athlete	bestow
antique	atom	bidder
antiquity	attain	biofuel
appall	attenuate	biography
apparatus	attic	birthright
appeal	attitude	bitter
applaud	attorney	bizarre
appraise	attribute	blackspot
appropriate	auction	blade
approve	auditorium	blast
approximately	authentic	blaze
aptitude	authorize	bleach
aquarium	autism	bleeding
arbitrary	automatically	blockade
archeology	autonomous	bloom
archive	avalanche	blunder
arduous	avenue	board
arena	aviation	bolt
arise	awake	bonus
aroma	awareness	booklet
arouse	awkward	boom
array		boost
arsenic	**B**	boulevard
articulate		boundary
artificial	babble	boutique
ascent	bachelor	brass
ascertain	backup	breadth
assassination	backward	breakdown
assault	balcony	breakthrough
assembly	bald	breed
assess	ballet	breeze
asset	ballistic	brim
assign	bankruptcy	brink
associate	barbarian	brisk
assort	barren	brittle
assure	basement	broadband
asteroid	bastion	broadcast
asthma	bazaar	brochure
astound	beacon	bronchitis

bronze
brutal
budget
bump
bunch
bureau
bustling
buzz

C

cabin
cabinet
cable
caffeine
calamity
calcium
calendar
calorie
canal
candidate
cane
cannon
canyon
capacity
cape
capsule
caption
cardiovascular
carousel
cart
carve
castle
casualty
catalyst
catastrophe
category
cater
cathedral
caution

cement
censorship
census
centennial
ceramics
champagne
chaos
chapel
charge
charity
charming
chase
chauffeur
checkout
chef
cherish
chew
chill
chimpanzee
cholera
cholesterol
chronic
chuckle
circular
circus
cite
citrus
civilian
clamor
clarify
clash
clearance
client
cliff
cling
clinician
clip
cloak
closure
clown

clue
clumsy
cluster
clutch
cocaine
cocktail
cognition
cohere
coincide
collaborate
collagen
collapse
collision
colony
colossal
coma
combat
comedy
comical
comma
commemorate
commence
commend
comment
commercial
commission
community
compact
compassionate
compatible
compel
compensate
competent
complement
compliment
comply
component
composition
comprehension
compress

comprise
compromise
compulsory
conceal
concede
conceive
concentrate
concession
concourse
concrete
condemn
condense
conducive
conference
confess
confine
confirm
conflict
conform
confront
congress
conscious
consecutive
consensus
consent
conserve
console
consolidate
conspicuous
conspiracy
constituent
constitute
consultation
contagious
contaminate
contemporary
contempt
contend
continent
continually

contour
contract
contribute
controversy
convention
convert
convict
coordination
cope
coral
cord
cordial
corporate
corresponding
cosmetic
cosmic
costume
council
courtesy
coverage
crack
crane
crank
crave
credit
creek
creep
crew
cripple
crispy
critical
crossroads
crucial
crude
cruise
crumby
crush
crutch
crystal
cuisine

cultivate
curb
current
curriculum
curse
cursor
custody
customs
cyber
cyclone

D

dairy
dale
damp
dam
dawn
dazzle
deadline
decay
deceive
decent
decibel
decline
dedication
deduce
defect
deficient
deficit
defy
degrade
deliberate
delicacy
delicate
delight
deliver
democrat
demonstrate
dentist

departure
depict
depletion
deploy
deprive
derive
descent
desert
deserve
desolate
dessert
destiny
destructive
detached
detain
detect
deter
detergent
deteriorate
detrimental
devastate
devise
devoid
devour
diabetes
diagnose
dignity
dilapidated
dilemma
dimension
diminish
diploma
diplomatic
disapprove
discard
discharge
disclose
discount
discriminate
disdain

disembark
disgrace
dismal
disparity
dispel
disperse
displace
dispose
dispute
disrupt
dissect
dissent
dissipate
distinct
distinctive
distinguish
distort
distract
ditch
divergence
diverse
diversity
divert
dizzy
dodge
domain
domestic
dominant
donate
donor
doom
dormouse
dose
drain
dramatic
drastic
dread
drill
drizzle
drought

drown
dump
duplicate
durability
dwell
dwindle
dynamic

E

earshot
ease
eatery
echo
economical
efficiency
elaborate
elapse
elastic
electron
elegance
elevate
elicit
eligible
eliminate
elite
ellipse
elude
emancipate
embark
embarrass
embrace
embryo
emerge
eminent
emit
empathy
enact
enchant
enclave

enclose
encounter
endanger
endeavor
endorse
endow
enforce
engrave
enhance
enlarge
enlighten
enlist
enormous
enroll
enthusiastic
entitle
entrepreneur
enzyme
epic
epidemic
equate
equivalent
eradicate
erase
erosion
erratic
erupt
escalator
escort
estate
esteem
eternal
euthanasia
evacuate
evade
evaluate
evaporate
everlasting
evolution
exceed
exceptional
excerpt
excessive
exclaim
exclude
execute
exert
exhaust
exodus
exotic
expand
expel
expertise
expire
explicit
exploit
explosive
exposure
exquisite
extend
exterior
external
extinct
extinguish
extract

F

fable
fabric
fabricate
fabulous
facilitate
faction
faculty
fade
faint
fairy
fake
famine
fantasy
fascinate
fatal
fatigue
feasible
feat
feeble
fend
ferocity
fertile
fervent
fiber
fiction
fidelity
fierce
filter
filthy
firearm
fiscal
flame
flare
flash
flaw
flee
fleet
flexible
flick
flock
flour
flourish
fluid
fold
folklore
footage
formulate
forthcoming
fortify
foster
foul
foundation

fraction
fracture
fragile
fragment
fragrance
frail
fraud
friction
frontier
frugal
frustrate
fulfill
fungus
funnel
furious
fury
futile
fuzzy

G

gadget
galaxy
gallery
gamble
gang
garbage
garlic
gasp
gauge
gear
generator
generous
genetics
genuine
gesture
ghetto
gigantic
giggle
ginger

gizmo
glacial
glamour
glare
glint
gloomy
glorious
gobble
gorgeous
gorilla
gossip
gourmet
gown
grab
graceful
gracious
graffiti
graphics
gratitude
gravity
graze
grease
grid
grief
grim
grin
grip
grocery
groove
grove
guardian
guilty
gulf
gulp
gust
gymnast

H

habitat

habitual
hail
hallmark
halt
hamper
handicap
handle
harbor
hardware
harsh
hasten
hatred
haunt
hawk
haze
heap
hearth
heedless
herb
herd
heritage
hermit
highlight
hike
hinder
hint
hive
hobble
hoist
holocaust
hook
horizon
hormone
horn
hospitality
hostility
household
hover
hub
hum

humanitarian
humble
humid
humiliation
hurdle
hurricane
hydrogen
hymn

I

iconic
identical
identify
identity
idyllic
illegible
illiteracy
illumination
immigrant
imminent
immoral
immune
impair
impede
impel
impending
imperial
implant
implement
implicate
implicit
impose
impoverish
inadequate
inalienable
inaugurate
incense
incentive
incline

incredible
incursion
indifferent
indigenous
indispensable
induce
indulge
ineligible
inevitable
infamous
infancy
infant
inferior
influenza
infrared
infrastructure
infringe
ingenuity
ingredient
inhabit
inherent
inherit
initiate
initiative
injection
inland
inmate
innocent
innovate
inquiry
inscribe
insert
insight
install
instinct
institute
insure
intact
integral
interact

interior
intermittent
intern
internal
internship
interpret
interstate
interval
intimate
intimidate
intractable
intricate
intrude
intuitive
invalid
invasion
inverse
irradiate
irrational
irritate
isolate
itch
ivory

J

jail
jam
jeopardize
journalist
jovial
judicial
jungle
junk
jury
justify

K

keen

kidnap
knee
knit

L

ladder
lag
landfill
landline
landmark
landscape
landslip
lane
lapse
laser
latent
latitude
lattice
laud
launch
lava
lavish
lawsuit
layman
leaflet
leak
leap
leather
legacy
legend
legible
legislation
leisure
lemon
lens
lentil
lesbian
lessen
lethal

lever
liable
license
lime
limp
linger
litter
livestock
loft
logging
longevity
longitude
lounge
loyal
lunar
lure
luster
luxury
lyric

M

magnet
magnify
magnitude
maid
mainstream
maintain
mall
malnutrition
maltreatment
mammal
mania
manipulate
mansion
manual
manufacture
manuscript
maple
marathon

march
margin
maritime
marvel
mask
massage
massive
maximize
medieval
melody
mend
mentor
menu
merchant
merge
mesh
messy
metabolism
metropolis
microscope
migrate
mild
milestone
minimal
minister
minivan
minor
mirage
miscellaneous
misery
mission
mitigate
mock
moderate
modify
moisture
molecule
monetary
monopoly
mortal

mosque
mosquito
motion
motivate
motive
mount
muffle
mute
mutual
myth

N

naive
naked
naval
navigate
negotiation
nitrogen
nominate
nonchalant
notary
notify
notion
notorious
nourish
novice
noxious
nudge
nuisance
null
nurture
nutrient

O

oath
obese
objection
obligatory

obscure
observatory
obsess
obsolete
occupation
occurrence
offence
olive
ominous
onset
opponent
oppression
opt
optimism
orchestra
ornament
orphanage
oust
outage
outbreak
outlaw
outlet
outlook
outrage
outskirts
overdose
overhear
overlap
overlook
oversee
overtake
overwhelm
oxygen
ozone

P

pace
package
pact

palette
pamphlet
pandemic
panel
panic
panorama
parachute
paralyze
parental
parliament
partial
particle
particulate
partition
passion
password
pastime
pasture
patriot
patrol
patron
pavement
paw
peculiar
pedal
pedestrian
peek
peep
pending
penguin
pension
perceive
perish
permanent
perpetual
persistence
perspective
pertain
pervasive
pessimistic

pesticide
pharmaceutical
phase
philanthropic
phobia
physician
physique
pillbox
pirate
pitfall
plague
plausible
pledge
plight
plot
plumage
plummet
plump
plunge
poach
pod
poise
polio
polish
polo
populous
portion
portray
pose
posture
potential
potion
prayer
precaution
precede
predator
predecessor
predicament
predominant
pregnancy

prejudice
preliminary
premature
premium
prescribe
preserve
prestige
presume
prevalent
previous
prey
priest
prime
primitive
principal
principle
prior
privilege
probe
procedure
proceed
proclamation
prodigy
profile
profound
prohibit
prolong
prominent
prompt
prone
propel
proportion
prose
prosecute
prospect
prospective
prosperity
protein
protest
proton

provision
provoke
proximity
prudent
pump
punch
punctual
pungent
purchase
pursuit

Q

quake
qualify
quarantine
quench
quest
quote

R

racism
radiation
radical
rage
raid
ramble
rampant
ranch
random
rapport
ratify
ratio
ration
ravage
raze
rear
reassure
rebellion

recede
recess
recipient
reciprocal
recline
recluse
recover
recruitment
recuperate
recur
redeem
redress
redundant
refine
refresh
refugee
regime
register
regulate
rehearsal
reinforce
release
relevant
reliant
relieve
relish
relocate
reluctance
remedy
reminder
renaissance
render
renewable
renovate
renowned
repeal
repel
represent
republican
resemble

resent
reserve
reservoir
reside
resolution
resolve
resort
respiratory
respond
restore
restraint
resume
retail
retain
retreat
reunion
reveal
revenue
revere
revision
revive
revoke
revolt
revolve
rhino
ridiculous
rigid
rigorous
riot
ritual
rival
roam
robbery
rogue
romance
rotary
routine
row
ruffle
ruin

rumor
rupture
rural
ruthless

S

sadden
sanction
sanitation
sarcastic
saturate
sauce
saunter
savor
scale
scam
scandal
scar
scarce
scarf
scary
scatter
scent
scheme
scooter
scope
scorch
scorn
scrap
scratch
scrawl
scream
scribble
scrutiny
sculpture
seal
seamless
seclusion
sector

sedentary	slump	spray
seduce	smash	spreadsheet
segment	smuggle	sprout
seismic	sneak	spur
seismograph	sneer	squander
semiconductor	snug	squeeze
senator	soak	squirrel
sensible	soar	stab
sensitive	sole	stable
serene	solicitor	stagger
session	solitude	stale
sever	soothe	stall
sewage	sophisticated	stammer
shabby	sore	stamp
shampoo	sour	stance
shatter	souvenir	startle
shed	sovereignty	startup
shelter	soybean	stationary
shepherd	spacious	stationery
shield	spark	statue
shift	sparse	stature
shortage	specimen	status
shovel	spectacular	statute
showcase	spectator	steady
shrink	spectrum	steer
shutter	speedometer	stem
shuttle	sphere	stereo
sigh	spice	stiff
signal	spike	stifle
signature	spill	stimulus
signify	spin	stir
silhouette	spire	stout
silicon	splash	straddle
skepticism	spoil	strain
sketch	sponsor	strategy
skyline	spotlight	stray
slam	spot	stream
slash	spouse	strenuous
slice	sprain	stretch
slide	sprawl	stride

strive
stroke
stroll
stubborn
stuffy
stumble
stun
stutter
submarine
submit
subscribe
subsequent
subsidy
substantial
substitute
subtle
suburban
successive
successor
succumb
suicide
summit
superb
superior
supervise
supreme
surge
surgeon
surgery
surmount
surname
surpass
surplus
surrender
survey
susceptible
suspect
suspense
suspicion
sustain

swallow
sway
swell
swing
swirl
switch
syllabus
sympathetic
symphony
symptom
synthetic
syrup

T

tablet
tackle
tactic
tailor
taint
tame
taskbar
tease
tedious
temperate
temper
temporary
tempting
tension
terminal
terminate
terrain
territory
testify
therapy
thigh
thirsty
thread
threat
threshold

thrifty
thrive
throne
thunderclap
tidal
tilt
timber
tinned
tissue
toil
tolerant
toothpaste
torch
torment
tornado
tournament
toxic
track
tragedy
trail
trait
trajectory
tramp
tranquil
transaction
transcend
transcript
transfer
transform
transistor
transition
transmit
transparent
transplant
trauma
traverse
trek
tremble
tremendous
tremor

trench
trial
tribe
trick
trigger
triple
triumph
trivial
tropical
trough
trunk
tsunami
tuberculosis
tug
tuition
tutor
twirl
twist
tycoon

U

ubiquitous
ultimate
unanimous
unaware
uncover
undercooked
undergo
underlie
underline
undermine
undertake
underway
underweight
undisguised
undue
unease
unfold
uniform

unity
universal
unprecedented
unrest
unveil
upcoming
updated
upgrade
upright
uprising
uproar
urban
usher
utility
utilize
utmost
utterly

V

vacant
vaccine
vacuum
vain
valid
valuable
vandal
vanilla
vanish
vanity
vapor
vendor
ventilate
venture
venue
verbally
verge
verify
versatile
vertical

vessel
veteran
veto
viable
vibrant
vicinity
victim
vie
vigor
violate
violent
virtually
virus
visa
visible
vista
vital
vitamin
vocation
void
volatile
volcano
volunteer
vow
vulnerable

W

wafer
wander
ward
wares
warfare
warranty
warrior
watershed
wavelength
wearisome
wedge
weird

welfare
whirl
whisper
wholesale
widespread
widow
wilt
windshield
witch
withdraw
wither
withstand
witness

workaholic
wrap
wreck
wrench
wrestler
wrinkle
wrist

X

xerox
X-ray

Y

yearn
yell
yield
yoga
yogurt

Z

zeal
zebra
zinc
zone